REA's Test Prep Books Are The Best!

(a sample of the hundreds of letters REA receives each year)

" I passed! Your book gave a great idea of the type of information that was to
be found on the PRAXIS PLT . . . I was prepared. "
Test-Taker, Richmond, VA

" The exams were right on target for the PRAXIS PLT. Excellent Book! "
Test-Taker, Atlanta, GA

" Your book was such a better value and was so much more complete than
anything your competition has produced—and I have them all! "
Teacher, Virginia Beach, VA

" Compared to the other books that my fellow students had, your book was
the most helpful in helping me get a great score. "
Student, North Hollywood, CA

" Your book was responsible for my success on the exam, which helped me get
into the college of my choice... I will look for REA the next time I need help. "
Student, Chesterfield, MO

" Just a short note to say thanks for the great support your book gave me in
helping me pass the test... I'm on my way to a B.S. degree because of you! "
Student, Orlando, FL

" The gem of the book is the tests. They were indicative of the actual exam.
The explanations of the answers are practically another review session. "
Student, Fresno, CA

(more on next page)

(continued from front page)

" I just wanted to thank you for helping me get a great score
on the AP U.S. History... Thank you for making great test preps! "
Student, Los Angeles, CA

" Your Fundamentals of Engineering Exam book was the absolute best
preparation I could have had for the exam, and it is one of the major
reasons I did so well and passed the FE on my first try. "
Student, Sweetwater, TN

" I used your book to prepare for the test and found that the advice and the
sample tests were highly relevant... Without using any other material, I earned
very high scores and will be going to the graduate school of my choice. "
Student, New Orleans, LA

" What I found in your book was a wealth of information sufficient to shore up
my basic skills in math and verbal.... The practice tests were challenging and the
answer explanations most helpful. It certainly is the Best Test Prep for the GRE! "
Student, Pullman, WA

" I really appreciate the help from your excellent book. Please keep
up with your great work. "
Student, Albuquerque, NM

" I used your *CLEP Introductory Sociology* book and rank it 99%– thank you! "
Student, Jerusalem, Israel

" The painstakingly detailed answers in the sample tests are the most helpful
part of this book. That's one of the great things about REA books. "
Student, Valley Stream, NY

Research & Education Association

The Best Teachers' Test Preparation for

PRAXIS™ PLT
Grades 5-9

2nd Edition

With REA's **TEST***ware*® on CD-ROM

Edited by
Anita Price Davis, Ed.D.
Charles Dana Professor Emerita of Education
Converse College, Spartanburg, S.C.

Staff of
Research & Education Association

Visit our Educator Support Center at:
www.REA.com/teacher

The competencies presented in this book were created and implemented by Educational Testing Service. For individual state requirements, consult your state education agency. For further information visit the PRAXIS website at *www.ets.org/praxis.*

PRAXIS® and The PRAXIS Series™ are trademarks of ETS®.

Research & Education Association
61 Ethel Road West
Piscataway, New Jersey 08854
E-mail: info@rea.com

The Best Teachers' Test Preparation for the PRAXIS™ PLT TEST: Grades 5-9 With TEST*ware*® on CD-ROM

Printed in the United States of America

Library of Congress Control Number 2008928727

ISBN-13: 978-0-7386-0477-0
ISBN-10: 0-7386-0477-1

Windows® is a registered trademark of Microsoft Corporation.

REA® and TEST*ware*® are registered trademarks of Research & Education Association, Inc.

About the Editor

Dr. Anita Price Davis was the Charles A. Dana Professor of Education and the Director of Elementary Education at Converse College, Spartanburg, South Carolina. Dr. Davis earned her B.S. and M.A. from Appalachian State University and her doctorate from Duke University. She also received a postdoctoral fellowship to Ohio State University for two additional years of study.

Dr. Davis worked over 35 years at Converse College, where she served as the faculty advisor for Kappa Delta Epsilon, a national education honor organization. She also worked 5 years as a public school teacher.

Dr. Davis has received wide recognition for her work, including a letter of appreciation from the U.S. Department of the Interior, inclusion in Contemporary Authors, and a citation of appreciation from the Michigan Council of the Social Studies. She has authored/coauthored 23 funded grants for Converse College. She has served as a mentor and was a two-time President of the Spartanburg County Council of the International Reading Association. The state of South Carolina twice named her an outstanding educator, and she was twice a nominee for the CASE U.S. Professor of the Year.

Dr. Davis has authored, co-authored, and edited more than 80 books, many for Research & Education Association. She has also authored numerous books in REA's MaxNotes® Literature Guides series.

Among her other publications, Dr. Davis has written two college textbooks titled Reading Instruction Essentials and Children's Literature Essentials. She has published several history books and is also the author of more than 80 papers, book reviews, journal articles, and encyclopedia entries.

Acknowledgments

In addition to our author, we would like to thank **Larry B. Kling**, Vice President, Editorial, for his overall direction; **John Cording**, Vice President, Technology, for coordinating the design, development, and testing of REA's TEST*ware*® software; **Pam Weston**, Vice President, Publishing, for setting the quality standards for production integrity and managing the publication to completion; **Heena Patel** and **Amy Jamison**, Software Project Managers, for software testing; **Dominique Won** for copyediting the manuscript; **Ellen Gong** for proofreading the manuscript; **Nancy Kopper** for indexing the book; **Diane Goldschmidt,** Senior Editor, for her editorial contributions to this edition; **Anne Winthrop Esposito**, Senior Editor, for coordinating revisions; and **Rachel DiMatteo**, Graphic Designer, for typesetting revisions.

We also extend thanks to **Julienne Empric**, **Erin Spanier-Evers**, **Christine Hudak**, **Paul Linnehan**, **Judy Downs-Lombardi**, **Donald Orlosky**, **Gail Platt**, **Gail Rae**, **Sally Stevens**, and **Christine Zardecki** for their editorial contributions.

 ## About Research & Education Association

Founded in 1959, Research & Education Association (REA) is dedicated to publishing the finest and most effective educational materials—including software, study guides, and test preps—for students in middle school, high school, college, graduate school, and beyond.

REA's Test Preparation series includes study guides for all academic levels in almost all disciplines. Research & Education Association publishes test preps for students who have not yet completed high school, as well as high school students preparing to enter college. Students from countries around the world seeking to attend college in the United States will find the assistance they need in REA's publications. For college students seeking advanced degrees, REA publishes test preps for many major graduate school admission examinations in a wide variety of disciplines, including engineering, law, and medicine. Students at every level, in every field, with every ambition can find what they are looking for among REA's publications.

REA presents tests that accurately depict the official exams in both degree of difficulty and types of questions. REA's practice tests are always based upon the most recently administered exams, and include every type of question that can be expected on the actual exams.

REA's publications and educational materials are highly regarded and continually receive an unprecedented amount of praise from professionals, instructors, librarians, parents, and students. Our authors are as diverse as the subject matter represented in the books we publish. They are well-known in their respective fields and serve on the faculties of prestigious high schools, colleges, and universities throughout the United States and Canada.

We invite you to visit us at www.rea.com to find out how "REA is making the world smarter."

CONTENTS

CHAPTER 1

Passing the PLT   1

About this Book and TEST*ware*® 3

About the Praxis Series...4

About the Principles of Learning and Teaching Tests 5

How to Use this Book and TEST*ware*® 8

Format of the PLT 5–9 8

About the Review Sections...11

Scoring the PLT 12

Score Reporting 13

Studying for the PLT 14

Test-taking Tips 15

The Day of the Test 17

PLT Study Schedule 19

Review for Content Category 1: Students as Learners (Chapters 2-5)

CHAPTER 2

Teaching Them All   25

Overview 25

Student Development and Maturation 26

Theories of Cognitive Development 28

Identity Achievement and Diffusion 31

Learning Factors 34

Maslow's Hierarchy of Needs 35

Effective Instruction 37

Metacognition 41

Motivation 42

Students as Learners 45

Jointly Constructed Meaning 52

Learning about the Community 58

Stabilizing Strengths of the Community 60

Coping with Problems in the Community 62

Nature and Nurture 65

Diversity 69

Special Education Legislation 72

Environmental Factors 77

Emotional Factors 79

References 82

CHAPTER 3

Substance Abuse by Students   85

Overview 85

Behaviors Tending Towards Substance Abuse 86

Physical and Behavioral Characteristics of Students
      Under the Influence of Drugs 91

The Use of Referrals 92

Teaching About the Dangers of Substance Abuse 93

References 94

CHAPTER 4

Physical Abuse of Students   95

Overview 95

Symptoms of Abuse 96

Visible Signs of Abuse 98

How to Report Suspicions of Abuse 99

References 101

CHAPTER **5**

Enhancing Comprehension and Mastery of Material   103

Overview 103

Questioning 104

Bloom's Six Levels of Taxonomy 106

Vary Practice Activities 108

Reinforce Retention of Specific Information 111

Provide a Variety of Activities to Promote Retention ... 112

Assist Students During Seatwork 113

Practice Activities Promote Long-Term Retention 115

References 117

Review for Content Category 2: Instruction & Assessment (Chapters 6-9)

CHAPTER **6**

The Physical and Emotional Environment of the Classroom   121

Overview 121

Physical Environment 122

Social and Emotional Climate 123

Academic Learning Time 125

Classroom Behavior 126

Behavior Patterns 128

References 130

CHAPTER 7

Managing Student Behavior in the Classroom   131

Overview 131

Cognitive Development and Moral Decision Making ... 133

Learning Styles and Personality Types 137

Standards for Classroom Behavior 138

Rules and the Student's Role in Decision Making 139

The Teacher's Role 142

Rules and School Safety Issues 147

"With it"-ness in the Classroom 151

Parent-Teacher Communication 153

References 155

CHAPTER 8

Assessment, Tests, and Measurement   157

Overview 157

Purposes of Assessment 159

Teacher-Made Tests 160

Authentic Assessments 161

Standardized Testing 164

Performance-Based Assessment 167

Classroom Tests 168

Principles of Test Construction 169

Test Blueprints 170

Test Items 172

Constructing Test Questions 175

Scoring the Test 180

Evaluating and Revising Tests 182

Preparation for Testing 185

Test Administration 187

Formative Feedback 189

Recording Student and Class Progress 190

Reporting Student and Class Progress 193

Maintaining Permanent Student Records 195

Understanding the Importance of Student Records 196

Summary 197

References 198

CHAPTER **9**

Technology in the Classroom   199

Overview 199

Educational Technology in the Primary Classroom 199

Educational Technology in the
        Secondary Classroom 202

Copyright Laws for Computer Programs.................... 207

References 208

Review for Content Category 3: Communication Techniques (Chapters 10-11)

CHAPTER **10**

Student Participation, Feedback, and Review   211

Overview 211

Effective Use of Language 214

Relationship Between Teachers and Students 214

Feedback 216

Digressions 217

Connected Discourse 218

Marker Expressions 218

Task Attraction and Challenge 219

Scrambled Discourse, Vagueness, and
   Question Overload 220

Provide Clear Feedback to Students 220

Make Specific Statements About
   Students' Responses 225

Methods of Correcting Students' Errors 227

Recapping Significant Points 232

Thesis, Antithesis, and Synthesis 234

Recapping Discussion and Reviewing
   Subject Matter 234

End of the Lesson Recap 236

Journal Writing 237

Cooperative Learning 237

Weekly and Monthly Reviews 239

Summary 241

References 244

CHAPTER 11

Communication in the Classroom   245

Overview 245

Principles of Verbal Communication 246

Voice.. 247

Nonverbal Communication 248

Eye Contact 248

Body Language 250

Media Communication 250

Summary 251

Planning Processes 251

Self-Directed Learning 254

References 255

Review for Content Category 4: Teacher Professionalism (Chapters 12-14)

CHAPTER 12

Goal-Setting 259

Overview 259

Identify Knowledge, Skills, and Attitudes 262

Construct or Adapt Short-Range Objectives 263

Organize and Sequence Short-Range Objectives 265

References 266

CHAPTER 13

Materials, Activities, Managing Time 269

Overview 269

Educational Resources 271

Planning for Resources 271

Print Resources 272

Visual Materials 273

Videodisc and Interactive Video 274

Human Resources 275

Procedures for Learning Success 276

Organizing Activities 277

Outcome-Oriented Learning..................................... 279

Planning and Performance of the
        Classroom Teacher 280

Beginning Classwork Promptly................................. 281

Student Activity 282

Transitions 284

Summary 286

References 286

CHAPTER 14

Methods & Implementation   287

Overview 287

Deductive Strategies 288

Inductive Strategies 290

Cooperative Strategies 294

Discussion Strategies 294

Comparison/Contrast 295

Teaching Styles 296

Directions 298

Objectives 299

Performance Standards 300

Supplies 301

Classroom Assessment 302

References 304

PLT GRADES 5-9 PRACTICE TESTS

Practice Test Answer Sheet   305

Practice Test 1   307

Case Study I 309

Constructed-Response Items 312

Case Study II 313

Constructed-Response Items 315

Case Study III 316

Constructed-Response Items 318

Contents

Case Study IV 319

Constructed-Response Items 322

Multiple-Choice Questions.....................................323

Answer Key..329

Detailed Explanations of Answers.............................330

Practice Test 2   363

Case Study I 365

Constructed-Response Items 368

Case Study II 369

Constructed-Response Items 371

Case Study III 372

Constructed-Response Items 375

Case Study IV 375

Constructed-Response Items 378

Multiple-Choice Questions.....................................379

Answer Key..386

Detailed Explanations of Answers.............................387

Index   419

Installing REA's TESTware®   430

PLT Grades 5–9

Passing the PLT

Passing
the PLT

About this Book and
TEST*ware*®

REA's *Best Teachers' Test Preparation for the PRAXIS PLT: Grades 5–9* provides you with an accurate and complete representation of the Principles of Learning and Teaching (PLT) 5–9 Test. This volume includes customized PLT reviews to provide you with the information and pinpoint strategies needed to pass the exam. We also provide two full-length practice tests based on the most recently administered examinations.

REA's practice tests replicate the actual two-hour PLT, carefully capturing every type of question—and the proper level of difficulty—that you can expect to encounter on the PLT. Following each practice test, you will find an answer key with detailed explanations designed to help you not just identify the correct answer, but also to understand *why* it's correct. Just as important, we explain why the remaining choices are incorrect.

Practice Tests 1 and 2 are included in two formats: in printed form in this book and in TEST*ware*® format on the enclosed CD. We recommend that you begin your preparation by first taking the computerized version of your test. The software provides the added benefits of enforced timed conditions and instantaneous, accurate scoring, making it easier to pinpoint your strengths and weaknesses.

About the Praxis Series

The Praxis Series™ is a group of teacher certification tests developed and administered by Educational Testing Service (ETS). There are three categories of tests in the series.

Praxis I includes the paper-based Pre-Professional Skills Tests (PPST) and the Praxis I Computer-Based Tests (CBT). Both versions cover essentially the same subject matter. These exams measure reading, mathematics, and writing skills. These tests are often a requirement for admission to a teacher education program.

Praxis II includes Subject Assessment/Specialty Area tests, Principles of Learning and Teaching (PLT) tests, and Teaching Foundations tests. These tests are taken after the classroom training, the coursework, and the practicums in most teacher-training programs.

Praxis III is different from the typical multiple-choice and essay tests normally used for assessment purposes. ETS-trained observers evaluate an instructor's performance in the classroom. The ETS assessors use nationally validated criteria for their evaluations. The observers may videotape the lesson, and other teaching experts may critique the resulting tapes.

About the Principles of Learning and Teaching Tests

What are the PLT Tests?

The Principles of Learning and Teaching Test you will be taking is one of three PLTs that come under the Praxis II: Subject Assessments umbrella. Praxis, by the way, is ETS's shorthand for Professional Assessments for Beginning Teachers®. The PLT tests use case studies, constructed-response items, and multiple-choice questions to gauge what ETS calls your "general pedagogical knowledge." Most people who take the PLTs are seeking initial licensure; check with your state's education agency to determine which PLT tests you should take. The four tests are as follows: Early Childhood, K–6, 5–9, and 7–12. The tests cover subject matter that is typically taught in teacher-education courses such as human growth and development, school curriculum, methods of teaching, and other professional development courses. **This book will prepare you to pass the PLT 5–9.**

Who administers the PLT?

The tests are developed and administered by Lawrence Township, N.J.-based ETS, the world's largest private educational testing and measurement organization.

When should I take the PLT 5–9?

The PLT 5–9 is a test for those who have completed or almost completed their teacher education programs. In some states the test is a requirement for initial certification; in other states the test is a requisite for beginning teachers during their first months on the job. Each state establishes its own requirements for certification; some states specify the passing of additional or different tests. Check with your state education agency for details.

When and where does one take the PLTs?

ETS offers the PLT tests six times a year at a number of locations across the nation. The usual testing day is Saturday, but examinees may request an administration on an alternate day if a conflict—such as a religious obligation—exists.

To receive information on upcoming administrations of the PLT, consult the ETS Registration Bulletin. Contact ETS at:

Educational Testing Service
Teaching and Learning Division
P. O. Box 6051
Princeton, NJ 08541-6051
Phone: (609) 771-7395
Website: www.ets.org/praxis
E-mail: praxis@ets.org

Special accommodations are available for candidates who are visually impaired, hearing impaired, physically disabled, or specific learning disabled. Telephone numbers for questions concerning disability services are available.

Disability Services: (609) 771-7780
TTY only: (609) 771-7714

Provisions are also available for examinees whose primary language is not English. The registration booklet includes directions for those requesting such accommodations.

The ETS registration bulletin includes information regarding available test sites; reporting test scores; requesting changes in tests, centers, and dates of test; purchasing additional score reports; and other basic facts. The bulletin also includes information on test retakes. There is even a listing of the more than 30 state certification agencies that require or accept Praxis tests.

Is there a registration fee?

To take a PLT test, the examinee must pay a registration fee which is payable by a check, money order, American Express, Discover, MasterCard, or Visa credit cards. Cash is not accepted for payment.

In certain cases, ETS offers fee waivers. The registration bulletin gives qualifications for receiving this benefit and describes the application process.

How to Use this Book and TEST*ware*®

What do I study first?

Read over our subject reviews and suggestions for test-taking. Studying the reviews thoroughly will reinforce the basic skills you will need to do well on the exam. Make sure to take the practice tests on CD-ROM so you'll be familiar with the format and procedures involved with taking the actual PLT. You can retake the tests printed in this book if you choose.

When should I start studying?

It is never too early to start studying for the PLT. The earlier you begin, the more time you will have to sharpen your skills. Do not procrastinate! Cramming is *not* an effective way to study because it does not allow you the time needed to learn the test material.

It is important, however, to review the material you need to study *one last time* the night before you take the test.

Format of the PLT 5–9

The PLT 5–9 Test contains 24 discrete multiple-choice questions. These questions assess a beginning teacher's knowledge of certain job-related skills and knowledge. Four choices are available for the test-taker to choose from; the options bear the letters A through D.

The PLT also contains four case studies. Three constructed-response questions follow each case study. You will be given two hours to complete the exam. Use the practice test to learn how to pace yourself. You should spend approximately 25 minutes on each case study and 20 minutes on the multiple-choice questions.

Our book contains two full-length model tests; both practice tests completely mirror the PLT 5–9.

The PLT contains four content categories: (1) Students as Learners, (2) Instruction and Assessment, (3) Communication Techniques, and (4) Teacher Professionalism.

The topics covered under the first category, "Students as Learners" include:

- Student development and the learning process

- Students as diverse learners

- Student motivation and the learning environment

This category accounts for approximately 35% of the total score.

The topics covered under the second category, "Instruction and Assessment," include:

- Instructional strategies

- Planning instruction

- Assessment strategies

This category accounts for approximately 35% of the total score.

The topics covered under the third category, "Communication Techniques," include:

- Effective verbal and nonverbal communication

- Cultural and gender differences in communication

- Stimulating discussion and responses in the classroom

This portion of the exam accounts for approximately 15% of the total score.

Finally, the "Teacher Professionalism" topics include:

- The reflective practitioner

- The larger community

This portion of the exam accounts for approximately 15% of the total score.

REA's model exams test the content included under each of the aforementioned topics. Individual test items require different thinking levels, ranging from simple recall to more complex evaluation and problem-solving.

About the Review Sections

The reviews in this book will 1) help you sharpen the basic skills needed to approach the PLT and 2) provide strategies for attacking the questions. By using the reviews in conjunction with the practice tests, you will better prepare yourself for the actual test.

This REA study guide covers each content category in the PLT in the review. When used in concert, the book's review sections and model tests will put you in the best possible position to succeed on the PLT.

Most of what you need to know to answer the questions on the test, you should have learned through your course work and your practical experience in the schools. The education classes you took should have provided you with the expertise to make important decisions about situations you will face as a teacher. Our review should help you fit the information you have acquired into its specific testable category. Reviewing your class notes and textbooks along with systematic use of this book will give you an excellent springboard for passing the PLT.

Scoring The PLT

How do I score my practice test?

The number of raw points awarded on the PLT tests is based on the number of correct answers given. Your scaled score is computed from your total number of raw points in a way that adjusts for the difficulty of the questions. The scoring of the constructed-response items is on a scale of 0-2. Your written response to each question is read and scored by two or more qualified scorers.

Your essay will receive a score of 2 if: The response appropriately answers all parts of the question. The response shows evidence of understanding the case study, the principles of learning and teaching, and how to apply the content categories to the answer.

Your essay will receive a score of 1 if: The response appropriately answers only parts of the question. It will show only some understanding of the case study, the principles of learning and teaching, and how to apply the content categories to the answer.

Your essay will receive a score of 0 if: The response is inappropriate. It does not answer the question nor does it show any understanding of the case study, the principles of learning and teaching, and how to apply the content categories to the answer.

Your passing score will vary depending on the state in which you are taking the test. The following table provides contact information and current passing scores for each of the states that administer the PLT tests. We recommend that you check with your state education agency for the latest information on the PLT battery.

STATE	CONTACT INFORMATION	PASSING SCORE PLT 5-9
AR	(501) 682-4475	164
HI	(808) 586-3276	157
ID	(208) 332-6884	162
KS	(785) 296-8010	161
KY	(502) 564-4606	161
LA	(877) 453-2721	154
MN	(651) 582-8691	155
MO	(573) 751-0051	160
MS	(601) 359-3513	152
OH	(877) 644-6338	168
SC	(803) 734-8466	165
TN	(615) 532-4885	154
UT	(801) 538-7500	160
WV	(304) 558-7826	159
WY	(307) 777-7291	157

Score Reporting

When will I receive my score report and in what form will it be?

ETS mails paper-based test-score reports for the Principles of Learning and Teaching (PLT) Tests four weeks after the test date.

Score reports will list your current score and the highest score you have earned on each test you have taken over the last 10 years.

Along with your score report, ETS will provide you with a booklet that offers details on your scores. For each test date, you may request that ETS send a copy of your scores to as many as three score recipients, provided that each institution or agency is eligible to receive the scores.

Studying for the PLT

It is critical to your success that you choose a time and place for studying that works best for you. Some people set aside a certain number of hours every morning to study; others may choose to study at night before retiring. Only you know what's most effective for you. Be consistent. Use your time wisely. Work out a study routine and stick to it. Don't let your personal schedule interfere and, most of all, don't try cramming the night before the test. There are any number of amazing tales about effective cramming. Don't kid yourself; most of them are false and the rest are about exceptional people who, by definition, aren't like most of us.

When you take the practice tests included on CD-ROM, try to make your testing conditions as much like the actual test as possible. Turn off your television, radio, and telephone. Sit down at a quiet table free from distraction.

As you complete the CD-ROM practice test, thoroughly review the explanations to the questions you answered incorrectly. Take notes on material you will want to go over again or research further.

Keep track of your scores. By doing so, you will be able to gauge your progress and discover your strengths and weaknesses. You should carefully study the material relevant to your areas of difficulty. This will build your test-taking skills, and your confidence!

Test-taking Tips

Although you may not be familiar with tests like the PLT, this book will help acquaint you with this type of examination and help alleviate your test-taking anxieties. Here are seven specific ways to help you become accustomed to the PLT.

1—Become comfortable with the format of the PLT. While you are practicing, simulate the conditions under which you will be taking the actual test. Stay calm and pace yourself. Wear a (noiseless) watch during the practice and during the actual test session. After simulating the test only once, you will automatically boost your chances of doing well. You will be able to sit down for the actual PLT with that much more grasp of the real exam.

2—Read all of the possible answers for the multiple-choice questions. Just because you think you have found the correct response, do not assume that it is truly the best answer. Read through each choice to be sure that you are not making a mistake by jumping to conclusions.

3—Use the process of elimination in selecting the correct answer to the multiple-choice questions. Go through each answer to a question and eliminate as many of the answer choices as possible. By eliminating even one answer choice, you have given yourself a better chance of getting the item correct. You would have a one out of three chance of getting the answer correct; without elimination, you had only a one of four chance. Mark your booklet to indicate the answer(s) you are sure is (are) wrong. Do not leave an answer blank; it is better to guess than not to answer a question on the PLT test.

4—Organize, answer, and review your response to the constructed-response test questions. Before you begin writing your answers to the constructed-response questions, make some notes as to the order you will follow and the supporting details you will include. This outline will help you express yourself well. Remember that anything you write in the section marked "Notes" will not receive a score. For a constructed-response question, give a **complete** answer. Your answer should include structure, appropriate concepts and terminology, and ample supporting details.

5—Work quickly and steadily. You will have two hours to complete the test. Avoid focusing on any one problem too long. Taking the practice tests in this book will help you learn to budget your precious time.

6—Learn the directions and format of the test. Familiarity breeds confidence. But knowing the directions and format is, at a very practical level, a real time-saver, as it will cut the chance of any unwanted surprises. When you sit for the test, it should be just as you thought it would be. By studying the directions and format ahead of time will help you avoid anxiety—and the mistakes a case of the jitters causes.

7—Be sure that the answer oval you are marking corresponds to the number of the question in the test booklet. Multiple-choice sections are machine-graded, and machines know nothing of your intention to mark on the line directly above or below. Marking one wrong answer can throw off your entire answer sheet and sink your score.

The Day of the Test

Before the test

On the day of the test, dress comfortably in layers. You do not want to be distracted by being too hot or too cold while you are taking the test. Plan to arrive at the test center early. This will allow you to collect your thoughts and relax before the test; your early arrival will also spare you the anguish that comes with being late. You should check your registration ticket to verify your arrival time.

Before you leave for the test center, make sure that you have your admission ticket and two forms of identification, one of which must contain a recent photograph, your name, and signature (e.g., a driver's license). You will not gain entry to the test center without proper identification.

You must bring several sharpened No. 2 pencils with erasers for the multiple-choice section and pens for the constructed-response questions. The proctor will not provide pencils or pens at the test center.

To apportion your testing time wisely, you may want to wear a watch to the test center. You may not, however, wear one that makes noise, which may disturb the other test takers. You may not take dictionaries, textbooks, notebooks, calculators, briefcases, or packages into the test center.

During the Test

The PLT includes four case studies, each of which presents a particular teaching situation. Three constructed-response questions relate to problems the case studies pose.

ETS administers the test in one sitting with no breaks. Proctors will enforce procedures to maintain test security.

Once you enter the test center, follow all of the rules and instructions that the test supervisor gives you. If you do not abide by the regulations, the proctor may dismiss you from the test and notify ETS to cancel your score.

When all the examinees have their test materials in hand, the test instructor will provide the directions for completing the test. Follow the directions carefully.

During the test, be sure to mark only one answer per multiple-choice question, erase all unwanted answer and marks completely, and fill in the answers darkly and neatly.

When you are completing the constructed-response sections, take a moment to organize your answer, use a pen, place the answers in the proper place in the test booklet, and track your time as you work.

After the Test

When you finish your test, the proctor will collect your materials and will dismiss the examinees. Go home and relax—you deserve it.

PLT Study Schedule

The following study course schedule allows for thorough preparation to pass the PLT 5–9. This is a suggested seven-week course of study. However, you can condense this schedule if you have less time to study or expand it if you have more time for preparation. You may decide to use your weekends for study and preparation and go about your other business during the week. You may even want to tape record information and listen to your tape in the car. However you decide to study, be sure to adhere to the structured schedule you devise.

Week	Activity
Week 1	*Take the first exam on CD-ROM as a diagnostic test. Your score will indicate your strengths and weaknesses. Make sure to take the test under simulated exam conditions. Review the explanations for the questions you answered incorrectly. Make careful notes of the information you need to use for extra review and study. Assess your essays carefully. Make sure that they meet the criteria detailed for you in the REA Study Guide.*
Week 2	*Study REA's PLT Review. Highlight key terms and information. Take notes on the reviews as you work through them. Writing may aid in your retention of the information. You may also want to record a cassette to listen to as you drive.*
Weeks 3 & 4	*Review other references and sources. Make sure that you also take time to review notes from your previous classes that might help you to prepare for the test. In addition to this guide, review the free ETS publication "Test at a Glance." Use any other supplementary guides and materials that are available to you and that your counselor recommends.*

Week	Activity
Week 5	*Condense your notes and findings. You should develop a structured outline detailing specific facts. You may wish to use index cards or audio tapes to aid you in memorizing important facts and concepts. Be sure to pay attention to the details on the essay.*
Week 6	*Test yourself using the index cards. You may want to have a friend or colleague quiz you on key facts and items.*
	Take the second full-length exam on CD-ROM. Review the explanations for the questions you answered incorrectly. Make notes of additional areas to study and review. Give particular attention to the essays you have written.
Week 7	*Study any areas you consider to be your weaknesses by using your study materials, references, and notes. You may want to retake the tests printed in this book and practice the answers to the constructed-response questions again. The REA study guide provides extra answer sheets for your additional study and practice.*

Week | Activity

End of Week 7 *The night before you take the test, lay out all your materials (pens, pencils, wristwatch, identification, admission ticket, keys, etc.). Review your notes and directions for the test one last time.*

Take the test! Do your best! Afterwards, make notes about the multiple-choice questions you remember and the essay question. You may not share this information with others, but you may find that the information proves useful on other exams that you take.

Relax! Wait for that passing score to arrive.

Content Category 1: Students as Learners

Chapters 2–5

Chapter

2

Teaching Them All

Overview

The teacher should employ a knowledge of physical, academic, and social developmental patterns representing individual differences in order to satisfy the instructional needs of all students in the classroom, and to counsel students about those needs.

This describes the importance of teachers having a basic understanding of the principles of human development in its many dimensions: physically, mentally, emotionally, and socially. It is also important that teachers appreciate a dynamic and interactive view of human development. This approach to understanding human development is one which recognizes that human beings do not develop in a vacuum. People exist in an environment which, friendly or unfriendly, supportive or non-supportive, evokes and provokes reactions from individuals; moreover, the environment is not the only formative factor in one's life People also act in certain ways to shape and form their environment. There is a constant interaction or interplay between people and their environments. Thus, effective teachers must be sensitive to and knowledgeable of both personal characteristics of students and characteristics of their environment.

A teacher enhances students' feelings of self-respect and the respect of other people including those from other cultural, economic, ethnic, and linguistic groups.

Student Development and Maturation

A teacher does not have to be an expert in anatomy and physiology to see the physical changes that accompany students' growth and maturity. The preschool child has trouble grasping pencils or crayons in a manner to facilitate handwriting; however, even most two-year olds can grasp crayons sufficiently to make marks on papers and, thus, enjoy the creative excitement of art.

Physiological changes play a significant role in the development of children as they increase their control of bodily movements and functions and refine their motor skills. Their ability to engage in simple to complex classroom and playground activities increases as they develop. Classroom and playground activities must be adjusted and adapted in order to be developmentally appropriate for the skill levels of the children.

As students enter junior high or begin their secondary education, they again experience important physiological changes with the onset of puberty. With puberty comes changes in primary sexual characteristics and the emergence of secondary sexual characteristics. In addition to bodily characteristics, there is a change in bodily feelings, and there is an increase in sex drive.

Girls, on average, reach maturational milestones before boys. Physical changes may cause embarrassment to both females and males when they draw unwelcome attention; moreover, these changes almost always create some discomfort as adolescents find the body they were familiar and comfortable with to be quite different, sometimes seemingly overnight.

David Elkind has noted two developmental characteristics of adolescence which share a relationship to the physiological changes accompanying maturation. These two characteristics are the *imaginary audience* and the *personal fable.* First, adolescents, preoccupied with their own physiological changes, often assume that others are equally intrigued by these changes in appearance and behavior; they may feel that others are staring at them, watching their every move, scrutinizing their behavior for one misstep or their appearance for any flaws. If everyone is watching, then it is imperative to be, to act, and to look just right. In today's culture, that means wearing the right clothes and having all the right brand names and status symbols. Because of adolescents' sensitivity to attention (especially the wrong kind of attention, that is, not fitting in, not being "right"), it is especially important that teachers of this age group be aware of the *imaginary audience* phenomenon and be sensitive to social interactions in the classroom. It, indeed, is important that teachers not contribute to creating unwanted attention or to stigmatizing or stereotyping students.

Personal fable refers to the belief that "My life is different from everyone else's; therefore, no one can understand how I feel or what I think. No one has ever felt or thought what I feel and think." This out-of-focus view tends to support both a feeling of isolation (which may be precipitated by the changing sensations from a body that is undergoing biological changes) and a willingness to engage in risky behaviors (thinking that only others have car accidents when they drive dangerously).

In sum, these two characteristics of adolescence are examples of how physical changes accompany, and perhaps even evoke, emotional and cognitive changes as individuals grow and mature. Both phenomena of imaginary audience and personal fable have emotional features (fear of rejection, fear of isolation, fear of difference, shame, guilt from increased sexual feelings, frustration, and so forth) and both describe a feature of adolescent cognitive ability: the ability to think about one's self as an object of one's own and of others' thoughts. The developmental epistemologist Jean Piaget explained that this way of thinking represents the cognitive stage of formal operations.

Cognition is a term commonly used to refer to all the processes whereby knowledge is acquired; the term can be used to cover very basic perceptual processes, such as smell, touch, sound, and so forth, to very advanced operations, such as analysis, synthesis, and critical thinking.

Theories of Cognitive Development

Until his death in 1980, Jean Piaget was a predominant figure in the field of cognitive psychology. It is safe to postulate that perhaps no other single individual has had greater influence on educational practices than Piaget. Basically, his theory of cognitive development is based on the notion that cognitive abilities (or one's ability to think) are developed as individuals mature physiologically, and they have opportunities to interact with their environment. Piaget described these interactions as the *equilibration of accommodation* and *assimilation* cycles or processes. In other words, when individuals (who, according to Piaget, are innately endowed with certain cognitive predispositions and capabilities) encounter a new or novel stimulus, they are brought into a state of *disequilibrium.*

That is a way of saying that they are thrown off balance; they do not know or understand that which is new or unfamiliar. However, through the complementary processes of *accommodation* (adjusting prior knowledge gained through former experiences and interactions) and *assimilation* (fitting together the new information with what has been previously known or understood), individuals come to know or understand that which is new. Once again, individuals are returned to a state of *equilibrium* where they remain until the next encounter with something unfamiliar. For Piaget, this is how learners learn.

Piaget also predicted that certain behaviors and ways of thinking characterize individuals at different ages. For this reason, his theory is considered a *stage* theory. *Stage* theories share the common tenet that certain characteristics will occur in predictable sequences and at certain times in the life of the individual.

According to Piaget, there are four stages of cognitive development, beginning with the *sensorimotor stage* describing individuals from birth to around the age of two. The second stage, *preoperational* (describing cognitive behavior between the ages of two and seven), is characterized by egocentrism, rigidity of thought, semilogical reasoning, and limited social cognition; some cognitive psychologists have observed that this stage seems to describe how individuals think more in terms of what they can't do than what they can do. This stage describes the way that children in preschool and kindergarten go about problem-solving; also, many children in the primary grades may be at this stage in their cognitive development.

The next two stages, however, may be most important for elementary and secondary school teachers since they describe cognitive development during the times that most students are in school. The third stage, *concrete operations,* is the beginning of operational thinking and describes the thinking of children between the ages of 7 and 11. Learners at this age begin to decenter. They are able to take into consideration viewpoints other than their own. They can perform transformations, meaning that they can understand reversibility, inversion, reciprocity, and conservation. They can group items into categories. They can make inferences about reality and engage in inductive reasoning; they increase their quantitative skills, and they can manipulate symbols if they are given concrete examples with which to work. This stage of cognitive development is the threshold to higher-level learning for students.

Finally, *formal operations* is the last stage of cognitive development and opens wide the door for higher-ordered, critical thinking. This stage describes the way of thinking for learners between the ages of 11 and 15 and, for Piaget, constitutes the ultimate stage of cognitive development (thus also describing adult thinking). Learners at this stage of cognitive development can engage in logical, abstract, and hypothetical thought; they can use the scientific method, meaning they can formulate hypotheses, isolate influences, and identify cause-and-effect relationships. They can plan and anticipate verbal cues. They can engage in both deductive and inductive reasoning, and they can operate on verbal statements exclusive of concrete experiences or examples. These cognitive abilities characterize the highest levels of thought.

Identity Achievement and Diffusion

Another theoretical approach to understanding human development is offered by Erik Erikson, another important stage theorist, who described psychosocial development. For each of eight stages, he identified a developmental task explained in terms of two polarities. For the purposes of this discussion, only those stages describing school-aged individuals will be included.

According to Erikson, preschoolers and primary-school aged children must be able to function in the outside world independently of parents; when children are able to do this, they achieve a sense of *initiative;* when children are not able to move away from total parental attachment and control, they experience a sense of *guilt.* Thus, this stage of psychosocial development is the stage of *initiative versus guilt.* The child's first venture away from home and into the world of school has considerable significance when viewed in light of this theory; it is imperative that teachers assist students in their first experiences on their own, away from parental control.

Erikson's next stage of development is one involving a tension between *industry* and *inferiority.* For example, if the child who enters school (thus achieving initiative) acquires the skills (including academic skills such as reading, writing, and computation, as well as social skills in playing with others, communicating with others, forming friendships, and so forth) which enable him or her to be successful in school, then the child achieves a sense of *industry;* failure to achieve these skills leads to a sense of *inferiority.*

Around the time students enter junior high, they begin the developmental task of achieving *identity.* According to Erikson, the struggle to achieve identity is one of the most important developmental tasks and one which creates serious psychosocial problems for adolescents. For example, even the individual who has successfully achieved all the important developmental milestones (such as initiative and industry) now finds him- or herself in a state of flux—everything (body, feelings, thoughts) is changing. The adolescent starts to ask, "Who am I?" Erikson believed that once adolescents find out what they believe in—what their goals, ideas, and values are—they can attain identity achievement; failure to discover these things leads to identity diffusion.

By the time many students reach high school, they are entering a stage of young adulthood—for Erikson, a psychosocial stage characterized by the polarities of *intimacy* and *isolation.* Individuals at this stage of development begin to think about forming lasting friendships, even marital unions. Erikson would argue that many psychosocial problems experienced by young adults have their origin in the individual's failure to achieve identity during the preceding stage; the young man or woman who does not know who he or she really is cannot achieve true intimacy.

For the classroom teacher, knowledge of psychosocial stages of human development can result in greater effectiveness. For example, the effective teacher realizes the importance of helping students achieve the skills necessary to accomplish crucial developmental tasks. According to Erikson's theory, teachers of elementary school-aged learners would do well to focus on teaching academic and social skills, helping students gain proficiency in skills that will enable learners to be productive members of society. On the other hand, secondary school teachers would do well to keep in mind, as they engage students in higher-ordered thinking activities appropriate to their stage of cognitive development, that students have pressing psychological and social needs in their struggle to achieve identity and to attain intimacy.

By understanding key principles of human development in its multiple dimensions, effective teachers provide students with both age-appropriate and developmentally-appropriate instruction. This, in sum, is the best instruction. It is instruction that addresses all the needs of students—physical, emotional, and social—as well as cognitive (or intellectual) needs.

Sample Multiple-Choice Question

Rueben Stein is a sixth-grade teacher who wants to teach his class about the classification system in the animal kingdom. He decides to introduce this unit to his class by having the students engage in general classification activities. He brings to class a paper bag filled with 30 household items. He dumps the contents of the bag onto a table and then asks the students, who will collaborate in groups of three or four, to put like items into piles and then to justify or explain why they placed certain items into a particular pile.

By assigning this task to his students, Mr. Stein is providing his students with a developmentally-appropriate task because

(A)   sixth-grade students like to work in groups.

(B)   the items in the bag are household items with which most students will be familiar.

(C)   the assignment gives students the opportunity to practice their skills at categorizing.

(D)   the assignment will give students a task to perform while the teacher finishes grading papers.

The correct response is **(C)**; According to Piaget's theory of cognitive development, students in sixth-grade would be at the stage of concrete operational thought.

Students at this stage of cognitive development would be able to categorize items. Choices (A), (B), and (D) are inappropriate for the following reasons. Choice (A) is a false statement. Although some students will like to work in groups, some students will prefer to work alone—at this and at any age group or cognitive stage. Preferring to learn in groups (or socially) or to learn alone (or independently) is a characteristic of learning style or preference, not a characteristic of cognitive or affective development. Choice (B) is irrelevant to the teacher's intent in assigning the task. Students could just as easily work with unfamiliar items, grouping them by observable features independent of their use or function. Choice (D) is not a good choice under any circumstances. Teachers should assiduously avoid giving students assignments merely to keep them busy while the teacher does something else. All assignments should have an instructional purpose.

Learning Factors

The teacher considers environmental factors that may affect learning by designing a supportive and responsive classroom community that promotes all students' learning and self-esteem. This competency addresses the need that teachers have to be able to recognize and identify both external and internal factors which affect student learning. The preceding discussion on human development primarily emphasized the characteristics of learners or what may be considered internal factors. Internal factors, beyond the general characteristics that humans share as they grow and mature, also include factors such as students' personality characteristics, their self-concept and sense of self-esteem, their self-discipline and self-control, their ability to cope with stress, and their general outlook on life.

External factors are not individual traits; however, they do have an impact on student learning and progress. These include the home environment and family relationships, peer relationships, community situations, and the school environment. In other words, external factors constitute the context in which the student lives and learns.

Maslow's Hierarchy of Needs

Abraham Maslow's hierarchy of human needs is a model applicable to many diverse fields, including education, business and industry, health and medical professions, and more. Maslow identified different levels of individuals' needs in a hierarchical sequence, meaning that lower-level needs must be satisfied before individuals can progress to higher levels of achievement. He identified the fulfillment of basic physiological needs as fundamental to individuals' sense of well-being and their ability to engage in any meaningful activity. Simply stated, students' physiological needs (to have hunger and thirst satisfied, to have sleep needs met, to be adequately warm, and so forth) must be met before students can perform school tasks. Today's schools provide students with breakfast and lunch when needed, and great effort and expense are often directed toward heating and cooling school buildings.

Maslow's second level of need concerns safety. Again, students must feel safe from harm and danger before they are ready to learn. Today, schools are often equipped with metal detectors to increase students' sense of safety. In some schools, guards and security officers patrol the halls.

The third level of need, according to Maslow's theory, is the need for affiliation or the need to belong and to be accepted by others. Although this need may, at first glance, seem less related to the student's environment, it does, indeed, refer to the student's social environment. Students need the opportunity to develop social relationships and to establish friendships among their peers. In essence, Maslow determined that environmental factors are important in education.

Another significant principle of human development arises from a long debate between experts who believe that innate characteristics (those the individual is born with) play the most important role in determining who the individual will become and what he or she will do versus those who believe that environmental characteristics are most important. This argument is referred to in the literature as the *nature versus nurture* debate.

Effective Instruction

The teacher understands how learning occurs and can apply this understanding to design and implement effective instruction. It is one thing for teachers to have command of their subject matter. It is a given that English teachers will be able to write well, that math teachers will be able to compute and calculate, that science teachers will know and understand science, and so forth. However, it is something else—and something at least as important—that teachers know how to teach.

When teachers understand developmental processes common to all learners, and how environmental features and learning styles—varied and diverse—affect learning, then they are better able to design and deliver effective instruction. Although there may be some intuitive aspects to teaching (and it seems that some people were born to teach), teaching skills can be acquired through processes of introspection, observation, direct instruction, self-evaluation, and experimentation.

How teachers teach should directly relate to how learners learn. Theories of cognitive development describe how students learn new information and acquire new skills. There are many theories of cognitive development, two of which will be included in this review; they are (a) Piagetian (or Neo-Piagetian) theory, and (b) information-processing theory.

Piagetian theory (including Neo-Piagetian theory) describes learning in discrete and predictable stages. Therefore, teachers who understand this theory can provide students with developmentally-appropriate instruction. This theory also describes how learners move from simpler ways of thinking, to more complex ways of problem solving and thinking. For teachers, there are many important implications of this theoretical perspective. For example, teachers must create enriched environments that present learners with multiple opportunities to encounter new and unfamiliar stimuli—whether they are objects or ideas. Teachers must also provide learners with opportunities to engage in extended dialogue with adults. According to Piaget's theory, conversational interactions with adults are a key component in cognitive development, especially for the acquisition of formal operations (or higher-ordered thinking skills). Moreover, it is important that adults (and teachers in particular) model desired behaviors; teachers must reveal their own complex ways of thinking and solving problems to students.

On the other hand, information-processing theories of human development take a different approach to describing and understanding how learners learn. Similar to a computer, information-processing theories determine the processing demands of a particular cognitive challenge (or problem to solve). They describe through a detailed task-analysis of how the human mind changes external objects or events into a useful form according to certain, precisely specified rules or strategies. This process is similar to the way a computer programmer programs a computer to perform a function. Thus, information-processing theories focus on the process—how the learner arrives at a response or answer.

A brief analysis of one information-processing theory will serve to illustrate this point. Sternberg's (1985) triarchic theory of intelligence is a theory that takes into account three features of learning. Those three features are (a) the mechanics or components of intelligence (including both higher-ordered thinking processes, such as planning, decision making and problem solving, and lower-ordered processes, such as making inferences, mapping, selectively encoding information, retaining information in memory, transferring new information in memory, and so forth); (b) the learner's experiences; and (c) the learner's context (including the adaptation to environments, and the shaping and selecting of those environments).

According to Sternberg, learners' use of the mechanics of intelligence is influenced by their experiences. To illustrate, some cognitive processes (such as those required in reading) become automatic as a result of continued exposure to and practice of those skills. Learners who come from homes where parents read and where there are lots of different reading materials, tend to be more proficient readers; certainly, students who read a lot become more proficient readers. Those learners who are exposed to reading activities and who have ample opportunities to practice reading have greater skill and expertise in reading; and, in a cyclical manner, students who have skills in reading like to read. Conversely, those who lack reading skills don't like to read. Students who don't like to read, don't read; thus, their reading ability fails to improve.

An information-processing approach acknowledges that not only are individuals influenced by their environments and adapt to those environments, but they also are active in shaping their own environments. In other words, a child who wants to read but who has no books at home may ask his or her parents to buy books, or may go to the library to read, or check out books to read at home.

Information-processing theory is of interest to educators because of its insistence on the idea that intelligent performance can be facilitated through instruction and direct training. In sum, intelligent thinking can be taught. Sternberg has urged teachers to identify the mental processes that academic tasks require and to teach learners those processes; he challenges teachers to teach students what processes to use, when and how to use them, and how to combine them into strategies for solving problems and accomplishing assignments.

Teachers who wish to follow Sternberg's advice might choose to begin teaching by identifying *instructional objectives,* that is, what students should be able to do as a result of instruction. Second, teachers would analyze the objectives in terms of identifying the *instructional outcomes,* those being the tasks or assignments that students can perform as a result of achieving the instructional objectives. Third, teachers would analyze instructional outcomes in terms of the *cognitive skills* or mental processes required to perform those tasks or assignments. After following these three steps the teacher is ready to conduct a *preassessment* (or pretest) to determine what students already know.

Instruction is then based on the results of the preassessment, with teachers focusing on directly teaching the cognitive skills needed in order for students to perform the task(s). Following instruction, teachers would conduct a *postassessment* (or post-test) to evaluate the results of instruction. Further instruction would be based on the results of the postassessment, which would reveal whether students had achieved expected outcomes, and whether teachers had achieved instructional objectives.

Regardless of which theoretical perspective teachers adopt—even if at times they find themselves taking a rather eclectic approach and borrowing elements from several theoretical bases—it is helpful for teachers to consider if they are structuring their classrooms to satisfy learners' needs or merely their own needs as teachers. Furthermore, if the teacher's goal is to enhance his/her effectiveness by facilitating learners' knowledge and skill acquisition, then he/she will engage continuously in a process of self-examination and self-evaluation.

Metacognition

Self-examination and self-evaluation are both types of *metacognitive* thinking. *Metacognition* is a term used to describe what, how, and why people know what they know when they know it. In short, it is thinking about thinking and knowing about knowing. Cognitive psychologists describe metacognition as a characteristic of higher-ordered, mature, and sophisticated thinking. Generally speaking, as learners achieve higher levels of cognitive skills, they also increase their metacognitive skills. Therefore, not only should teachers engage in metacognitive thinking, they should model this thinking for their students, and encourage their students to develop metacognitive skills.

According to J.H. Flavell, metacognition can be understood in terms of (a) metacognitive knowledge and (b) metacognitive control. Basically, metacognitive knowledge is what learners need to know, and metacognitive control is what learners need to do. Metacognitive control, therefore, is in the hands of the learner. Teachers cannot control learners' behavior, although they can encourage or admonish the behavior. The best that teachers can do is help learners expand their metacognitive awareness and knowledge.

Awareness can be increased by talking about metacognition. Flavell has explained that there are three kinds of metacognitive knowledge: (a) person knowledge, (b) task knowledge, and (c) strategy knowledge.

Person knowledge falls into one of three categories: (a) intraindividual knowledge, (b) interindividual knowledge, and (c) universal knowledge. First, intraindividual knowledge is what the learner knows or understands about him- or herself. Therefore, it is important that learners have opportunities to learn about themselves, their interests, abilities, propensities, and so forth. For this reason (among others), it is important that learners have opportunities to learn about their own learning style and their perceptual strengths. It is also helpful for them to have opportunities to examine their personalities, values, and goals.

Furthermore, in a model that recognizes the dynamic nature of instruction, that is, one which recognizes that the learner also knows certain things and can contribute to the classroom, the teacher realizes that he or she is a learner, too. Teachers, then, can benefit from examining their own learning style, perceptual strengths, personalities, values, and goals. Moreover, it can be extremely beneficial for teachers to consider their own instructional style.

Motivation

The teacher understands how motivation affects group and individual behavior and learning and can apply this understanding to promote student learning. Students often say that they like teachers who can motivate them when, in fact, teachers are not the sole reason for students' motivation. Motivation is a student's responsibility; motivation comes from within the student. However, effective teachers will help students develop self-discipline, self-control, and self-motivation. These skills of self-management can be taught, yet they require a great deal of effort and practice in order for students to gain true proficiency.

When students say that they like or want teachers who motivate them, they are probably referring to some characteristics that teachers possess that are attractive and interesting to them. It is also true that teachers can influence motivation—that teachers can promote and/or inhibit motivation in the classroom by their attitudes and their actions.

One researcher, M.B. Baxter-Magolda, has offered three guiding principles that will lead to greater teaching effectiveness in the classroom. Interestingly, each of these principles leads to empowering students and, thus, are motivational in nature.

The first principle is to validate students as knowers. This principle is based on the idea of the active learner who brings much to the classroom (the dynamic view of human development). How can teachers validate students? Baxter-Magolda suggests that teachers display a caring attitude toward students. This means that it is appropriate for teachers to take an interest in students, and to learn about their likes, dislikes, interests, and hobbies, both in school and outside school. This also means that it's acceptable for teachers to show enthusiasm and excitement for their classes, not only for the subject-matter they teach, but for the students they teach as well. It also means, as Carol Tavris noted, that it is good for teachers to show empathy for students' emotional needs.

Baxter-Magolda also recommends that teachers question authority by example and let students know that they, as teachers, can also be questioned. This means that teachers model critical thinking skills in the classroom. Teachers can question authority when they examine and evaluate readings—whether from textbooks or other sources. Teachers can question authority when they teach propaganda techniques, exposing advertising claims and gimmicks. Teachers can question authority when they discuss the media and how so-called news sources shape and form public opinion. There are numerous opportunities for teachers to integrate current affairs and public opinion into the curriculum, and to inculcate their students with both critical thinking and higher-ordered reasoning skills.

Also, when teachers allow students to question them, teachers are acknowledging that everyone is a learner. Everyone should participate in a lifelong process of continuous learning. It is no shame or disgrace for the teacher to admit that sometimes he or she doesn't know the answer to every question. This gives the teacher the opportunity to show students how adults think, how they have a level of awareness (metacognition) when they don't know something, and how they go about finding answers to their questions. Teachers who admit that they don't have all the answers have the opportunity to show students how answers can be found and/or can reveal to students that there are no easy answers to some of life's most difficult questions.

Third, to validate students as knowers, teachers can value students' opinions, ideas, and comments. Teachers' affirmations include smiles and nods of approval, positive comments (such as, "That's a good answer."), and encouraging cues (such as, "That may seem like a reasonable answer, but can you think of a better answer?" or, "Can you explain what you mean by that answer?"). Validating students as knowers also means supporting students' voices, that is, giving them ample opportunities to express their own ideas, to share their opinions, and to make their own contributions to the classroom. These opportunities can include times of oral discussion as well as written assignments.

Students as Learners:

Behaviorism, John B. Watson, and B. F. Skinner

Behaviorism has its emphases on experimental methods and on variables that one can observe, measure, and manipulate. Experiments often focus on managing one variable and measuring the effects on another variable. This theory of personality suggests that one's environment can affect one's behavior.

John B. Watson and B. F. Skinner (1904-1990) are two psychologists who outline some of the basic theories and terms associated with behaviorism. John Broadhus Watson advanced the behaviorist position in his book *Behavior: An Introduction to Comparative Psychology* (1914); he suggested that reflexes, stimulus-response associations, and reinforcers could explain human behavior.

Operant conditioning is the basis of B. F. Skinner's entire system. While the organism is "operating," it receives a reinforcer, or a reinforcing stimulus. Some of its basic premises are:

1.   A reinforcing stimulus may increase the operant, or the behavior occurring just before the reinforcer; this is operant conditioning.

2.   A behavior may be followed by a consequence; the nature of the consequence may modify the tendency of the organism to repeat the behavior in the future.

3.   A reinforcing stimulus following a behavior results in the increased probability of that behavior occurring again.

4.   A behavior no longer followed by a reinforcing stimulus results in a decreased probability of that behavior occurring again.

5.   An aversive stimulus following a behavior results in a decreased probability of that behavior occurring again.

6.   If the experimenter removes an aversive stimulus that is in effect, it is negative reinforcement.

7.   The removal of an aversive stimulus following a behavior may result in an increased probability of that behavior repeating.

Skinner began his experiments with continuous reinforcement, which meant that every time the organism performed the behavior, it received positive reinforcement. Skinner also used fixed ratio scheduling, which meant there was a fixed ratio between the behaviors and their reinforcers. With a fixed interval schedule, he used a timing device; Skinner found the organism tended to speed up the behavior when the time for reinforcement was near and slowed down the behavior right after the reinforcement. With a variable schedule, extinction of the behavior in the organism is not likely.

There are limitations to implementing theories of behaviorism in the classroom.

1.   It is often difficult to determine positive and negative reinforcement for individuals.

2.   Variables in a classroom are often difficult to control.

3.   It may be difficult for the teacher to produce internal changes.

4.   Positive and negative reinforcements are not always possible—or perhaps even desirable.

5.   Varying the intervals between the behavior and the reward/punishment may affect the response.

The therapy technique based on Skinner's work is behavior modification. This therapy suggests extinguishing an undesirable behavior by removing its reinforcement; a desirable behavior should replace the undersirable behavior as a result of the absence of reinforcement.

Students as Learners: Albert Bandura

Albert Bandura added to the principles of behaviorism. His theory of reciprocal determinism suggests that behavior, the environment, and a person's psychological processes may change.

Bandura ceases to be a strict behaviorist and begins to resemble a cognitivist when he introduces the images and the language of the individual into the experiments. Bandura helped to begin the cognitivist movements.

Bandura also found that an individual may learn by observing. People may, therefore, change their behavior without rewards for approximation. Bandura calls the phenomenon of observing a behavior and approximating that behavior by the name *modeling.*

Bandura noted that attention, retention (remembering), and a reproduction of the behavior were often steps in modeling. He also noted that practice and even imagining the reproduction of a behavior may enhance one's ability to perform it. Motivation helps bring about imitation.

Students as Learners: L. S. Vygotsky

Comparable to Bandura's work is the work of L. S. Vygotsky. Vygotsky asserts that social interaction plays a fundamental role in cognition development. He emphasizes that in the child's cultural development, every function appears twice: on the social level and (later) on the individual level.

Another theory he advances is the zone of proximal development (ZPD). Vygotsky insists that the potential for cognitive development is limited to a time span—the ZPD. Vygotsky purports that the zone depends upon full social interaction and that adult guidance and/or peer collaboration can advance the range of skill.

Vygotsky explains consciousness as a product of socialization. One's first word serves the purpose of communicating; once one masters this speech (brought about through socialization), it becomes internal and allows for inner speech.

Students as Learners: Howard Gardner

Howard Gardner suggests that the traditional notion of intelligence, based on testing for IQ, is too limited; he proposes eight different intelligences:

- Linguistic Intelligence,

- Logical-Mathematical Intelligence,

- Spatial Intelligence,

- Bodily-Kinesthetic Intelligence,

- Musical Intelligence,

- Interpersonal Intelligence,

- Intrapersonal Intelligence, and

- Naturalist Intelligence.

Gardner advises teachers to present instruction in a wide variety of ways. He also encourages adults to develop their sense of self in a variety of ways.

Students as Learners: Jerome Bruner

A main theme suggested by Jerome Bruner is that learning is an active process. Learners, in his opinion, can construct new ideas or concepts from their past or present knowledge. Bruner stated in 1996 (*Theory of Instruction*) that there are four major aspects to instruction:

- creating a predisposition towards learning,

- structuring a body of knowledge so that the learner can easily grasp it,

- determining the best sequences for presenting the material; and

- presenting the stimuli, reinforcing stimuli, aversive stimuli, rewards, and punishments appropriately.

Students as Learners: John Dewey (1859-1952)

Influenced by G. Stanley Hall (a prominent American experimental psychologist) and George Sylvester Morris (a Hegelian philosopher), John Dewey focused his philosophical interests on "the theory of inquiry" or "the theory of knowledge." Dewey's education philosophy is *instrumentalism,* or pragmatism. Dewey de-emphasized rote learning and dogmatic instruction; he emphasized learning-by-doing.

Students as Learners: Educational Scaffolding

Educational scaffolding is a technique used to provide guidance to students as they conduct research, but the technique does not limit the student in the investigation. Ideally, educational scaffolding will

1. Provide direction.

2. Clarify purpose.

3. Keep students on task.

4. Offer the assessment (the rubric) to clarify expectations.

5. Supply some suggestions for sources.

6. Make available a lesson/activity without problems because the teacher has prepared well.

7. Be an efficient instructional technique.

8. Generate thinking.

Students as Learners: Gagné-Ausubel Pattern of Lecture (GAP)

Robert Gagné and Davis Ausubel sought to devise a way to make the lecture method more effective. There are ways to help the students benefit from this teaching method. Their plan to improve the lecture method is GAP. The steps are to:

1. Begin the lecture by focusing on an event to gain the attention of the students and introducing a question that can only be answered with the lecture content.

2. Present the new content. The lecturer should limit the lecture sessions to about 15 minutes; the lecturer may wish to also use questioning to measure if learning is occurring.

3. Allow the students to practice the new content. Working in groups may be an effective way to practice some content.

4. The teacher should monitor the students as they practice the content. The instructor may provide feedback on their work and perhaps even discuss the work.

5. The teacher may conclude the session by having the groups/ individuals present their results and by calling attention to the differences in results.

6. Make an assignment for some part of the content.

GAP will help students:

- to be active learners,

- to learn from their peers,

- to profit from group work,

- to continue the work outside of class,

- to receive feedback on their work in the lecture session.

Jointly Constructed Meaning

Another principle in Baxter-Magolda's guidelines for teaching effectiveness is for teachers and students to recognize that learning is a process of jointly-constructing meaning. To explain, Baxter-Magolda says that it is important for teachers to engage in dialogue with students (also an important concept in Piagetian theory), and that teachers emphasize mutual learning. Also in agreement with Piagetian principles, Baxter-Magolda recommends that teachers reveal their own thinking processes as they approach subjects, as they analyze and understand new subjects, and as they solve problems and reach decisions. She further advises that teachers share leadership and promote collegial learning (group work), acknowledging that individual achievement is not the sole purpose or focus for learning. By allowing students to collaborate, they also will learn significant lessons directly applicable to work situations where most accomplishments are the result of team efforts, not the sole efforts of individuals.

Baxter-Magolda's final principle for teachers is to situate learning in the students' own experiences. She suggests that this be done by letting students know that they are wanted in class by using inclusive language (avoiding ethnic and cultural bias and stereotyping, and instead using gender-neutral and inclusive language), and focusing on activities. Activities are important for motivation because they give learners things to become actively involved in—arousing their attention and interest, and giving them an outlet for their physical and mental energy. Activities can have an additional benefit in that they can serve to connect students to each other, especially when students are given opportunities to participate in collaborative learning, and to work in groups. Finally, in situating learning in students' own experiences, it is important to consider the use of personal stories in class as appropriate (that is, without violating anyone's right to privacy and confidentiality). Moreover, teachers can share personal stories which allow them to connect with students in a deeper and more personal way.

Robert Coles, the child psychologist, Harvard professor, and author of numerous scholarly and popular books, wrote of his experiences teaching in a Boston inner-city high school. He told of his disillusionment and his struggle to claim students' respect and attention so that he could teach them. Finally, there was a classroom confrontation, followed by a self-revelation (that he was able to show his students what he was like as a person). He shared some of his thoughts and feelings about loneliness. He spoke about his own boyhood experiences of visiting museums with his mother and what she taught him about art. In the end, he too had a revelation. He concluded that when teachers share what we have learned about ourselves with our students, we often can transcend the barriers of class and race. A teacher can change a "me" and a "them" (the students) into an "us." Building camaraderie this way then becomes an optimal starting point for teaching and learning. Dr. Coles' experience was that telling his story to the class was a step toward helping his students claim some motivation of their own.

When students assume responsibility for their own motivation, they are learning a lesson of personal empowerment. Unfortunately, although personal empowerment is probably one of the most important lessons anyone ever learns, it is a lesson infrequently taught in classrooms across the country.

Empowerment has at least four components, one of which is *self-esteem*. A good definition of self-esteem is that it is my opinion of me, your opinion of you. It is what we think and believe to be true about ourselves, not what we think about others and not what they think about us. Self-esteem appears to be a combination of self-efficacy and self-respect as seen against a background of self-knowledge.

Self-efficacy, simply stated, is one's confidence in one's own ability to cope with life's challenges. Self-efficacy refers to having a sense of control over life or, better, over one's responses to life. Experts say that ideas about self-efficacy are established by the time children reach the age of four. Because of this early establishment of either a feeling of control or no control, classroom teachers may find that even primary grade students believe that they have no control over their life—that it makes no difference what they do or how they act. Therefore, it is all the more important that teachers attempt to help all students achieve coping skills and a sense of self-efficacy.

Control, in this definition of self-efficacy, can be examined in regard to external or internal motivators. For example, external motivators include such things as luck and the roles played by others in influencing outcomes. Internal motivators are variables within the individual. To explain, if a student does well on a test and is asked, "How did you do so well on that test?," a student who relies on external motivators might reply, "Well, I just got lucky," or "The teacher likes me." If the student failed the test and is asked why, the student dependent on external motivators might answer, "Well, it wasn't my lucky day," or "The teacher doesn't like me," or "My friends caused me to goof off and not pay attention so I didn't know the answers on the test." A student who relies on internal motivators and who does well on a test may explain, "I am smart and always do well on tests," or "I studied hard and that's why I did well." On the other hand, even the student who relies on internal motivators can do poorly on tests and then may explain, "I'm dumb and that's why I don't do well," or "I didn't think the test was important and I didn't try very hard." Even though students have similar experiences, in regard to issues of control, what is important is how students explain their experiences. If students have external motivators, they are likely to either dismiss their performance (success or failure) as matters of luck or to credit or blame the influence of others. If students have internal motivators, then they are likely to attribute their performance to either their intelligence and skills (ability), or their effort.

Students who have external motivators need help understanding how their behavior contributes to and influences outcomes in school. Students need clarification as to how grades are determined and precise information about how their work is evaluated. Students who have internal motivators but low self-esteem (such as thinking, "I'm dumb") need help identifying their strengths and assets (something that can be accomplished when students are given information about learning styles). In this way, self-efficacy can be enhanced.

Another factor in empowerment is *self-respect*. Self-respect is believing that one deserves happiness, achievement, and love. Self-respect is treating one's self at least as nicely as one treats other people. Many students are not aware of their internal voices (which are established at an early age). Internal voices are constantly sending messages, either positive or negative. Psychologists say that most of us have either a generally positive outlook on life and our inner voice sends generally positive messages ("You're okay," "People like you," "Things will be all right," and so forth), or a generally negative outlook on life and an inner voice sending negative messages ("You're not okay," "You're too fat, skinny, ugly, stupid," and so forth).

Many students need to become aware of their inner voice and how it can be setting them up for failure. They need to learn that they can tell their inner voice to stop sending negative messages, and that they can reprogram their inner voice to be kinder, gentler, and to send positive messages. However, it does require effort, practice, and time to reprogram the inner voice.

Two tools which can help students in the reprogramming process are *affirmations* and *visualizations*. Affirmations are statements describing what students want. Affirmations must be personal, positive, and written in the present tense. What makes affirmations effective are details. For example, instead of saying, "I am stupid," students can be encouraged to say, "I am capable. I do well in school because I am organized, I study daily, I get all my work completed on time, and I take my school work seriously." Affirmations must be repeated until they can be said with total conviction.

Visualizations are images students can create whereby they see themselves the way they want to be. For example, if a student wants to improve his or her typing skills, then the student evaluates what it would look like, sound like, and feel like to be a better typist. Once the student identifies the image, then the student has to rehearse that image in his or her mind, including as many details and sensations as possible. Both visualization and affirmation can restructure attitudes and behaviors. They can be tools for students to use to increase their motivation.

Finally, the fourth component of empowerment is *self-knowledge*. Self-knowledge refers to an individual's strengths and weaknesses, assets and liabilities; self-knowledge comes about as a result of a realistic self-appraisal (and can be achieved by an examination of learning styles). Achieving self-knowledge also requires that students have opportunities to explore their goals and values.

Students who know what their goals and values are can more easily see how education will enable them to achieve those goals and values. Conversely, students cannot be motivated when they do not have goals and values, or when they do not know what their goals and values are. In other words, without self-knowledge, motivation is impossible. Therefore, teachers who follow Baxter-Magolda's guidelines for effective instruction and who teach their students about personal empowerment are teachers who realize the importance of motivation and who set the stage for students to claim responsibility for their own successes and failures. Such teachers help students to become motivated to make changes and to accomplish more.

Sample Multiple-Choice Question

Ben Douglas is a high school history teacher. His class is studying the Korean Conflict when a student brings up a question about the morality of the war in Vietnam. This is not a subject that Mr. Douglas is prepared to teach at the time.

In response to the student's question, Mr. Douglas

(A)   tells the student that the day's topic is the Korean Conflict and suggests that the student bring up the question later on in the term.

(B)   invites the class to respond to the student's question.

(C)   gives the student a cursory response, eliminating the need for any further discussion.

(D)   disciplines the student for not paying attention to the topic under discussion.

The correct response is **(B)**. This is the best answer because it acknowledges the student's curiosity and legitimizes the student's right to pursue information by asking questions. It gives approval and recognition to the student's voice of inquiry, and it allows other students to voice their opinions and/or to make relevant comments. The teacher does not have to have a ready answer to every question, and this answer choice recognizes that also. The other three choices—(A), (C), and (D)—all have the opposite effect; by ignoring students' voices and missing an opportunity for students to become active learners, they will fail to learn something about which they may be genuinely interested. All three of the incorrect choices reflect an autocratic attitude toward teaching, which is the opposite of what Baxter-Magolda recommends for teaching effectiveness.

Learning about the Community

The first staff development for new teachers in a school district is often based upon providing insight into the makeup of the community. Many larger districts have developed videotapes about their communities. Information to help the teacher adjust to a new employment situation, and possibly a new residential and shopping area, are most vital. Sometimes, the school district busses the teachers on a tour of the immediate neighborhood of the school in which they will be teaching, often with helpful commentary by an experienced professional. If such orientation is not provided, the teacher should solicit at least an informal tour of the community, preferably by someone who has lived there several years. If other new teachers have joined the staff, together they may solicit a tour guide from staff members themselves—a teacher, a secretary, a paraprofessional. Sometimes a volunteer from the organized parents' group of a campus may have the orientation of new staff members as one of their goals.

Chamber of Commerce information can always provide data about the community. This public relations material is important since it projects the image of the community that the community values. Directly or indirectly reflected therein will be the expectation for the school. Real estate brochures are equally informative. Are the schools used as an attracting agent for people considering moving into the general area? What positive factors in the community are used to lure prospective home-buyers or apartment-leasers? If the new teacher is planning to buy or lease living accommodations within the community, calling upon a real estate agent to learn more about the area, as well as assisting in locating potential residential areas, will be useful.

Once the students have started school, the teacher may ask the students to talk about their community. Their perceptions, although certainly reflecting their age biases, still provide insights not otherwise available to a new teacher. Perhaps the teacher will find several students who will spend an hour or two one afternoon or Saturday morning touring the community and pointing out special places—the neighborhood library, nearby public parks, shopping areas, any favorite hangouts of the teenagers. If the teacher is an elementary school teacher, a parent, with one or two of the students, may provide the tour.

Finally, becoming a patron of a few businesses within the community can serve as a source of information about the community, as well as its expectations of and attitudes toward the school. The teacher can take cleaning to a local cleaning establishment, or shop at a grocery store or drugstore, exchanging a few words about the school with the persons who provide service at such establishments. Visiting the local library and talking with the librarian will always provide help as well. If the teacher attends a local church or synagogue, certainly talking to the members can be very informative.

Learning as much as possible about the community that a school serves will assist the teacher in numerous ways throughout the teaching assignment in that community. The teacher, at the same time, may be building allies upon whom to call if a need arises.

Stabilizing Strengths of the Community

Every community will have established sources of support for the school. Parents' groups such as the Parent-Teacher Association, the Dads' Club, the Band Boosters, the Sports Club, and dozens of other groups have been formed to provide both financial and philosophical support. These groups are often searching for projects to undertake as part of their yearly program of goals.

Retired teachers in the community may provide information that can be invaluable to the new teacher. Finding out the names of respected former teachers can be accomplished by asking other teachers or by seeking names from parents and students. In some cases, the retired teachers not only have advice, but also have an abundance of teaching suggestions, and even materials for an earnest new teacher in search of assistance.

Using the community as subject matter for writing experiences can provide additional information for the teacher's use, while it teachs the students to do a variety of activities to gather primary and secondary information about their home area. Students can research the history of the area in several ways. A very young student can interview and record older members of the community as they talk about the past. Often, the elders welcome an invitation to visit a class and talk about their earliest days in the area and retell the stories that their parents may have told them. Gathering letters, photographs, magazines, maps, toys, and other artifacts of days gone by can provide primary documentation that is often quite interesting to students and also to parents when displayed at open house.

Sometimes special interest groups within the community welcome the opportunity to share aspects of their interest with a class. A local story-telling group may visit a class and demonstrate techniques to make a story's retelling truly exciting for the listeners; a writing group may judge creative writing of the students and offer tips for expressive writing. Parents will often attend elementary classes and share work experiences to begin the students' awareness of the world of work. More formal Career Days, frequently planned on secondary campuses, utilize a variety of local people to talk about their vocational choices and respond to students' questions.

All subject areas can find useful activities centered in the community to teach the content more effectively and realistically.

Teaching early stages of reading, the teacher requests students to bring in slogans and advertisements associated with popular breakfast cereals. Often, students who do not formally read have become acquainted with such sayings. Sharing them with the class becomes a stimulating activity for everyone. Older language learners can use the community for a variety of language study assignments. Finding errors in spelling or mechanics in the newspaper or on commercial signs, defining the methods used for naming streets in various residential areas of town, collecting the phrases on signs posted about the town—all make reading a real-life activity, not one merely restricted to a textbook in a classroom.

In social studies and literary study especially, as heroes and heroic values are discussed, the teacher can use the community patterns as well to identify contemporary local heroes and heroic values. Open discussion of differences in opinion and style of dress and haircut, conducted in a nonjudgmental environment, allows for the variety of values often found in any community today. Living safely and sanely together is surely an accepted value promoted by most school curricula and cannot be postponed until problems arise.

Coping with Problems in the Community

Each community, along with the strengths that can be identified, will have deterrents to the educational process. Some of these negative aspects are not merely local problems, but symptomatic of many communities today—drug and alcohol abuse, unemployment, heavy mobility within the community, and crime and violence, especially as reflected in gang conflicts. Accompanied by the apparent apathy of adults in regard to the educational process, the toll of these problems upon the effectiveness of the schools can be heavy, for students of any age may be affected adversely by one or more of these conditions of contemporary society.

Often when a school exists in an environment affected by one or more of the societal ills of today, the in-service programs for teachers will focus on the relevant problems obviously affecting the student population. The teacher will learn ways to help students in the classroom and will find out about sources of even greater assistance for students through these staff training sessions. The teacher's good judgment will always be required, however, to know to what extent he or she can help with a pervasive problem area. Working at intervention, before a problem area becomes a critical factor affecting the educational process in the classroom, is always a wise course of action.

Young people's familiarity with drugs and alcohol begins very early in some communities. Children as young as nine or ten have become addicted to illegal drugs or alcohol. Certainly by middle-school age, most students have had some personal involvement with alcohol or drugs; either he/she has experimented or knows a classmate who has.

Another major factor creating an unstable family structure is the family's employment situation. More and more adults are finding changes in their work necessary. Finding new employment opportunities is seldom easy, and the time during which a parent is searching for work can be most stressful upon all family members. The greater mobility of families throughout the United States is often related to employment changes. Certainly as children move to new schools in new communities, adjustment to a different school can create a problem.

Teachers need to find out what a new student has been studying in each content area and try to build upon that familiar base. Records from the former campus often take months to be transferred and may be of little help if the student has moved frequently.

Any community is now vulnerable to greater crime and violence within its boundaries. Such an atmosphere will affect the youth and, therefore, the school environment. Not uncommon today is the requirement for students to enter a school building by passing through a metal detector, one attempt to keep weapons out of the school building. If the community is unfortunate enough to have gangs attracting the teenagers, the rival attitudes and behaviors cannot be blocked out of the building as easily as knives or guns. Staff training in multicultural understanding will assist the new teachers in understanding the characteristics of different ethnic groups. In the classroom, intervention may be successful by studying literary works based upon prejudice. Class discussion may defuse potentially volatile situations in real life as students read about conflicts between rival groups, as in *Light in the Forest, When the Legends Die, The Chosen, Flowers for Algernon,* or other novels based upon religious or ethnic prejudices. The classics can also illustrate groups in conflict, such as in *Romeo and Juliet, A Tale of Two Cities,* or *Animal Farm.* Actual historical incidents, as well as contemporary news stories, provide other examples to discuss in class. The teacher, making good judgment calls, can successfully intervene before a problem occurs in class.

The effective teacher can make a difference, even when the problems in the community seem insurmountable. Using the time and talent available, the teacher can address the problems that seem to affect his or her students in an appropriate way in the classroom and be familiar with sources of more extensive help available on campus and in the community.

Nature and Nurture

After experts on both sides of the argument stated their positions, the conclusion seemed to be that both *nature* (the internal variables) and *nurture* (the environment) play equally important roles in determining the outcome of individuals' growth and maturation. Again, it is important to remember the interaction of the individual with his or her environment, and recall that this view is the *dynamic* view of human development.

Before proceeding, teachers would do well to understand that perception plays an important role for learners to the extent that perception creates our individual reality. The world as we know it is a result of our selective perception. We cannot attend to all events and variables in our environment. We select certain events and variables to notice and attend to, and these phenomena which we observe form our perceptions; thus, we create our own reality. External and internal phenomena grab our attention and shape reality for each of us.

Thus, it is one thing for teachers to be aware of and sensitive to the student's environment; it is, however, impossible for teachers to see, feel, and understand the individual's environment in exactly the same way that it is seen, felt, and understood by the student.

Carol Tavris, a social psychologist and author of the book, *Anger: The Misunderstood Emotion,* notes that emotion plays a significant role in students' perceptions. For example, guilt is an emotion aroused by thoughts such as, "I should study or my parents will kill (be disappointed in) me." This is easily contrasted with the emotion of fear generated by the thought, "I should study or I will be a failure in life." Furthermore, guilt and fear can be compared to the emotion of anger which is prompted by thoughts such as, "Why should I study when my teacher is out to get me?" Today's student often sees the teacher as an enemy, not as an authority figure or a friend. Tavris has identified anger as a primary emotion experienced by many students today and one which plays a significant role in shaping their academic perceptions which, in turn, forms their reality of classroom experiences.

Explaining further, Tavris observes that unfulfilled expectations lead to anger. For example, if a student is led to believe (by teachers, school administrators, peers, or parents and siblings) that attending class is somehow irrelevant to academic achievement, then the student who is frequently absent still has the expectation of being successful. The student's perception is that absenteeism is compatible with academic achievement. If, because of absenteeism, the student fails to master essential elements of the curriculum and does not succeed, then the student will feel anger, the appropriate and anticipated emotion.

Anger, however, can be diffused by addressing perceptions, correcting false impressions, and establishing appropriate and realistic expectations. To illustrate, if all those individuals significant to the student emphasize the importance of class attendance, then students acquire the correct perception (in this case) that attendance is important for academic achievement and that absenteeism leads to academic failure.

For the sake of illustration only, let's consider what might happen if the teacher stresses attendance and the parents do not. In this case, the best route for the teacher to take is to show empathy for the student's dilemma. The teacher can acknowledge how difficult it is for the student to attend class when the parents are not supporting attendance, but the teacher also must seek to empower the student to make choices and to take responsibility for his or her own behavior.

In the situation described here, the student undergoes stress because of conflicting messages, and stress is faced by students and faculty alike. In fact, in the above example, the teacher is stressed too, because he/she faces the conflict between supporting the parents of the student and supporting that which is in the best educational interests of the student.

Stress is the product of any change; both negative and positive changes produce stress. Environmental, physiological, and psychological factors cause stress. For example, environmental factors such as noise, air pollution, and crowding (among others) create stress; physiological factors such as sickness and physical injuries create stress; and, finally, psychological factors such as self-deprecating thoughts and negative self-image cause stress. In addition to the normal stressful factors that everyone experiences, some students are living in dysfunctional families; some students are dealing with substance abuse and addictions; some are experiencing sexual abuse. There are numerous sources of stress in the lives of students.

Since life is a stressful process, it is important that students and faculty learn acceptable ways to cope with stress. The first step in coping with stress is to recognize the role that stress plays in our lives. A teacher might lead a class through a brainstorming activity to help the students become aware of the various sources of stress affecting them. Next, the teacher could identify positive ways of coping with stress, such as the importance of positive self-talk, physical exercise, proper nutrition, adequate sleep, balanced activities, time-management techniques, good study habits, and relaxation exercises.

Students who are stressed often become angry rather easily; however, students are not just angry. They experience a wide range of emotions and may be sad, depressed, frustrated, afraid, and, on the positive side, happy and surprised. Effective teachers realize that students' emotions as explained in this section and the preceding section on human development, play a significant role in their classroom performance and achievement. Thus, effective teachers seek to create a classroom environment supportive of students' emotional needs. They have appropriate empathy and compassion for the emotional conflicts facing students, yet their concern is tempered by a realistic awareness of the importance of students attaining crucial academic and social skills that will grant them some control over their environment as they become increasingly independent and, eventually, come to the point where they need to become productive citizens.

Effective teachers recognize the effects of students' perceptions on the learning process and the effects of many environmental factors; as a result, they plan instruction to enhance students' self-esteem and to promote realistic expectations. It is important that teachers be able to differentiate positive and negative environmental factors, maximizing the positive variables and minimizing the negative ones. The teacher has the primary responsibility of creating a classroom environment that recognizes the different environmental factors affecting each student and that encourages each learner to excel, to achieve his or her personal best. Effective teachers work hard at creating learning environments in which all students are ready to learn—where students feel safe, accepted, competent, and productive.

Diversity

The effective teacher appreciates human diversity, recognizing how diversity in the classroom and the community may affect learning and creating a classroom environment in which both the diversity and uniqueness of individuals are recognized and celebrated. Effective teachers realize that students bring to the classroom a variety of characteristics, both personal and social, that create within the classroom a microcosm reflective of American society at large. Indeed, America has long had the characteristic of being a "melting pot," whereby members of various racial, ethnic, religious, and national origin groups contribute to the wealth of our culture.

Ethnocentrism is a sociological term used to describe the natural tendency of viewing one's own cultural or familial way of doing things as the right, correct, or best way. Because ethnocentrism is a natural tendency, all people are likely to engage in ethnocentric thinking and behaviors at times.

Some social critics have pointed out that ethnocentrism has played a notable role in American education. They assert that educational institutions often have been guilty of assuming a Eurocentric viewpoint, that is, solely recognizing the contributions of European writers, artists, scientists, philosophers, and so forth, at the expense of those from other cultures. These critics have also noted that the contributions of men often are disproportionately recognized over similar achievements of women.

In fact, David and Myra Sadker (1994) have found that teachers, both male and female, at all grade levels, are more likely to call on male than female students, are more likely to give positive reinforcement to males' correct responses than to those of females, and to provide more coaching or instructional help to males when their responses are incorrect than to females. Their research has led them to conclude that teachers are usually unaware of gender bias in their teaching, but that such bias is pervasive in American schools. Their research also has persuaded them that bias can be eliminated once teachers become sensitive to its debilitating effects on students.

The point made here is that ethnocentrism, in any form, can be damaging because it is exclusive rather than inclusive. Eurocentric, Afro-centric, and other ethnocentric perspectives are equally limited in that they narrowly focus attention on one set of ideas at the neglect of others. Therefore, effective teachers will wisely expend a degree of effort in avoiding ethnocentric thinking and behaviors. Effective teachers will attempt to include all students in all classroom activities. The race, ethnicity, religion, national origin, and gender of learners will be viewed as strengths which enable students to learn with and from each other.

Historically speaking, educational experiments have demonstrated the importance of teachers avoiding bias and ethnocentric thinking. The *Hawthorne effect*, or the phenomenon whereby what teachers expected became reality, was demonstrated when teachers were told that some students in their classes were extremely intelligent whereas others were extremely slow or mentally retarded. In fact, all students had normal-range intelligence. Nonetheless, at the end of the experiment, students who had been identified to the teachers as being extremely intelligent all had made significant academic progress and were not only at the top of their class, but also performing at the top on national achievement tests. Those students who had been identified as retarded had made no progress at all; in fact, they had lost previously-made gains. Thus, it was demonstrated that teachers' expectations for students often become self-fulfilling prophecies.

In today's society, there is a considerable reference to multiculturalism. Multiculturalism, if it serves merely to separate and distinguish the accomplishments of select cultural and ethnic groups, has the potential of separating and alienating Americans. To view multiculturalism in a positive light is to acknowledge a kind of multiculturalism which embraces the accomplishments of all cultural and ethnic groups, thereby strengthening our country and society instead of fragmenting it.

Because multiculturalism and/or cultural diversity can be a controversial issue with many sides to consider, a reasonable approach to diversity for the classroom teacher is to distinguish between cultural diversity and learning diversity, and to focus on diversity in learning. This approach transcends cultural boundaries and recognizes that all people have distinct learning preferences and tendencies. Furthermore, this approach acknowledges that all preferences and tendencies are equally valid and that each style of learning has strengths. The teacher who understands learning styles can validate all students in the class.

Special Education Legislation

Diverse Learners and Public Law 94-142 (Individuals with Disabilities Education Act—IDEA)

Diverse learners and those with disabilities have always existed. Historically, however, it was more convenient to remove them from the social mainstream than to integrate them into the schools and provide jobs or training. Case law and federal legislation has helped bring about progress for diverse learners.

Before the 1970 Education for all Handicapped Children Act and the passage in 1975 of the Individuals with Disabilities Education Act (IDEA), many students missed the opportunity for learning in our public institutions. Over one million students had found exclusion from the public school system.

PL 94-142, however, helped put into the "regular" classrooms students with

- emotional disturbance;

- speech or language impairments;

- specific learning disabilities;

- autism;

- health impairments;

- mental retardation, including severe disabilities and multiple disabilities;

- orthopedic impairments;

- traumatic brain injury;

- hearing impairments; and

- visual impairments.

To implement PL 94-142, teachers must

- practice nondiscriminatory testing;

- create an individual education plan for the student;

- develop educational objectives and a means for implementation;

- monitor the progress of the students;

- integrate these students;

- work to accommodate their needs;

- practice speaking about the child before discussing the disability.

The federal government has responsibility to IDEA. It should

- assist the states in funding these programs;

- encourage the growth of diversity;

- provide technology services to assist in educating diverse students; and

- support professional development for those who work with those with disabilities.

Diverse Learners and Americans with Disabilities Act (ADA, 1990)

Signed into law on July 26, 1990, the Americans with Disabilities Act attempted to make American Society more accessible to people with disabilities. ADA attempts to provide accommodations for those with disabilities in employment, public services, public accommodations, and telecommunications. Title V of ADA prohibits coercing, threatening, or retaliating against the disabled or those who assist people with disabilities in asserting their rights under the Americans with Disabilities Act.

Diverse Learners in the Educational Environment

Students with needs and exceptionalities may require different types of accommodations. Some may have

- their placement in a regular classroom and receive program modifications;

- their placement in a regular classroom, receive program modifications, and receive additional support from the special education teacher;

- their placement with a special education teacher for part of the day and their placement in a regular classroom for part of the day;

- placement in a special education classroom but may receive direct and indirect support from consultative staff and other special education teachers;

- their placement in a residential program or treatment program with ongoing, complete support from a variety of staff.

Regardless of placement, students with exceptionalities and special needs will have in place an Individual Education Plan (IEP).

Diverse Learners and the Individual Education Plan (IEP)

Each student in the classroom is unique and has unique needs. To meet the needs in the academic program, the teacher must recognize and plan for the exceptional students and those with special needs. All educators want each student to function as effectively as possible in the school environment. To help ensure that the educational environment meets the needs of diverse learners and especially those with special needs, all exceptional students—and perhaps others in the class—must have an Individual Education Plan (IEP).

The Individual Education Plan (IEP) is a planning document that a teacher uses in conjunction with the daily and the long-range plans. The programming details may vary from state to state and country to country. Most require, however,

- the date of the implementation of the plan;

- the date that the placement of the individual became effective;

- the signature of the adult responsible for the care of the student;

- the signature of the student (depending on the student's age);

- the exceptionality/exceptionalities of the student;

- health issues;

- list of equipment that is required and that is personalized or on loan;

- list of equipment—like a feeding chair or a walker—that is used regularly;

- list of personnel (like vision specialist or speech therapist) that may be necessary;

- an indication of the curricular modifications or accommodation;

- a listing of the amount of support (30% of the day, 20 minutes a day) necessary;

- information about the strengths and interests of the student;

- results of standardized tests and assessments;

- academic functioning information;

- information about the modifications necessary for all subject areas;

- grade levels for every subject;

- details and identification of goals, expectations, and performance;

- *clear* and *detailed* information on strategies for helping the student achieve the goals and expectations;

- evaluation comments throughout the year;

- copies for adult caregivers/parents and (if applicable) the students; and

- copies stored in a secure place at the school.

Environmental Factors

Many factors play a role in determining a student's learning style. Among those most often cited in the research literature on learning style are environmental, emotional, sociological, physiological, and psychological factors. Although there are several different models for understanding learning differences and many good instruments for assessing learning styles, the Dunn and Dunn (1993) model is one widely used in public schools with versions suitable for students in elementary and secondary classrooms. It will serve as the basis for the following discussion.

Environmental factors include students' reactions to stimuli such as sound, light, temperature, and room design. Do students prefer to study and learn with or without sound, with bright or soft lights, in warm or cool rooms, and/or with standard classroom furniture or alternative seating? Classroom teachers observe that some students are easily distracted by any noise and require absolute quiet when studying or working on assignments. On the other hand, some students seem to learn best when they can listen to music. Some researchers have found evidence that students who prefer sound learn best when classical or instrumental music is played in the background.

Light is another environmental factor, with students' preferences for it appearing to be basically inherited, with family members often exhibiting the same preference. Some students prefer bright, direct illumination, while others prefer dim, indirect lighting.

Temperature and design are two other environmental factors affecting learning style. Some students will prefer warmer temperatures whereas others will prefer cooler temperatures. Finally, some students will prefer to sit in straight-backed chairs at desks while others may prefer to sit on soft, comfortable chairs or to sit or recline on the floor.

Although traditional classrooms are structured to provide quiet, brightly illuminated study and work areas with straight-backed chairs and desks, classroom teachers will observe that this environment meets the needs of only some of the learners in the class.

An effective teacher will take into consideration the learning styles of all students and experiment with different room designs and study centers creating different environments in the classroom. Although classroom temperature may seem to be beyond the control of the teacher, students can be advised to dress in layers so that they can remove outer garments when they are too warm and put on more layers when they are too cool.

Emotional Factors

According to Rita and Kenneth Dunn, emotional factors include motivation, persistence, responsibility, and structure. To explain, some students are motivated intrinsically: they undertake and complete tasks because they see the value in doing so. Other students are motivated extrinsically: they undertake and complete tasks because they desire to please others or to earn good marks. In regard to persistence, some students, when they undertake assignments, become totally and completely engaged in their work; they seem to lose track of time and can work for long periods without interruption or without feeling fatigued. Other students seem to work in short spurts of energy, and need to take frequent breaks.

When it comes to responsibility, some students are nonconforming, always doing the unexpected (and sometimes unwanted), whereas other students are conforming, always following the rules. Structure refers to whether or not students need detailed and precise instructions. Some students have lots of questions about how assignments should be done, and they desire detailed, step-by-step instructions on each phase of the assignment. Other students, however, seem to work from general concepts and are usually eager to begin assignments, often beginning their work before the directions have been given.

Sociological factors include whether or not students are social learners—preferring to work in pairs or in groups—or whether they are independent learners—preferring to work alone. Another sociological factor is whether or not students work best under the close guidance and supervision of an authority figure, be it teacher or parent, or whether they work best with a minimum of adult guidance and are best left primarily on their own to do their work.

Physiological factors include students' preferences for food or drink while they study, what time of day they learn best, their mobility needs, and their perceptual strengths. Briefly, some students may need to eat or drink in order to effectively and efficiently learn. Rita Dunn says that to make sure that students do not abuse this privilege, she allows them to eat only carrot or celery sticks (cooked so that the snacks will not crunch when eaten by students) and to drink water. This way, she is certain that only students who really need to eat when they are learning will take advantage of this concession.

Some students may learn best early in the morning, some later in the morning, some in early afternoon, and some later in the afternoon. Researchers have found that merely manipulating the time of day that certain students take tests can significantly affect their test performance.

Mobility needs refer to the fact that some students need to move around when they study, whereas other students can sit still for longer periods of time. Although all of these factors are important, and a growing body of literature tends to support the idea that these factors play a significant role in increasing students' performance and in increasing teachers' effectiveness with students, perhaps one of the most important elements in understanding learning style is to identify students' perceptual strengths. Perceptual strengths refer to students' learning modalities, such as whether they are visual, auditory, tactile, or kinesthetic learners. Basically, these perceptual modalities refer to whether students learn best by seeing, hearing, or doing.

Some students can be given a book or handout to read and then perform a task well, based on what they have read. These students tend to have visual (iconic or semantic) perceptual strength. Other students are visual learners, too, but they tend to learn best from images. These are the students who seem to recall every event, even minor details, from films, videos, or classroom demonstrations.

Although evidence indicates that less than 15 percent of the school-age population is auditory, much of the classroom instruction takes the form of teachers telling students information. Most students do not learn auditorially. Therefore, these students must be taught how to listen and learn from oral instructions and lecture.

Teachers who rely on telling students the information that is important would do well to remember that females are more likely to learn auditorially than males. Teachers should also keep in mind that whether or not students benefit from lectures is likely to depend on several other elements as well, such as whether or not the students are auditory learners, whether or not the students like the teacher, whether or not they think the information being presented is important, or whether or not they think that listening to the teacher will help them to achieve their goals.

On the other hand, there are students who do not seem to benefit much from lectures, textbook assignments, or visual aids. These students' perceptual strengths are tactile and kinesthetic. They learn from movement and motion—being able to touch, handle, and manipulate objects. Often these students may have been identified as having learning disabilities. Sometimes they have been relegated to shop or cooking classes or have found their success in athletics, music, or art. Interestingly, many of the "hands on" skills that often identify a student for a career as an auto mechanic are also important skills for mechanical engineers and surgeons.

References

Further reading of these references may enhance understanding of the chapter and may also increase performance on the examination.

Baxter-Magolda, M. B. *Knowing and Reasoning in College: Gender-Related Patterns in Students' Intellectual Development*. San Francisco: Jossey Bass, 1992.

Coles, R. "Point of View: When Earnest Volunteers are Solely Tested." *Chronicle of Higher Education*. Vol. A52, May, 1993.

Elkind, D. "Egocentrism in Adolescence." *Child Development*. Vol. 38, p. 1025-34, (1967).

Ellis, D. *Becoming a Master Student*. Rapid City, South Dakota: College Survival, 1991.

Erikson, E. *Childhood and Society*. New York: Horton, 1963.

Flavell, J. H. "Speculations about the Nature and Development of Metacognition." *Metacognition, Motivation, and Learning*. Hillsdale, New Jersey: Erlbaum, 1987.

Maslow, A. *Toward a Psychology of Being*. New York: Horton, 1963.

Piaget, J. *The Psychology of Intelligence*. London: Routledge and Kegan Paul, 1950.

Sternberg, R. J. *Beyond IQ: A Triarchic Theory of Human Intelligence.* Cambridge: Cambridge University Press, 1985.

Tavris, C. Presentation on Coping with Student Conflict Inside and Outside the Classroom at Texas Junior College Teachers Conference, San Antonio, Texas, February 25, 1994.

Dunn, R. Presentation on the Productivity Environmental Preferences Scale (PEPS) at Learning Styles Institute, Lubbock, Texas, June 5–9, 1993. (Sponsored by Education Service Center, Region XVII).

Dunn, R. & K. Dunn. Presentation on Using Learning Styles Information to Enhance Teaching Effectiveness at Learning Styles Institute, Lubbock, Texas, June 5–9, 1993. (Sponsored by Education Service Center, Region XVII).

Sadker, M. & D. Sadker. *Failing at Fairness: How America's Schools Cheat Girls.* New York: Charles Scribner's Sons, 1994.

Chapter

3

Substance Abuse by Students

Overview

The teacher distinguishes signs of alcohol and drug abuse in students and demonstrates awareness of appropriate intervention and referral procedures.

Dr. Elaine M. Johnson, Director of the Center for Substance Abuse Prevention, recently wrote, "...We must prevent substance abuse if we really hope to reduce crime, violence, school failure, teen pregnancy, unemployment, homelessness, HIV/AIDS, diminished productivity and competitiveness, highway death, and escalating health care costs." This statement communicates the risks of substance abuse to society.

Substance abuse prevention focuses on the promotion of healthy, constructive lifestyles for individuals without the use of drugs. Prevention reduces the risk of danger in society and fosters a safer environment. Successful prevention programs have led to reductions in traffic fatalities, violence, HIV/AIDS and other sexually transmitted diseases, rape, teen pregnancy, child abuse, cancer and heart disease, injuries and trauma, and many other problems associated with drug abuse.

The backbone of substance abuse prevention is education. Every professional educator should be aware of the behaviors and characteristics that indicate a tendency toward the use of drugs and/or alcohol, and the physical and behavioral signs indicating that students are under the influence of drugs and/or alcohol. Moreover, teachers must be able to make immediate referrals when any student is suspected of using drugs and/or alcohol in order to protect other students, and to secure assistance for the abuser. Finally, teachers must be equipped to provide accurate information to students concerning substance abuse.

Behaviors Tending Toward Substance Abuse

Drug and alcohol problems can affect anyone, regardless of age, sex, race, marital status, place of residence, income level, or lifestyle. However, certain risk factors for substance abuse have been identified. Risk factors are those characteristics that occur statistically more often for those who develop alcohol and drug problems, either as adolescents or as adults, than for those who do not develop substance abuse problems. Recent research studies have identified a number of such factors, including individual, family, and social/cultural characteristics.

Individual Characteristics

Studies have shown that certain personality characteristics or traits are associated with problems of substance abuse. These personality characteristics include the following: a) aggressiveness; b) aggressiveness combined with shyness; c) decreased social inhibition; d) emotional problems; e) inability to express feelings appropriately; f) hypersensitivity; g) inability to cope with stress; h) problems with relationships; i) cognitive problems; j) low self-esteem; k) difficult temperament; and i) over-reaction to certain situations.

Other important personal factors are whether the individual is the child of an alcoholic or other drug abuser, whether there is less than two years between the child and older/younger siblings, and whether the child has any birth defects, including possible neurological and neurochemical dysfunctions. The presence of physical disabilities, physical or mental health problems, and learning disabilities can also add to the student's vulnerability to substance abuse. In many ways, students who are at risk academically are also susceptible to substance abuse problems.

In adolescence, other factors emerge that are statistically related to problems with substance abuse. These factors are a) school failure and attrition (dropping out); b) delinquency; c) violence; d) early, unprotected sexual activity; e) teen pregnancy/parenthood; f) unemployment or underemployment; g) mental health problems; and h) suicidal tendencies. Teachers should be alert to these factors as they may be symptomatic of a number of negative adolescent behaviors and experiences, including: a) a failure to bond with society through family, school, or community; b) rebellion and nonconformity; c) resistance to authority; d) a strong need for independence; e) cultural alienation; f) feelings of failure and a fragile ego; g) lack of self-confidence and low self-esteem; and h) the inability to form positive, close relationships and/or an increased vulnerability to negative peer pressure.

Family Characteristics

Many family characteristics are also associated with substance abuse among youth. First, and perhaps most important, is the alcohol or other drug dependency of a parent or both parents. This characteristic might be linked with another significant factor—parental abuse and neglect of children. Antisocial and/or mentally ill parents are also factors that put children at risk for drug and/or alcohol abuse. In addition, high levels of family stress (including financial strain), large, overcrowded family conditions, family unemployment or under-employment, and parents with little education or socially isolated parents are also risk factors. Single parents without family or other support, family instability, a high level of marital and family conflict or violence, and parental absenteeism due to separation, divorce, or death can also increase children's vulnerability. Finally, other important factors to consider are the lack of family rituals, inadequate parenting, little child-to-parent interaction, and frequent family moves. These factors describe children without affiliation or a sense of identity with their families or community. All of these family factors can present risks for substance abuse.

Social and Cultural Characteristics

Living in an economically depressed area with high unemployment, inadequate housing, a high crime rate, and a prevalence of illegal drug use are social characteristics that can put an individual at risk of substance abuse. Cultural risk factors include minority status involving racial discrimination, differing generational levels of assimilation, low levels of education, and low achievement expectations from society at large.

While these are recognized as risk factors, they are only indicators of the potential for substance abuse. Although these factors can be helpful in identifying children who are at risk or vulnerable to developing substance abuse problems and useful to teachers in helping them develop prevention education strategies, they are not necessarily predictive of an individual's proclivity to drug or alcohol abuse. Some children who are exposed to very adverse conditions grow up to be healthy, productive, and well-functioning adults. Yet, if teachers recognize these risk factors in some of their students, there are certain things that teachers possibly can do to increase the chances that the youngster or adolescent will resist the lures of illegal and dangerous alcohol and drug abuse.

Experts suggest that children have a better chance to grow up as healthy adults if they can learn to do one thing well that is valued by themselves, their friends, or their community. Teachers certainly can help assure that students achieve this goal by teaching them the crucial reading, writing, and math skills that will enable them to become independent learners. By presenting lessons that require the development of effective communication and critical thinking skills, teachers can help students acquire important life skills.

Other important strategies for educators to consider are listed below:

- Require children to be helpful as they grow up;

- Help children learn how to ask for help themselves (develop assertiveness skills);

- Help children elicit positive responses from others in their environment (enable children to develop a sense of community in their classrooms, and to work collaboratively and/or in cooperation);

- Assist children in developing a healthy distance from their dysfunctional families so that the family is not their sole frame of reference;

- Encourage children to form bonds with the school, and to identify with the school as an important and integral part of the community.

Finally, the teacher can be a caring adult who provides students with consistent positive responses and messages. Researchers have identified this as a crucial element in preventing substance abuse among children exposed to multiple risk factors.

Physical and Behavioral Characteristics of Students Under the Influence of Drugs

Sometimes it can be difficult to tell if someone is using illegal drugs or alcohol. Usually, people who abuse drugs or alcohol (including young people) go to great lengths to keep their behavior a secret. They deny and/or try to hide the problem. However, there are warning signs that can indicate if someone is using drugs or drinking too much alcohol.

Some of the signs that substance abuse is a problem include: a) lying; b) avoiding people who are longtime friends or associates; c) giving up activities that once brought pleasure and positive feedback (ranging from failing to turn in homework assignments to giving up extracurricular activities such as sports, drama, band, and so forth); d) getting into legal trouble; e) taking risks (including sexual risks, and driving under the influence of alcohol and/or drugs); f) feeling run-down, hopeless, depressed, even suicidal; g) suspension from school for an alcohol-or drug-related incident; and h) missing work or having poor performance.

Teachers should be alert to these signs in their students' behavior at school. When students stop coming to class, stop doing their work (or start performing poorly), avoid making eye contact with the teacher, have slurred speech, smell of alcohol or drugs (such as marijuana), complain of headaches, nausea, or dizziness, fall asleep in class, and/or have constant difficulty in staying awake and participating in class activities—a teacher's suspicions should be awakened. These examples, in and of themselves, are insufficient to confirm a substance abuse problem, but in combination and when displayed with consistency over time, they are strong indicators. Teachers should record their observations, keeping written reports of the behavioral changes they witness. Moreover, they should report their suspicions to the appropriate school authorities.

The Use of Referrals

Schools should adopt zero tolerance policies for guns and drugs. For safer schools and a higher quality of education, schools should provide effective anti-drug and substance-abuse prevention programs, including programs that teach responsible decision making, mentoring, mediation, and other activities aimed at changing unsafe, harmful, or destructive behaviors.

Teachers should not delay in taking action, since substance abuse has the potential for great harm. Authorities can investigate and verify or allay the teacher's concerns.

In addition to school resources, students with substance abuse problems can find help in a number of community resources. These community resources can include community drug hotlines, community treatment centers and emergency health care clinics, local health departments, Alcoholics Anonymous, Narcotics Anonymous, Al-Anon and Alateen, and hospitals.

Teaching About the Dangers of Substance Abuse

Teachers will find a number of helpful resources for teaching students about the dangers of substance abuse and for promoting prevention by contacting different agencies or organizations, including those listed below:

American Council for Drug Education
164 West 74th Street
New York, NY 10023
(800) 488-DRUG
acde@phoenixhouse.org

The National Center on Addiction and Substance Abuse at Columbia University
633 Third Avenue, 19th Floor
New York, NY 10017-6706
(212) 841-5200

National Clearinghouse for Alcohol and Drug Information
11426-28 Rockville Pike, Suite 200
Rockville, MD 20852
(800) 729-6686

In addition, the Internet offers a number of sites with useful information. The National Clearinghouse for Alcohol and Drug Information (http://www.health.org) and the National Institute on Drug Abuse (http://www.nida.nih.gov/) have excellent web sites with links to updated statistics, reports, and educational materials.

Prevention education promotes healthy and constructive lifestyles that discourage drug abuse, and fosters the development of social environments that facilitate and support drug-free lifestyles. Successful prevention means that underage youth, pregnant women, and others at high risk do not use alcohol, tobacco, or other drugs. Education for prevention does work. Research studies show that in 1979, 37 percent of all adolescents aged 12–17 drank alcohol in the past month; by 1992, that number dropped to 16 percent. The incidence of cirrhosis of the liver, a product of alcohol abuse, has dropped significantly, and 14,000 lives have been saved that would have been lost in alcohol-related traffic fatalities, with credit given to minimum drinking age laws. Teachers play an important role in drug and alcohol education, and abuse prevention.

References

Further reading of these references may enhance understanding of this chapter and may also increase performance on the examination.

Breaking New Ground for Youth at Risk: Program Summaries. OSAP Technical Report 1 BK 163, 1990.

Florida State Law, Chapter 232.277.

Johnson, Elaine M. *Making Prevention Work.* Center for Substance Abuse Prevention, 1998.

National Clearinghouse for Alcohol and Drug Information. *Straight Facts About Drugs and Alcohol,* 1998.

4

Physical Abuse of Students

Overview

The teacher is aware of the overt physical and behavioral indicators of child abuse and neglect, knows the rights and responsibilities regarding reporting, and understands how to interact appropriately with a child after a report has been made.

During an observation, you see that the teacher is getting nowhere with Belinda, the child who sits in the third row, center, of the classroom. No matter how many times her teacher, Mr. Smith, smiles at her, she flinches. If he waves his hands while illustrating a point, she flinches. If he raises his voice to ask for quiet, she flinches. He's taken the few extra minutes he finds in his teaching day to sit with her independently, but she doesn't seem to want this. Is it his fault? Is it the child's? Maybe there's another question to ask: Is it the fault of another who may be abusing or neglecting her?

Despite all the media attention given to child abuse and neglect, many teachers still believe that it can't happen to their students. They may think, "This is a nice neighborhood," or "Most of these students have both a mother and father living at home with them," or "The children are too outspoken to allow that to happen." However, abuse and neglect happen to children all the time, possibly even to some students who will be in your classroom.

Symptoms of Abuse

Contemporary research has led scientists to believe that modifications of both the chemistry of the brain and a child's neurological structure may be caused during abuse and, worse yet, that these effects are permanent. The child suffers from chronic shock, which is a result of increased hormones and electrical impulses. Each time the child is abused, a modification in the child's brain and its systems occur. It's the stress accompanying the abuse that causes the child to become hypersensitized to the abuse; this hypersensitizing then causes brain and body modification.

This process may also explain why Belinda involuntarily flinches when her teacher smiles at her—she may believe he's singling her out and, in her experience, not necessarily in a positive way. When he makes sudden motions with his hands—as is done when striking a person—or raises his voice, which may also be a precursor to rage, Belinda associates these behaviors with patterns of abuse. The effects of child abuse may not be as evident when dealing with an older child (possibly as a result of being told he or she "asked for it" or being threatened with dire consequences if he or she tells), but may be clearer in the child's peer interactions. At times, the teacher may become overly sensitive and may see child abuse/neglect in every bruise and mood change. But, through practice and by discussing suspicions with other teachers, one can become adept at recognizing signs that suggest child abuse.

While the abused child may be angry, "wired," unruly, and/or belligerent (in a word, "overstimulated"), the neglected child acts differently. He or she may want to be left alone. Common symptoms of neglect include being unsociable, sedate, withdrawn—all of which point to understimulation. It is thought that this behavior is taught at home during periods of neglect. The child's affect has been changed by the neglect, but the range is wide, varying from almost flat—registering no emotion—to anger. While poor attention, tears, violence, and languid behavior may be indicators of either abuse or neglect, the children usually have feelings of hopelessness and cannot adequately control their thoughts. Students either become obsessed by the neglect or refuse to acknowledge that the neglect is really happening.

Consider the following example: Darnell looks as though he isn't getting enough to eat, yet he eats everything—including the other children's leftovers at lunch—but remains underweight. He's a loner who seems shy and always looks rundown. He seems oblivious to his appearance, but the teacher notices he is often absent due to colds and other minor ailments. What the teacher may not know is that these are symptoms of neglect; it's poor nutrition that causes these illnesses. It's important for the teacher to see that Darnell's immunizations are up-to-date since he is so susceptible to illness. Darnell's sad affect may be another clue to the neglect he has experienced.

Visible Signs of Abuse

There are visible signs of child abuse. Among those are red welts on the body that are caused by being hit. This may be proof that the child is being abused and teachers must report the evidence. It is also one of the ways teachers separate the real abuse cases from those which are unfounded. While marks from the hand, fist, or belt are usually recognized, other marks in geometric shapes—eating utensils, paddles, coat hangers, and extension cords—can signify child abuse. If, for example, a boy in your class has unrecognizable bruises on his arms and legs, they could be the result of whippings; furthermore, if he constantly has bruises on his neck and head and always tells you they are from falling, be prepared to report suspicion of child abuse—this could be the result of hitting, possibly even choking. Teachers need a basis for their reports, so they must notice capillary ruptures (reddened areas) in any bruise, which indicate a strong hit. If a bruise is shaded on its outer borders, it may still be a result of hitting—just a softer hit. It may help to establish the charge of abuse if the teacher also reports the size and shape of the bruises, since they may indicate what was used to create such bruises. Teachers should be alert to any suspicious marks or signs of abuse and neglect.

Teachers must be aware of children who are prematurely interested in sex acts. Children who are prepubertal and act in a sexual manner have been taught, by example, to act this way. They are possible victims of sexual abuse. For example, young children who have been known to masturbate in the classroom or to attempt to foist sexual behavior on their classmates are simply not sexually developed nor mature enough to understand the consequences of their actions. A sudden show of promiscuity may follow molestation. Kissing, usually seen as a positive interaction between parent and child, if done in a sexual manner, is also abuse, as are leers and sexual stares. Parents are not the only ones to commit sexual abuse of children; grandparents, family friends, and siblings may also be the perpetrators of criminal abuse.

How to Report Suspicions of Abuse

Teachers may want to comfort the child after he or she admits to being sexually abused. However, they must be careful not to interview the child, but to wait for the professional trained to deal with abuse. Otherwise, teachers may inadvertently delay or even damage the possibility of a conviction and potentially cause more harm to the child. As a state-licensed teacher, you must report suspicion of child abuse/neglect. Reports are required of anyone—but especially educators—in such cases. The child is the one who needs help. Teachers must report suspicions so that an investigation can be made. Failure to report suspicions may adversely affect the child's life. Teachers have the right to have the report kept confidential, but including their name may save time and effort if more information becomes necessary. Failure to file a report of suspicion of child abuse/ neglect has consequences; it may result in a fine, criminal charges, or revocation of teacher certification or license to teach.

A delay in reporting solid suspicions of child abuse/ neglect may be cause for action against the teacher. Solid suspicion does not mean proof; it means that the suspicion is reasonable. Once again, the onus of deciding if this is child abuse/neglect is on the counselor—not the teacher. If it is deemed necessary—by the counselor, not the teacher who reports the suspicion—an investigation will be immediately initiated. If an immediate threat to the child is not found, an investigatory team will be sent out within 24 hours to collect further evidence.

Once the report is made, the teacher may want to interact with the child. The teacher should realize that the child—already needing support—may feel that his/her private life has been exposed. While accepting the child's feeling of betrayal, the teacher can explain that the report had to be filed. The teacher should assure the child that he/she can be protected against reprisals for telling about the abuse. Sometimes the child may benefit from just knowing that an adult does care about his/her well-being.

Once the report is filed, the teacher should avoid the person suspected of the abuse/neglect. Should the teacher be harassed or persecuted by this person, the teacher should go to the police. If the report turns into a legal issue, the teacher would be wise to retain an attorney. While the teacher's rights as the reporter are protected, legal matters can take unusual directions and a teacher may require legal advice to avoid becoming another victim of criminal behavior.

Teachers need to know that suspected sexual abuse creates special situations for the teacher. The teacher should ask for permission before patting a student on the back or holding a student's hand. The student has the right to decide whether he or she wants to be touched, and the teacher must acknowledge this decision. Often, the most important action for the teacher to take after reporting suspected abuse is to offer his/her support.

References

Further reading of these references may enhance understanding of the chapter and may also increase performance on the examination.

Child Abuse Prevention Foundation
    http://www.preventchildabuse.com

National Clearinghouse of Child Abuse and Neglect Information
    http://nccanch.acf.hhs.gov/index.cfm

Enhancing Comprehension and Mastery of Material

Overview

A teacher stimulates and guides student thinking, and verifies student comprehension through suitable questioning techniques.

The teacher provides appropriate practice to promote learning and retention.

It is obvious that in virtually any human activity we learn by practice. Whether we are trying to learn to play tennis or to speak a second language, we quickly realize how much we need to practice in order to make progress in the new skill. And yet, it is sometimes easy for teachers to neglect the importance of practice because they themselves are so familiar with the material they teach. It is so clear and plain to them that they forget what is was like to learn it as new and different. However, it became clear and plain only through long familiarity and practice.

Students not only need to understand a lesson; they need practice in using and applying their new knowledge. A child may "learn" one day that $4 \times 25 = 100$, but may not fully master that knowledge until he or she has several times given or received four quarters for a dollar. He or she may learn that *valiant* means brave, but the child may not remember the meaning or use the word until he or she has seen or heard it used many times.

The practice a teacher provides must be appropriate— that is, it must promote the objective established by the teacher or the prescribed curriculum. For example, if the objective is for students to be able to locate specific states on a map of the United States, practice in spelling the names of the states is inappropriate for that particular objective. The student must have practice in trying to do the very thing that is expected. To take another example, if the objective is to enable students to carry on simple conversations in Spanish, they must practice listening to and speaking Spanish; practice in reading Spanish would not be appropriate for that objective.

Questioning

There are many ways that teachers can ask questions that elicit different levels of thinking, although studies of teachers' skills in questioning often reveal frequent use of lower-level questions and infrequent use of higher-level ones.

A simple method is to divide questions into two types, closed and open. An example of a closed question is, "What was the main character's name?" There is usually only one right answer to a closed question. Often students can point to a phrase or sentence in a book to answer a closed question.

An open-ended question requires students to think carefully about the answer. There may be more than one appropriate answer to an open-ended question. An example is, "What do you think was the most important contribution of Pascal to the field of mathematics?" Teachers who ask open-ended questions are not looking for one specific answer, rather they are looking for well-supported responses. Asking an open-ended question but requiring one specific answer will discourage rather than encourage thinking.

An example of a closed math question is, "What is 5×5?" An example of an open-ended math question is, "What is the best way to solve this problem?" The open-ended question assumes that the teacher will accept all reasonable methods of solving the problem, provided the students can explain why their method is best.

There are other ways to categorize questions. Benjamin Bloom, et al., developed a taxonomy of educational objectives for the cognitive domain. Teachers have used this taxonomy for a variety of purposes in addition to writing objectives, including categorizing questions and activities.

Bloom's Six Levels of Taxonomy

There are six levels in Bloom's taxonomy, each one building on the previous level. The first level is **knowledge**. This is similar to the closed question, with one right answer which should be obvious to students who have read or studied. Words which often elicit recall or memory answers include who, what, when, and where. Examples of knowledge-level questions include: Who developed the first microscope? What were the names of Columbus' ships? When was South Carolina first settled? Where is Tokyo?

The next level is **comprehension**, which also elicits lower-level thinking and answers. The primary difference from the first level is that students must show that they understand a concept, perhaps by explaining in their own words. The question "What does *obfuscate* mean?" would be answered on a knowledge level if students repeat a memorized definition from the dictionary and on a comprehension level if students explain the term in their own words.

The first higher-level category is **application**. Students take what they've learned and use this knowledge in a different way or in a different situation. A simple example of this level is using mathematics operations—add, subtract, multiply, and divide—to solve problems. Another example is translating an English sentence into Spanish, or applying what the students have learned about Spanish vocabulary and grammar to develop an appropriate and correct response. Another form of application is changing the format of information, e.g., create a graph from a narrative description of a survey. The key to this level is the use or application of knowledge and skills in a similar but new situation.

The next level is **analysis**, which involves taking something apart, looking at all the pieces, and then making a response. An example of an analytical question is, "How are these two characters alike and how are they different?" This question requires students to examine facts and characteristics of each individual, then put the information together in an understandable comparison. Another example is, "What are the advantages and disadvantages of each of these two proposals?" Another example might be, "Compare the wolves in *The Three Little Pigs* and *Little Red Riding Hood.*"

The next level is **synthesis**, which involves putting information together in a new, creative way. Developing a new way of solving problems, writing a short story, and designing an experiment are all creative ways of synthesizing knowledge. For example, fourth-grade science students may develop and conduct research on food waste in the cafeteria and make recommendations for changes. An example of a synthesis question is, "What do you predict will happen if we combine these two chemicals?" This question assumes students will have factual knowledge. Their predictions must be reasonable and based on prior reading and/or discussion.

The highest level is **evaluation**. This level involves making value judgments and very often involves the question "Why?" or a request to "justify your answer." For example, students may be asked to use their analysis of two possible solutions to a problem to determine which is the better solution. Their response must be reasonable and well supported.

Evaluation-level activities must build on previous levels. Skipping from knowledge-level to evaluation-level questions will result in ill-conceived and poorly supported responses. Although teachers might use an evaluation question to provoke interest in a topic, they should make sure that students have opportunities to work at other levels as they develop their responses.

This type of questioning promotes risk-taking and problem-solving, whereby the teacher has established a safe environment in which students are encouraged and not ridiculed for creative or unusual responses. The teacher does not expect only one specific answer, but allows students to ponder several reasonable possibilities.

Effective teachers also appreciate cultural dimensions of communication and are aware that some cultures teach their children not to question adults. These teachers explain to students that they expect questions, encourage students to ask them, but do not force the issue if students are very uncomfortable. Sometimes students may be willing to write down and turn in questions for the teacher. Teacher attitude can promote or deter questions, even by so simple a tactic as changing, "Does anybody have any questions?" to "What questions do you have?" The first question implies that no one should have questions; the second assumes that there will be questions.

Vary Practice Activities

Numerous studies have shown that variety in teaching methods and styles promote student achievement and help maintain attention.

The nature of practice activities, therefore, should be varied. At one time, the teacher may have the students respond in unison; at another time, the teacher may have students work in pairs, where they ask one another questions; still another time, he or she may call on individuals or have all the students do written exercises at their seats.

Perhaps the most common of all practice activities is recitation, whereby the teacher poses questions to the class and calls on individuals to answer. Once a pupil has answered, the teacher responds to the answer and either calls on another pupil in the event that the question has been answered incorrectly, or goes on to another question if the student's answer is correct.

There are, however, many alternatives to recitation that teachers can and should use:

✔ **demonstrations by the teacher of a student,**

✔ **oral reports,**

✔ **slides,**

✔ **movies,**

✔ **television,**

✔ **radio, and**

✔ **recordings.**

Small-group activities, such as the following, can all help provide practice in newly learned material:

✔ **debates,**

✔ **role-playing sessions,**

✔ **panel discussions,**

✔ **project construction, and**

✔ **discussions of test answers.**

The duration of practice should be varied according to the difficulty of the material. Grammatical concepts of subject-verb-object may need considerable repetition and practice exercises, while the concept of size (large/small) may need only brief practice before it is mastered.

The duration of practice should vary also according to the ability of the learner. Some students will catch on right away to the idea of subject-verb-object; others will need considerable practice with it. Teachers need to determine which students are "getting it" quickly and which ones need to spend more time learning the material so that they grasp it fully. This may mean that the teacher gives most of the class a new activity while he or she works individually or in small groups with those who require help and practice.

One of the teacher's weightiest responsibilities is to pay close attention to the progress of individual students, providing more practice for those who have not yet mastered the material and introducing new or related challenges to those who have mastered it.

Reinforce Retention of Specific Information

A geography teacher is trying to help his/her students learn the names and locations of the major regions and countries in Africa. He or she can ask the students individually to come up to the map and point to Egypt or South Africa. The teacher can also ask individuals to name the country or the region to which he/she points. Or, the teacher can have the whole class call out the names of the countries and regions as he/she points to them in turn. If the teacher uses a variety of these methods, he/she is more likely to keep students' attention longer, and hence increase the learning that takes place in that session.

Varying the method is important for another reason—each method has its own benefits. Individual student responses give the spotlight to particular students, increasing their involvement in the class, and developing their ability and comfort in speaking in a group. Group response ensures that everyone is involved. Of course, the teacher should watch for the student who is not responding and encourage him or her to participate.

In calling on and responding to individual students in class, teachers must be especially mindful of personal biases to which everyone is susceptible. Do you tend to call on boys more than girls, or vice versa? Do you tend to call only on those who raise their hands? Should you ignore "call-outs"? The last question has no easy answer. If a student who is usually nonparticipatory calls out an answer on one occasion, it may be better to reward that student's willingness to participate by acknowledging the response. On the other hand, if a student frequently calls out without raising his/her hand, it is probably better to ignore the response until the student raises his/her hand and waits to be recognized.

Provide a Variety of Activities to Promote Retention

Repetition is the mother of learning. Unfortunately, it can also be the father of boredom. To prevent practice exercises from becoming monotonous and unproductive, the teacher needs to vary the kinds of repetitive practice.

If, for example, students are to learn 20 new vocabulary words, the teacher may use some or all of the following practice activities:

> ✔ **fill in the blanks in sentences with the appropriate vocabulary words,**
>
> ✔ **create your own sentences using the vocabulary words,**
>
> ✔ **match the vocabulary words to synonyms or antonyms,**
>
> ✔ **match the vocabulary words to definitions,**
>
> ✔ **find the vocabulary words in a word-search puzzle,**

✔ **complete a crossword puzzle whose answers are the vocabulary words, and**

✔ **write a brief story or speech using the vocabulary words.**

To practice material that has been explained by the teacher and discussed in class, students can work in pairs or small groups, asking questions of one another. In foreign language classes, for example, students can practice simple conversations in pairs, using newly learned words and phrases.

In mathematics classes, practice need not be limited to homework assignments of number problems and word problems. If, for example, students are learning to add fractions, they might be asked to make up their own word problems using real-life situations, exchanging problems with their classmates, and solving one another's problems. Such an activity not only gives the students practice in adding fractions, it also engages their imaginations since they have to think about situations in their own lives where fractions are used and need to be added.

Assist Students During Seatwork

One common and potentially effective way to give students practice in the material is to assign them seatwork—reading, writing, or some other individual activity done by the student at his or her desk. It is estimated that elementary school students spend 300-400 hours a year doing seatwork in language arts alone. It is obviously important, then, that seatwork be well designed and appropriate to the learning goal and the learner, and that the teacher explains clearly:

✔ **what is to be done,**

✔ **how to do it, and**

✔ **what the student should learn from doing it.**

Unfortunately, many teachers neglect the last two instructions, telling the students only what they are to do.

With seatwork, the teacher's job is to make sure that individual students are:

✔ **staying on task,**

✔ **understanding what they are doing (not just going through the motions), and**

✔ **receiving help when they need it.**

The teacher should be especially watchful for low achievers who often do poorly on seatwork assignments, answering questions without really understanding the material. For example, a student may perform arithmetical operations with the numbers in word problems without having any idea what particular operation (addition, subtraction, multiplication, or division) is called for.

The teacher can prevent children from wasting time by carefully overseeing what they are doing in their workbooks or on their activity sheets. Also, since these practice materials often fail to require higher levels of comprehension, such as reasoning and drawing conclusions, the teacher would be well advised to use them sparingly.

For seatwork, some good alternatives to workbooks and worksheets are the following:

✔ **silent reading,**

✔ **answering open-ended questions,**

✔ **writing an alternate ending to a story, and**

✔ **writing an ending for another student's story.**

Sometimes it is good to have students work together on seatwork. You may want to have them debate an issue in a story, compare endings that they have written, and so forth.

Practice Activities Promote Long-Term Retention

One way to vary practice exercises is to alternate between massed and distributed activities. A massed activity is a single activity done by the whole class; a distributed activity is one that is divided into a number of parts, each part assigned to a different group or individual.

Let us suppose, for example, that you have been teaching your class about the elements of a story: plot, character, setting, theme, conflict, and so on. You could have the whole class first do a massed activity—all pupils write out in their own words what is meant by plot, character, setting, etc. Once they have done that, you could have them do a distributed activity by dividing the class into as many groups as there are elements of a story. Each group would be assigned a story element and would describe that element in a story they have recently read. Group A would describe the plot of the story, Group B would name and describe the main characters, and so forth.

Once all the groups have completed their work, a spokesperson for each group could read to the whole class the description his/her group wrote. This last activity would combine massed and distributed activities: the whole class is listening, but each group is reporting on a different story element.

The combination of massed and distributed activities promotes long-term retention through repetition (several activities all about the elements of a story) and variation (individual, small-group, and whole-class activities). The teacher who limits him- or herself to either massed or distributed activities is less likely to have students who achieve the same degree of understanding and retention as students who practice using both methods.

References

Further reading of these references may enhance understanding of the chapter and may also increase performance on the examination.

"Comprehension" Chapter 10, pages 131-148 *Reading Instruction Essentials* by Anita Price Davis (Third Edition) Boston, Massachusetts: American Press, 2004.

Content Category 2: Instruction and Assessment

Chapters 6-9

The Physical and Emotional Environment of the Classroom

Chapter

6

Overview

The teacher organizes the physical environment to facilitate instruction and ensure the safety of his or her students.

A teacher can detect overt signs of emotional distress in students and has knowledge of suitable intervention and referral procedures.

Physical Environment

While there are certain physical aspects of the classroom that cannot be changed (size, shape, number of windows, type of lighting, etc.), there are others that can be. Windows can have shades or blinds which distribute light correctly, and which allow for the room to be darkened for video or computer viewing. If the light switches do not allow some of the lights to remain on, sometimes schools will change the wiring system. If not, teachers can use a lamp to provide minimum lighting for monitoring students during videos or films.

Schools often schedule maintenance, such as painting and floor cleaning, during the summer. Often, school administrators will accede to requests for a specific color of paint, given sufficient time for planning.

All secondary school classrooms should have a bulletin board used by the teacher and by the students. The effective teacher has plans for changing the board according to units of study. Space should be reserved for display of student work and projects, either on the bulletin board, the wall, or in the hallway. (Secondary teachers who need creative ideas can visit elementary classrooms.)

Bare walls can be depressing; however, covering the wall with too many posters can be visually distracting. Posters with sayings that promote cooperation, study skills, and content ideas should be displayed, but the same ones should not stay up all year because they will seem invisible when they become too familiar.

Most classrooms have movable desks, which allow for varied seating arrangements. If students are accustomed to sitting in rows, this is sometimes a good way to start the year. Harry K. Wong has described his method of assigning seats on the first day of school, which is to assign each desk a column and row number, then give students assignment cards as they come into the room. Another method is to put seating assignments on an overhead, visible when students enter the room. Once students are comfortable with classroom rules and procedures, the teacher can explain to students how to quickly move their desks into different formations for special activities, then return them to their original positions in the last 60 seconds of class.

The best place for the teacher's desk is often at the back of a room, so there are few barriers between the teacher and the students, and between the students and the chalkboards. This encourages the teacher to walk around the classroom to better monitor the students.

Social and Emotional Climate

The effective teacher maintains a climate that promotes the lifelong pursuit of learning. One way to do this is to practice research skills that will be helpful throughout life. All subject areas can promote the skills of searching for information to answer a question, filtering it to determine what is appropriate, and using what is helpful to solve a problem.

Here is an example. Most English teachers require some type of research project, from middle school through the senior year. Ken Macrorie's books on meaningful research can guide English teachers as they develop a project that can answer a real-life issue for students. For instance, a student who is trying to decide which college to attend could engage in database and print research on colleges that have the major characteristics he or she is interested in, conduct telephone or written interviews with school officials and current students, review school catalogs and other documents, and find magazine or journal articles that deal with the school. At the end of the process, students will have engaged in primary as well as secondary research, plus they will have an answer to a personal question.

The English teacher and any other subject area teacher can team up to collaborate on a joint research project. The resulting product satisfies both the need of the English teacher to teach research skills, and the need of the subject area teacher to teach content knowledge as well as research skills. Primary research can be done through local or regional resources such as business owners, lawyers, physicians, and the general public. Research questions could include: (1) What effects do artificial sweeteners have on the human body's functioning (biology)? (2) What process is used to develop the platform of a political party (history)? (3) What happens when a business is accused of Title IX violations (business)? (4) What effects have higher medical costs had on family budgets (economics)? (5) How has the popularity of music CDs affected the music industry and businesses that sell records and tapes (music and business)?

The effective teacher also facilitates a positive social and emotional atmosphere, and promotes a risk-taking environment for students. He or she sets up classroom rules and guidelines for how he or she will treat students, how students will treat him or her, and how students will treat each other. In part, this means that he or she doesn't allow ridicule or put-downs, either from the teacher or among the students. It also means that the teacher has an accepting attitude toward student ideas, especially when the idea is not what he or she was expecting to hear. Sometimes students can invent excellent ideas that are not always clear until they are asked to explain how they arrived at them.

Students should feel free to answer and ask any questions that are relevant to the class, without fear of sarcasm or ridicule. Teachers should always avoid sarcasm. Sometimes teachers consider sarcasm to be mere teasing, but because some students often interpret it negatively, effective teachers avoid all types and levels of sarcasm.

Academic Learning Time

The effective teacher maximizes the amount of time spent for instruction. A teacher who loses five minutes at the beginning of class and five minutes at the end of class wastes ten minutes a day that could have been spent at educational activities. Ten minutes may not seem like a lot of time to lose. However, this is equivalent to a whole period a week, four classes a month, and 36 periods a year.

Academic learning time is the amount of allocated time that students spend in an activity at the appropriate level of difficulty with the appropriate level of success. The appropriate level of difficulty is one which challenges students without frustrating them. Students who have typically been lower achievers need a higher rate of success than those who have typically been higher achievers.

One way to increase academic learning time is to teach students procedures so they will make transitions quickly. Another way is to have materials and resources ready for quick distribution and use. Teachers can also give students a time limit for a transition or an activity. In general, time limits for group work should be slightly shorter than students need, in order to encourage time on task and to prevent off-task behavior and discipline problems. It is essential for the teacher to have additional activities planned should the class finish activities sooner than anticipated. As students complete group work, they should have other group or individual activities so they can work up until the last minute before the end of class.

Classroom Behavior

The effective teacher realizes that having an interesting, carefully planned curriculum is one of the best ways to promote desired student behavior and to prevent most discipline problems. Teachers maintain a system of classroom rules, consequences, and rewards to guide students toward proper classroom behavior with the goal of keeping them engaged and on-task. Inevitably, students misbehave and test the techniques and procedures that teachers use to guide students back on-task. Some student behaviors will not respond to the standard procedures used by the effective teacher. If a student continues to misbehave frequently or in a disturbing manner, the effective teacher observes the student with the intent of determining if any external influences are causing the misbehavior that may require additional intervention from the student's teacher and family.

When under stress, students may be inclined to act out or to behave differently for the duration of the stress-inducing event. Students may react to events in the classroom or in their homes in a manner that violates the established policies of the classroom. For example, nervousness caused by a test or a school play audition may cause a student to speak out of turn or appear skittish. The loss of a loved one may cause a student to become depressed. Such behaviors are normal reactions to stress. However, teachers must pay attention to these situations and observe if the misbehavior occurs for an extended period of time. Unusual and/or aggressive student behavior may indicate that the student is suffering from severe emotional distress. Teachers must be careful to note the frequency, duration, and intensity of the student's misconduct.

Atypical behaviors, such as lying, stealing, and fighting, should be recorded if they transpire frequently. The teacher should attempt to determine the motivation behind the behavior. Is the child lying to avoid a reprimand? Is the student telling false stories to hide feelings of insecurity? Does the student cry during a particular subject, or at random moments during the school day? These are some of the many questions the teacher needs to consider.

Misbehaving may be a sign that a student is losing control of his or her actions and is looking for help. The role of the teacher in these situations is to help determine if the student is acting out as a reaction to a particular issue, or if there is a deeper emotional problem. Some students may require various forms of therapy to treat the emotional disturbances that cause the misbehavior. Therapy can also be used to examine the possibilities of a more severe cause for the student's behavior.

If concerned that a student is suffering from emotional stress, the teacher should contact, and then remain in constant discussion with, the student's parents. It is particularly important in these situations to establish an open dialogue with the student's family to facilitate the student's treatment. When combined, the parents and teacher will be able to provide important and unique insights into the student's situation.

Chapter 6

School professionals are another valuable resource for advice, assistance, and support when dealing with students' emotional disturbances. Guidance counselors, school psychiatrists, and other specialists are able to aid in the counseling of these students and make recommendations for the parents and teacher. Together with the student's family, these professionals may develop or recommend a particular program or therapy for treatment.

When working with a class of students with emotional disorders, the management of the classroom must be flexible to aid in the student's development. While the goal of any management system is to prevent misbehavior, the teacher must be prepared to provide an area or opportunity for the student to regain control, should an emotional episode occur.

Teachers should also be aware that drug therapy is often used as a form of treatment. Prescribed by medical doctors, the drug treatments available can help students gain independence from their disorder. However, these drugs treat the symptoms, rather than the cause of the disorder, and can have severe side effects. Drug treatments should not be taken lightly. Their use should also be closely monitored by the classroom teacher and the school nurse.

Behavior Patterns

Established behavior patterns that teachers must be aware of include mood disorders, psychotic disorders, and autism.

Mood Disorders

Mood disorders are characterized by various emotional and physical signs. Depression can manifest itself in an overall lack of interest in activities, constant crying, or talk of suicide. Anxiety or obsessive thoughts are another indication of a possible mood disorder. Physical signs include a disruption in eating or sleeping patterns, headaches, nausea and stomach pain, or diarrhea. These difficulties need to be addressed by the teacher as a cause for serious concern and treatment.

Psychotic Disorders

Psychotic disorders, such as schizophrenia, are serious emotional disorders. These disorders are rare in young children and difficult to diagnose. One of the warning signs for this disorder is a student who experiences a complete break from the reality of his or her surroundings. Schizophrenics may have difficulty expressing themselves, resulting in unusual speech patterns or even muteness. Schizophrenics, who are more likely to be boys than girls, may also exhibit facial expressions that are either markedly absent of emotion or overly active.

Early Infantile Autism

Infantile autism is a serious emotional disorder that appears in early childhood. It is characterized by withdrawn behavior, and delayed or absent language and communication skills.

Symptoms of autism can appear in children between four and eighteen months of age. Autistic children will usually distance themselves from others and may be unable to experience empathy. In addition, they often cannot distinguish or appreciate humor. These symptoms are frequently misdiagnosed as mental retardation, hearing/ auditory impairment, or brain damage.

Autistic children may have a preoccupation with particular objects, or may perform particular activities repeatedly. While autistic children can range in all levels of intelligence, some children can be extremely skilled in particular and focused areas, such as music or math.

Treatment for autistic children may involve therapy, drugs, or residential living. However, only five percent of autistic children becomes socially well-adjusted adults.

References

Further reading of these references may enhance understanding of the chapter and may also increase performance on the examination.

"Physical Environment of the Classroom", pages 157-160. *Reading Instruction Essentials* by Anita Price Davis (Third Edition) Boston, Massachusetts: American Press, 2004.

Maslow's Hierarchy of Needs
    http://chiron.valdosta.edu/whuitt/col/regsys/maslow.html

    http://web.utk.edu/~gwynne/maslow.HTM

Managing Student Behavior in the Classroom

Overview

The teacher develops a standard for student behavior in the classroom.

Jaime Escalante, called "America's greatest teacher" by President Reagan and the subject of the motion picture *Stand and Deliver,* tells a story about having two students named Johnny in his class. He says that one, "good Johnny," was a dedicated and responsible student, courteous, polite, and high-achieving. The other Johnny, "bad Johnny," seldom came to class, and when he did, he created discipline problems. "Bad Johnny" wouldn't listen, wouldn't do his work, and wouldn't cooperate.

On the night of the annual open house, a very nice woman came to Mr. Escalante's classroom and introduced herself, "I am Johnny's mother." Mr. Escalante assumed she was "good Johnny's" mother. He said, "Oh, I am so glad to meet you. You must be very proud of your son. He is an exceptional student, and I am pleased to have him in my class."

The next day, "bad Johnny" came to class. After class, he approached Mr. Escalante and asked, "Hey, why did you tell my mother those things last night? No one has ever said anything like that about me." It was then that Mr. Escalante realized his mistake.

He didn't admit his error to Johnny, and the strangest thing happened next. "Bad Johnny" stopped being bad. He started coming to class. He started doing his work. He started making good grades. Mr. Escalante concludes his story by saying, "I ended up with two 'good Johnnys' in my class."

This anecdote emphasizes an important aspect of teaching: Teacher perception is ultimately significant. Students may be what their teachers think them to be. What's more, students may also become what their teachers believe them to be. Teachers report that when they treat their students like responsible young adults, most students rise to the occasion. This is the "Pygmalion in the Classroom" phenomenon as Rosenthal studied.

A teacher deals with various misconduct in a manner that promotes and maintains instructional momentum.

Teachers must be "with it" in a classroom to prevent misbehavior that will interrupt the flow of learning. The level of "with it"-ness must extend beyond the obvious events of the classroom. A teacher needs to understand the dynamics behind the actions that occur in the classroom, and then proceed accordingly.

There are many factors that influence student behavior. Young children will generally follow the rules of the classroom out of a desire to please their teachers. Misbehavior that occurs in a classroom may be the result of a conflict that is occurring elsewhere. Teachers should be aware that these conflicts can occur between peers, between students and the teacher, or as a result of events in the student's family or out-of-classroom experiences.

Cognitive Development and Moral Decision-Making

Of course, teachers of young children may have to contend with some different issues, but all teachers should be aware of age and maturational differences among students. Jean Piaget, whose ideas on cognitive development have greatly influenced American education, thought that children younger than eight years of age (because of their egocentric thought) were unable to take the perspective of another individual. Thus, Piaget concluded that children under the age of eight made decisions about right and wrong on the basis of how much harm was caused. For example, children might say that a child who ate two forbidden cookies was less guilty than the child who ate six forbidden cookies. Children over the age of eight, however, were able to take into consideration whether or not the individual acted purposely or accidentally. For example, a child who broke a toy by accident was not as guilty of misbehavior as the child who broke the toy on purpose. Researchers who have tested Piaget's ideas have found that children younger than age eight are able to engage in moral reasoning at much more complex levels than Piaget thought possible.

The term *standards*, when used with regard to behavior, evokes issues of right and wrong, sometimes referred to as ethical or moral decisions. With regard to moral development, teachers should be familiar with the concepts of Lawrence Kohlberg. Kohlberg, following the example of Piaget, developed a scenario to quiz children and teens. Kohlberg told a story about a man whose wife was so seriously ill that she would die without medication, yet her husband had no money to buy her medicine. After trying various legal means to get the medicine, her husband considered stealing it. Kohlberg asked if it were wrong or right to steal the drug, and to explain why it was either wrong or right. Kohlberg did not evaluate whether the respondent said it was wrong or right to steal the drug; he was interested in the reasons given to justify the actions.

On the basis of the responses he received, Kohlberg proposed six stages of moral development. Stage one, punishment and obedience, describes children who simply follow the rules so as to escape punishment. If these children, for example kindergarten-age students, are told not to talk or they'll lose their chance to go outside for recess, they will not want to lose their playground privileges, so they will not talk. On the other hand, stage two, individualism and change, refers to children who follow the rules, not only to escape punishment, but also when they think there is some reward in following the rules. These children, for example older primary-grade children, seek not only to escape punishment, but also to receive a reward or benefit for their good behavior.

Kohlberg's stage three is described as mutual interpersonal expectations and interpersonal conformity; at this stage, children want to please the people who are important to them. Junior high students, for example, may behave in a manner that gains the approval of their peers or their idols.

At stage four, Kohlberg said that adolescents become oriented to conscience, and they recognize the importance of established social order. Teens at this stage obey the rules unless those rules contradict higher social responsibilities. In other words, most high school students realize that rules are necessary, and they will obey most rules if the rules are based on basic social values, such as honesty, mutual respect, courtesy, and so forth.

Post-conventional morality was the term Kohlberg gave to stages five and six. At stage five, individuals recognize the importance of both individual rights and social contracts, but believe that people should generally abide by the rules to bring the greatest good to the majority. Kohlberg believes that about one-fifth of adolescents reaches stage five. Therefore, Kohlberg would have expected that few high school students would be operating at this level.

Finally, Kohlberg would not have expected high school students to reach stage six, since he believed that very few individuals ever reached this stage. Stage six is characterized by universal principles of justice. Individuals at this stage believe that most rules should be obeyed because most rules are based on just principles; however, if rules violate ethical principles, then individuals have a greater obligation to follow their conscience even if that means breaking the rules. Social reformers, such as Martin Luther King, Jr., would be an example of stage six moral reasoning.

Kohlberg's theory describes the progression of children's moral reasoning from school entry at kindergarten (stage one) to graduation from high school (stages four, and five for some). Kohlberg's theory has been widely taught and applied in school settings, but not without controversy.

Some have contended that Kohlberg's theory is limited and biased because of his research techniques (getting reactions to a scenario), and because his theory was based on a study of white, middle-class males under the age of 17. Many would say that his ideas have limited application to other ethnic groups, socioeconomic groups, or females.

One theorist interested in applying Kohlberg's theory to women is Carol Gilligan, a student of Kohlberg's, who developed an alternative theory of moral development in women. Gilligan found that women, unlike the men at Kohlberg's stages five and six, tend to value caring and compassion for others above abstract, rational principles. Therefore, when women make decisions, they base their conclusions on how others will be affected by their choices and actions.

Gilligan posited that women pass through three levels of moral reasoning, although like Kohlberg, not all reach the third level. At the first level, the individual is concerned only about herself. At level two, the individual sacrifices her own interests for the sake of others. Finally, at the third level, the individual synthesizes responsibilities to both herself and to others.

An effective teacher may want to consider the implications of these theories for the behavior of students in their classes, in particular, how students will respond to rules of behavior. Although students taking the exam will not be tested on these specific theorists, they are, nonetheless, valuable resources for assessing student behavior. For example, according to Kohlberg, younger students are more concerned about punishments and rewards; older students are more concerned about reasonable rules based on principles of fairness and equality. According to Gilligan, female students may be thinking about how rules affect their friendships. To illustrate, according to these theorists, a male student might be offended by someone cheating (because cheating is wrong) and report the individual to the teacher. Female students, on the other hand, might value their friendship with the cheater more than the principle of honesty; therefore, females might be less likely to report cheating to the teacher.

Learning Styles and Personality Types

Information about learning styles and personality types essential to effective teaching can also shed light on how individuals make ethical and moral decisions. For example, research indicates that the population is fairly evenly distributed between people who make decisions based on rational, logical, and objective data—thinking types—and those who make decisions based on feelings—feeling types. Slightly more males than females are thinking types.

The "feeling" half of the population tends to make decisions based on how those decisions may affect others, avoiding conflict and promoting harmony; slightly more females than males are feeling types.

In addition to this aspect of type, that is, how people make decisions, is the aspect of type that deals with how people learn or process information. Most people (approximately 76 percent) are the "sensing type", those who learn through sensory experiences; they are linear learners who enjoy facts and details. They like sequential organization and memory tasks. They often work slowly and methodically, taking great care to finish each project before beginning another one.

On the other hand, however, is the minority (approximately 24 percent) which is the intuitive type. This type learns not through experience, but by insight and inspiration. These students are bored by facts and details, and prefer global concepts and theories. They dislike memory work. Generally, they are quick to grasp ideas and catch on to the gist of things; this means they can be disruptive because they have already learned their lesson or finished their assignment. While they generally perform well on tests, they also daydream and lose interest quickly in the things that they deem uninteresting or dull. They like to do several things at once and find it tedious to have to slow down or wait for others to finish.

Standards for Classroom Behavior

Teachers who understand these characteristics and ways of thinking, whether it is in regard to information processing or moral decision making, can use this information to establish standards for classroom behavior. Standards should reflect community values and norms, and should take into consideration students' ethnicity (i.e., what language they speak at home), socioeconomic status, and religious beliefs. These factors are important when formulating a dress code, determining how to address authority figures, defining the use of appropriate language, examining interactions between males and females, or developing school safety procedures. An important part of the teacher's role is to educate the students about school policies, and/or district and state policies with regard to these issues.

What are common values across cultural, ethnic, religious, and social strata? Honesty, mutual respect, consideration, and courtesy are among those virtues that have widespread acceptance. Students (and their parents) should know about standards for attendance, grades, and student behavior. Students should know how to dress for school, how to address their teachers and other school employees, and what is appropriate language for school (limiting the use of slang or vulgarities). They should know rules for turning in homework, rules for making up missed assignments, and rules for handing in work late (if it is accepted). They should know what they can and cannot bring to school (certain kinds of materials and tools). They should know what will happen if they break the rules.

Psychological research on behavior modification and reducing aggression shows that modeling acceptable and nonaggressive behaviors is more effective than catharsis and punishment. Teachers are most effective when they follow the rules and exemplify the standards of conduct themselves. Teachers who are courteous, prompt, enthusiastic, in control, patient, and organized provide examples for students through their own behavior. They send the message "Do as I do," not "Do as I say."

In addition to modeling appropriate behaviors, another effective way of treating misbehavior (that is, more effective than catharsis and punishment) is the use of incompatible responses. Effective teachers learn how to employ these responses. Some studies have even suggested that open body language (arms open, not crossed) and positive facial expressions (smiling) can be used by teachers to diffuse student anger.

Rules and the Student's Role in Decision-Making

Some educational experts have suggested that standards and rules are most effective if students play a role in formulating them. This doesn't mean that students make all the rules, but it means that they can contribute ideas. Stephen Covey, author of the best-selling *The Seven Habits of Highly Effective People,* suggests that people who desire to be effective or successful should be proactive. He explains that being proactive means anticipating everything that can go awry before it does; teachers can think about what could go wrong in class concerning a student's conduct and be prepared if it ever happens. Of course, a teacher may not be able to predict everything that a student may attempt, but trying to analyze many possibilities may provide a teacher some level of comfort in dealing with misbehaviors. Covey also uses the term *proactive* to stress the importance of self-direction, not only for teachers, but for students, as well.

Allowing students to have a voice in establishing standards and formulating codes provide students with an excellent opportunity to exercise their problem-solving skills and critical-thinking abilities. Although one key purpose of education is to teach students to become responsible citizens capable of participating thoughtfully in a democratic society, educational practices have had a tendency to foster dependency, passivity, and a "tell me what to think and do" complacency.

Older students especially can benefit from participating in the decision-making process. American industries and businesses have attained greater success, efficiency, and effectiveness through principles of Total Quality Management (TQM). Many TQM principles have also been applied to American education with great success.

One of the key ingredients of TQM is information sharing, so that all partners in an endeavor are aware of goals and objectives. If education is the endeavor, then applying TQM principles means that teachers and students, parents and principals, and other supporting players are all partners in the endeavor. Following TQM principles also means that if all partners have information concerning goals and objectives, then they can form a team to work cooperatively with greater efficiency and effectiveness to achieve goals and objectives.

These ideas require teachers to share authority with students, allowing students a voice in decision making. For some teachers, learning to share control with students may be difficult. Helping students to make some of their own decisions will conflict with some teachers' training, as well as their own ideas and expectations about being in charge. But the many benefits of shared decision making as described above, are worth the struggle to adjust.

Although this may not sound like the perfect classroom to every teacher, Covey describes what, for him, was his most exciting learning experience:

> As a teacher, I have come to believe that many great classes teeter on the very edge of chaos.... There are times when neither the teacher nor the student knows for sure what's going to happen. In the beginning, there is a safe environment that enables people to be really open and to learn and to listen to each other's ideas. Then comes the brainstorming, where the spirit of evaluation is subordinated to the spirit of creativity, imagining, and intellectual networking. Then an absolutely unusual phenomenon begins to take place. The entire class is transformed with the excitement of a new thrust, a new idea, a new direction that's hard to define, yet it's almost palpable to the people involved.

Covey describes a dynamic classroom, not one in stasis; however, there are important requirements for the classroom. First, the students have to feel safe, not only safe from physical harm, but safe from mental harm—from mockery, intimidation, unfair criticisms, threats—from teachers or, especially, other classmates. These features describe a classroom in which there is mutual respect and trust between teacher and students and among the students themselves.

The Teacher's Role

One experienced teacher of seventh- and eighth-grade students has suggested the following guidelines for teachers in managing their classes:

- ✔ **Let students have input whenever you can, and when you can't, let them think they are giving input;**

- ✔ **Listen to students; they have surprising insights and viewpoints;**

- ✔ **Be consistent with expectations and consequences;**

- ✔ **Don't make exceptions to school rules, even if you don't agree with them;**

- ✔ **Don't correct or reprimand a student in front of a class. Quickly establish that your classroom is a safe place and can be a fun place, but that disrespect for learning, others, or property will not be tolerated and there will be no further warnings;**

- ✔ **Do not begin teaching until everyone is ready to learn;**

- ✔ **Do consult with colleagues and administrators for advice;**

- ✔ **Make sure that students know their rights and their responsibilities.**

Blanchard and Johnson, the authors of *The One Minute Manager*, another best-selling book for those wanting to achieve success, suggest using one-minute goal-setting. This can be attained by: a) deciding on goals; b) identifying what good behaviors are; c) writing out goals; d) reading and re-reading goals; e) reviewing goals every day; and f) determining if behaviors match goals. This list is applicable to the classroom teacher who needs to decide on behavioral goals, and identify behaviors both expected and unacceptable.

Another good technique offered by these authors is the "one-minute praise," by which they encourage catching people (in this case, students) doing something right. Blanchard and Johnson suggest to praise people immediately, telling them what they did right. In applying this principle to students, the teacher would tell students how he or she feels about their behavior, how it has helped others in class, and helped the success of the class. The teacher would stop for a moment after the praise to let the student feel good about the praise. Finally, the teacher would encourage the student to continue behaving in this manner, shaking hands with the student.

Likewise, the one-minute reprimand could also be useful. However, the teacher should reprimand the student after class, avoiding interrupting a lesson whenever possible. Specifically, the teacher should tell the student what was done wrong. After correcting the student, the teacher should stop and let the student think about the situation for a moment. Then, the teacher should shake hands with the student, and remind the student that he or she is valued and affirmed as a person, even though his or her behavior was inappropriate. It is important to distinguish between the individual student (who deserves respect) and the individual's actions (which may be disrespectful and/or unacceptable).

As final advice, Blanchard and Johnson admonish, "When it's over, it's over." After correcting the student, the teacher should not harbor a grudge or ill-will toward the student or dwell on the infraction, but move on to the next task at hand. The authors conclude their book by stating, "Goals begin behaviors, consequences maintain behaviors."

When teachers discipline students, they should remember that the word *discipline* comes from the Latin word for teaching. The whole point of disciplining a student should be to teach the student what is right and correct, not to embarrass, humiliate, or shame a student.

Teachers should make sure that students understand the rules and that they understand the consequences for breaking the rules. Teachers, like parents, should carefully choose their battles. They should not make rules that they do not want to enforce. Consequences for breaking rules should be certain and swift. Consequences should be appropriate in scope and severity to the infraction.

Budd Churchward, creator of *The Honor Level System: Discipline by Design*, describes a system of discipline with four stages. Step one is a reminder. He explains that a reminder is not a reprimand. A reminder can be directed at an individual or the entire class. Churchward stresses that many students will learn quickly to respond to reminders, but he points out, "Some teachers may complain that they should not have to remind children over and over. We remind the children because they ARE children."

Step two is a reprimand, approaching a student and issuing a verbal or written reprimand. Verbal warnings are not given across the room, but delivered personally to the student. The teacher comes close to the student and tells him or her what to do; the student is asked to identify the next step (step three). Written warnings, however, are described as being even more effective. The teacher approaches the student and gives the student an infraction slip. The teacher has checked an item on the slip and tells the student that if no further problem occurs, the student can throw the slip away at the end of the class or period. If the misbehavior continues, the slip will be collected and turned in (to the principal's office). Churchward emphasizes that it is important that the child have possession of the slip, and knows that he or she is in control of the slip and what happens to it next (fostering and encouraging internal locus of control, or a feeling of being in charge, being self-directed, or proactive, as Covey would say).

Step three is collecting the infraction slip. If the student is approached again, he or she is reminded that a warning already has been issued. If the student received a verbal warning, an infraction slip now is sent to the office. If the student has the infraction slip, it is taken up. The student is then asked to identify the next step.

The next step, the final step, is to send the offender to the office, removing the student from class. Churchward advises that if the first three steps are followed faithfully, the last step is rarely required. However, if things do go this far, he insists that the teacher can stay calm and unemotional, perhaps saying something such as, "Tomorrow we will try again. I'm sure that we can work this out."

Churchward recommends that these steps be posted in several places in the classroom, in addition to posting three to five selected classroom rules important to teaching. The list should be short and stated in a positive way. For example, instead of writing, "Students will not ask for repeated directions," the teacher should write, "Students will follow directions the first time they are given." By taking time to go over the rules and the steps with students, they will know that they can always look on the wall if the teacher asks them what the next step will be. Churchward says it is important to let students know that they may be asked to identify the next step if they get in trouble; also, students should know that the teacher has the right to skip steps in extreme cases if there are certain behaviors that cannot be tolerated. Teachers should be specific about the behaviors that are not tolerated and give students exact examples of what is meant.

Some other practices, which may encourage good classroom behaviors, are a) monitoring; b) low-key interventions; c) "I" messages; and d) positive teaching. Briefly, monitoring refers to walking around the room to monitor what students are doing. After a teacher gives an assignment, he or she should wait a few minutes to give students time to get started and then the teacher should move around the room, checking to make sure that all students have begun their work. Thus, the teacher can also give individualized instruction as needed. Students who are not working may be motivated to begin as they see the teacher approaching. The teacher should not interrupt the class during monitoring, but should use a quiet voice to show personal attention.

Low-key interventions are quiet and calm. Effective teachers are careful that students are not rewarded for misbehavior by becoming the focus of attention. By being proactive, teachers have anticipated problems before they occur. When teachers correct misbehaving students, the teachers are inconspicuous, making sure not to distract others in the class. When they lecture, effective teachers know to frequently mention students by name to bring their attention back to class.

"I" messages are an effective communication technique, whatever the situation; however, they can be used with particular success in the classroom. The message begins with the word "I" and contains a message about feelings. For example, a teacher might say, "I am very frustrated about the way you are ignoring instruction. When you talk while I am talking, I have to stop teaching and that is very frustrating."

Finally, positive discipline refers to the use of language to express what the teacher wants instead of the things that students cannot do. Instead of saying, "No fighting," a teacher can say, "Settle conflicts using your words." Taking a positive approach with language also means using lots of praise. An effective teacher is quick to praise students for their good behavior, using lots of smiles and positive body language, as well as laudatory words.

Rules and School Safety Issues

The importance of a safe school environment for promoting good behavior has been mentioned already. According to a 1999 report issued jointly by the National Center for Education Statistics and the Bureau of Justice Statistics, in 1996-1997 10 percent of all public schools reported to authorities at least one serious violent crime—including murder, rape or other type of sexual battery, suicide, physical attack or fight with a weapon, or robbery. "Another 47 percent of public schools reported a less serious violent or nonviolent crime," while the remaining 43 percent reported no crime at all. The report observes that despite an overall decline in school crime rates in recent years, "students seem to feel less safe at school now than just a few years ago." In particular, the presence of street gangs on school property is cited as contributing to these fears. Thus, the fear—as much as the reality—of victimization presents a serious challenge for the teacher.

Research shows that the following factors contribute to school violence and antisocial behaviors: overcrowding, poor design and use of school space, lack of disciplinary procedures, student alienation, multi-cultural insensitivity, rejection of at-risk students by teachers and peers, and anger or resentment at school routines. On the other hand, the following characteristics contribute to school safety: positive school climate and atmosphere, clear and high performance expectations for all students, practices and values that promote inclusion, student bonding to school, high levels of student participation and parent involvement in school activities, and opportunities to acquire academic skills and develop socially.

Effective teachers need to be alert to the signs of potentially violent behavior, acknowledging that signs can easily be misinterpreted and misunderstood. Warning signs should be used to get help for children, not to exclude, punish, or isolate them. Experts also emphasize that warning signs should not be seen as a checklist for identifying, labeling, or stereotyping children, and that referrals to outside agencies based on early warning signals must be kept confidential and, except for those suspected of child abuse or neglect, must have parental consent.

The American Psychological Association has identified four "accelerating factors" that increase the risk of violence. These four factors are a) early involvement with drugs and alcohol; b) easy access to weapons, especially handguns; c) association with antisocial, deviant peer-groups; and d) pervasive exposure to media violence. Longitudinal studies (studies following groups over time) have shown youth violence and delinquency to be linked with situations in which a) one or more parents have been arrested; b) the child has been the client of a child-protection agency; c) the child's family has experienced death, divorce, or another serious transition; d) the child has received special-education services; and/or e) the youth exhibits severe antisocial behavior.

Along somewhat analogous lines, the U.S. Department of Education and Department of Justice have compiled a long list of possible early warning signs. These signs include a) social withdrawal (often associated with feelings of depression, rejection, persecution, unworthiness, and lack of confidence); b) excessive feelings of isolation and isolating oneself; c) excessive feelings of rejection; d) being a victim of violence—including physical or sexual abuse; e) feelings of being picked on and persecuted; f) low school interest and poor academic performance; g) expression of violence in writings and drawings; h) uncontrolled anger; i) patterns of impulsive and chronic hitting, intimidating, and bullying behaviors; j) history of discipline problems; k) history of violent and aggressive behaviors; l) intolerance for differences and prejudicial attitudes; m) drug use and alcohol use; n) affiliation with gangs; o) inappropriate access to, possession of, and use of firearms; and p) serious threats of violence.

In addition to these early warning signs are what the Departments of Education and Justice called imminent warning signs, which require an immediate response. Imminent warning signs are a) serious physical fighting with peers or family members; b) serious destruction of property; c) rage for seemingly minor reasons; d) detailed threats of lethal violence; e) possession and/or use of firearms and weapons; and f) other self-injurious behaviors or threats of suicide. Immediate intervention by school authorities and possibly by law enforcement officials are required if a child has presented a detailed plan to harm or kill others, or is carrying a weapon—particularly a firearm—and has threatened to use it. Parents should be informed immediately about situations in which students present other threatening behaviors.

Violence prevention strategies at school range from adding social-skills training to the curriculum to installing metal detectors at the entrances to buildings. Educational experts recommend that schools teach all students procedures in conflict resolution and anger management, in addition to explaining the school's rules, expectations, and disciplinary policies.

The federal Gun-Free Schools Act of 1994 required every state to pass zero-tolerance laws on weapons at school or face the loss of federal funds. Every state has complied with this law and requires school districts to expel students for at least a year if they bring weapons to school.

The U.S. Department of Education and the Department of Justice have produced a joint report recommending actions to promote school safety. First, an open discussion of safety issues is essential. "Schools can reduce the risk of violence," the report says, "by teaching children about the dangers of firearms, as well as appropriate strategies for dealing with feelings, expressing anger in appropriate ways, and resolving conflicts. Schools also should teach children that they are responsible for their actions and that the choices they make have consequences for which they will be held accountable." Also recommended is treating students with equal respect, creating ways for students to share their concerns, and helping children to feel safe when expressing their feelings.

In review, effective and safe schools develop and enforce consistent rules that are clear, broad-based, and fair. Effective schoolwide disciplinary policies include a code of conduct, specific rules, and consequences that can accommodate student differences on a case-by-case basis when needed. School policies need to include anti-harassment and anti-violence policies, and due process rights. Rules should reflect the cultural values and educational goals of the community. School staff, students, and families should be involved in the development, discussion, and implementation of fair rules, written and applied in a nondiscriminatory manner, and accommodating cultural diversity. Consequences for violating rules must be commensurate with the offenses, and negative consequences must be accompanied by positive teaching for socially appropriate behaviors. Finally, there must be zero-tolerance for illegal possession of weapons, drugs, or alcohol.

"With it"-ness in the Classroom

The goal of "with it"-ness is to prevent misconduct in the classroom. Through everyday interactions, the teacher develops a sense of an individual student's normal behavior and general mental state. The "with it" teacher also develops a sense of the relations between the students in a class and within the school. If the beginning of a conflict between individuals in a class is noticed, the "with it" teacher is able to mediate the students to a resolution that avoids the disruption of class time.

The desired behavior for the students should be well-explained and clearly displayed in a classroom. Posted rules provide a constant guide and reminder of classroom rules. Teachers can also use these displays as a reference when discussing expected behavior, either individually or with the class as a whole.

Teachers should self-monitor their interactions with the misbehaving students. Children may act out if they feel they are threatened, disliked, or treated unfairly. A "with it" teacher knows which particular students are causing the class disruption and works to curb this behavior without punishing the class as a whole. The class momentum can be disrupted either by the teacher's response to the behavior or by the teacher allowing the misbehavior to persist.

Both the individual student and the class as a whole are affected by how the teacher handles classroom misconduct. The effective approach is when the teacher compliments the positive behavior modeled by other students in the classroom, rather than individually reprimanding student misbehavior. If certain students are not properly addressing the task at hand, the teacher can say, "I like the way Glen is working in his math book" or "Belinda, I like the way you are quietly raising your hand and waiting your turn." By doing so, the teacher is reinforcing the desired behavior for the class without directly addressing and calling attention to the misbehavior. The individual student has an opportunity to monitor his or her own behavior, and class momentum is not lost.

Teachers can also guide a student toward appropriate behavior by stating the student's name, or explaining what task he or she should currently be working on. Non-verbal cues include walking toward the student, making eye contact, or gently touching the student's desk or shoulder. These techniques can be used without disrupting the flow of the classroom.

Teachers must clearly voice their expectations without yelling or being angry. Quiet and controlled reprimands have been shown to be very effective. Maintaining control without involving punitive measures lowers the tension in the entire classroom. Students should not be made to feel uncomfortable because the teacher is angry. This is especially important when teachers are working with small groups, or when working on simultaneous tasks. Individualized instruction should not suffer when the teacher must reprimand another student. When a teacher demonstrates "with it"-ness, students do not feel that they have an opportunity to misbehave just because the teacher's attention is not focused directly on them.

Parent-Teacher Communication

If a student is misbehaving, the teacher should examine if the misbehavior is caused by a conflict in the classroom. If the cause cannot be determined based on classroom experience, there may be a problem at home. When a child is not responding to the teacher's efforts to stop the behavior, the teacher should contact the parents. This will allow the teacher and parents to discuss any problems that may help explain the misbehavior. The parents may be facing similar difficulties at home, or may not even be aware of a problem. Such a discussion enables the teacher and parents to work together at getting the child back on track. It is important for the teacher to express his or her feelings of concern to the parents. The parents should also be assured that the child's educational welfare and personal well-being are continuing primary concerns of the teacher.

The teacher can contact the parents using a written note, a telephone call, a meeting outside of school hours, or even a home visit if the administration approves. During the conference, the teacher should mention the incidents of misbehavior, the record of the student's daily effort if failure to accomplish assignments is the problem or part of it, the attempts made to change the negative performance, and the suggestions for solving the problem. In turn, the teacher should ask the parents about the child's attitude toward school, comments, and behavior at home. Having the student present is sometimes a useful strategy, especially if the student is omitting part of the story when talking about it at home. The parents and teacher must develop a partnership to focus on the student's well-being.

The end of any conference should include writing down the actions each participant—teacher, parent, and student—will take to improve the situation. A tentative date for meeting again, or at least for communication between the teacher and parents, should be established before the meeting ends. Within a few days, the teacher must try to find an opportunity to provide feedback to both the parents and the student about the matters discussed, especially if improvement of a negative situation is noted.

If the initial consultation with the parents is not successful at ending the misbehavior, there are a few techniques that the teacher and parents can try. A daily report may be used to provide frequent contact between the teacher and the student that allows the parents to monitor the student's behavior in the classroom. The teacher sends home a report of the student's behavior, positive and/or negative, for the parents to review, sign, and return back to the teacher the next day. This also provides the parents with a way to add their own feedback to the situation. If the behavior improves, the reports can be sent less frequently, until the student's behavior is consistently positive.

If the combined efforts of the parents and the teacher are unable to resolve the situation, they may need to consult with a school or community professional. Family or individual counseling may be another route to end the student's conflict, and guide him or her back into the classroom momentum.

References

Further reading of these references may enhance understanding of this chapter and may also increase performance on the examination.

Blanchard, K. and S. Johnson. *The One Minute Manager.* New York: Berkley Books, 1981.

Border, L. *Morphing: A Quintessential Human Capability.* National Teaching and Learning Forum, Vol. 7 (4).

Churchward, B. *The Honor Level System.* 1995.

Covey, Stephen. *The Seven Habits of Highly Effective People.* New York: Simon and Schuster, 1989.

ERIC Clearinghouse on Educational Management. *Trends and Issues: School Safety and Violence Prevention.* 1998.

Florida State Board of Education. *The Code of Ethics and the Principles of Professional Conduct of the Education Profession in Florida.* 1998.

Gilligan, C. *In a Different Voice: Psychological Theory and Women's Development.* Cambridge, Massachusetts: Harvard University Press, 1982.

Kaufman, P., Chen, X., Choy, S. P., Ruddy, S. A., Miller, A. K., Chandler, K. A., Chapman, C. D., Rand, M. R., and Klaus, P. *Indicators of School Crime and Safety, 1999.* U.S. Departments of Education and Justice, National Center for Education Statistics and Bureau of Justice Statistics, Washington, D.C.: 1999.

Kohlberg, L. "The Psychology of Moral Development: The Nature and Validity of Moral Stages." *Essays on Moral Development* (Vol. 2), 1984.

McDaniel, T. R. "A Primer on Classroom Discipline." *Phi Delta Kappan* September 1986, pags 63-67.

Myers, I. B. *Gifts Differing.* Palo Alto, California: Consulting Psychologists Press, 1980.

Rosenthal, R. and Jacobson, L. *Pygmalion in the Classroom* New York:Rinehart and Winston, 1968.

Sternberg, R. *In Search of the Human Mind.* Ft. Worth, Texas: Harcourt Brace, 1995.

U.S. Departments of Education and Justice. *Early Warning, Timely Response.* Washington, D.C.: U.S. Government Printing Office, 1998.

Assessment, Tests, and Measurement

Overview

A teacher determines the entry-level understanding and ability of students for a given set of educational objectives using diagnostic tests, teacher observations, and/or student records.

A teacher creates classroom tests and tasks to measure students' accomplishments of the teacher's and the school's objectives.

A teacher should create a testing environment for students in which they can display their knowledge and skills, and obtain sufficient information about the quality of their test performance.

Considerable effort is necessary to develop tests and other procedures to evaluate students. However, if the testing environment in which the student is expected to perform is neglected, the evaluative information obtained on students will be suspect. The purpose of this narrative is to describe and explain procedures for establishing a proper testing environment. The discussion in this chapter provides information about administering teacher-made, pencil-paper tests. In the case of standardized testing, the information provided to the proctor should be strictly followed to make certain the conditions under which the test was normed are also the conditions under which the students take the test. Performance tests that measure skill acquisition call for demonstration of proficiency in a given task. Some of the discussion that follows can be generalized to skill testing and standardized tests, but that is not the primary focus of this chapter. Thus, this chapter describes the procedures to follow in the administration of teacher-made, paper-pencil tests.

The three phases of testing described in this chapter are (1) preparation for testing; (2) test administration; and (3) formative feedback.

The teacher establishes an effective system for maintaining student records.

Teachers will develop a sense of what progress their class has made based on their many hours of interaction with the students. It is very important, however, to keep accurate records of student achievement in addition to the more business-related tasks of attendance and inventory. Reviewing these records provides the teacher with the opportunity for self-evaluation: Is the class performing better in some areas than in others? Are the students being graded on a variety of tasks? Am I meeting the requirements of the curriculum? Careful recording will allow for detailed report cards and a more reliable assessment of the individual students and the class as a whole. This knowledge will facilitate meaningful and specific conferences with students and parents.

This chapter will review different forms of recordkeeping, grade reporting, and the laws surrounding the maintenance of permanent student records.

Purposes of Assessment

The effective teacher understands the importance of ongoing assessment as an instructional tool for the classroom and uses both informal and formal assessment measures. Informal measures may include observation, journals, written drafts, and conversations. More formal measures may include teacher-made tests, district exams, and standardized tests. Effective teachers use both formative and summative evaluation. Formative evaluation occurs during the process of learning, when the teacher or the students monitor(s) progress in obtaining outcomes, while it is still possible to modify instruction. Summative evaluation occurs at the end of a specific time period or course, usually by a single grade used to represent a student's performance.

Teacher-Made Tests

The effective teacher uses a variety of assessment techniques. Teacher-made instruments are ideally developed at the same time as the goals and outcomes are planned, rather than at the last minute after all the lessons have been taught. Carefully planned objectives and assessment instruments serve as lesson development guides for the teacher.

Paper and pencil tests are the most common method for evaluation of student progress. There are a number of different types of questions: multiple-choice, true/false, matching, fill-in-the-blank, short answer, and longer essay. The first five types tend to test the knowledge or comprehension levels. Essays often test at the lower levels, but are suitable for assessing learning at higher levels. Projects, papers, and portfolios can provide assessment of higher-level thinking skills.

If the purpose is to test student recall of factual information, a short objective test (multiple-choice, true/false, matching, fill-in-the-blank) would be most effective and efficient. The first three types of questions can be answered on machine-scorable scan sheets to provide quick and accurate scoring. Disadvantages are that they generally test lower levels of knowledge and don't provide an opportunity for an explanation of answers.

If the purpose is to test student ability to analyze an event, compare and contrast two concepts, make predictions about an experiment, or evaluate a character's actions, then an essay question would provide the best paper/pencil opportunity for the student to show what he or she can do. A teacher should make the question explicit enough so that students will know exactly what he or she expects. For example, "Explain the results of World War II" is too broad; students won't really understand what the teacher expects. It would be more explicit to say, "Explain three results of World War II that you feel had the most impact on participating nations. Explain the criteria you used in selecting these results."

Advantages of an essay include the possibility for students to be creative in their answers, the opportunity for students to explain their responses, and the potential to test for higher-level thinking skills. Disadvantages of essay questions include the time needed for students to formulate meaningful responses, language difficulties of some students, and the time needed to evaluate the essays. Consistency in evaluation is also a problem for the teacher, but this can be alleviated by using an outline of the acceptable answers or a scoring rubric. Teachers who write specific questions and who know what they are looking for will be more consistent in grading. Also, if there are several essay questions, the effective teacher grades all student responses to the first question, then moves on to all responses to the second, and so on.

Authentic Assessments

A paper-and-pencil test or an essay is only one method of assessment. Others include projects, observation, checklists, anecdotal records, portfolios, self-assessment, and peer assessment. Although these types of assessments often take more time and effort to plan and administer, they can often provide a more authentic measurement of student progress.

Projects are common in almost all subject areas. They promote student control of learning experiences and provide opportunities for research into a variety of topics, as well as the chance to use visuals, graphics, videos, or multimedia presentations in place of, or in addition to, written reports. Projects also promote student self-assessment because students must evaluate their progress along each step of the project. Many schools have science or history fairs for which students plan, develop, and display their projects. Projects can also be part of business, English, music, art, mathematics, social sciences, health, or physical education courses.

The teacher must make the requirements and the criteria for evaluation of the projects clear before students begin them. He or she must also assist students in selecting projects which are feasible, for which the school has learning resources, and which can be completed in a reasonable amount of time with little or no expense to students.

Advantages of projects are that students can demonstrate their visual, graphic, art, or musical abilities; students can be creative in their topic or research; and the projects can appeal to various learning styles. Disadvantages include difficulty with grading, although this can be overcome by devising a checklist for required elements and a rating scale for quality.

Observations may be made for individual or group work. This method is very suitable for skills or for effective learning. Teachers usually make a list of competencies, skills, or requirements, then check off the ones that are observed in the student or group. An office skills teacher wishing to emphasize interviewing skills may devise a checklist that includes personal appearance, mannerisms, confidence, and addressing the questions that are asked. A teacher who wants to emphasize careful listening may observe a discussion with a checklist that includes paying attention, not interrupting, summarizing another person's ideas, and asking questions of other students.

Anecdotal records may be helpful in some instances, such as capturing the process a group of students uses to solve a problem. This formative data can be useful during feedback to the group. Students can also be taught to write an explanation of the procedures they use for a project or a science experiment. An advantage of an anecdotal record is that it can include all relevant information. Disadvantages include the amount of time necessary to complete the record and difficulty in assigning a grade. If used for feedback, then no grade is necessary.

Advantages of checklists include the potential for capturing behavior that can't be accurately measured with a paper-and-pencil test, i.e., shooting free throws on the basketball court, following the correct sequence of steps in a science experiment, or including all important elements in a speech in class. One characteristic of a checklist that is both an advantage and a disadvantage is its structure, which provides consistency but inflexibility. An open-ended comment section at the end of a checklist can overcome this disadvantage.

Portfolios are collections of students' best work. They can be used in any subject area where the teacher wants students to take more responsibility for planning, carrying out, and organizing their own learning. They may be used in the same way that artists, models, or performers use them to provide a succinct picture of their best work. Portfolios may be essays or articles written on paper, video tapes, multimedia presentations on computer disks, or a combination. English teachers often use portfolios as a means of collecting the best samples of student writing over the whole year. Sometimes they pass on the work to the next year's teacher to help assess the needs of his or her new students. Any subject area can use portfolios, since they contain documentation that reflects growth and learning over a period of time.

Teachers should provide or assist students in developing guidelines for what materials should be placed in portfolios, since it would be unrealistic to include every piece of work in one portfolio. The use of portfolios requires the students to devise a means of evaluating their own work. A portfolio should be a collection of the student's own best work, not a scrapbook for collecting handouts or work done by other individuals, although it can certainly include work by a group in which the student was a participant.

Some advantages of portfolios over testing are that they provide a clearer picture of a student's progress, they are not affected by one inferior test grade, and they help develop self-assessment skills in students. One disadvantage is the amount of time required to teach students how to develop meaningful portfolios. However, this time can be well spent if students learn valuable skills. Another concern is the amount of time teachers must spend to assess portfolios. However, as students become more proficient at self-assessment, the teacher can spend more time in coaching and advising students throughout the development of their portfolios. Another concern is that parents may not understand how portfolios will be graded. The effective teacher devises a system which the students and parents understand before work on the portfolio begins.

Standardized Testing

In *criterion-referenced tests*, each student is measured against uniform objectives or criteria. CRTs allow the possibility that all students can score 100 percent because they understand the concepts being tested. Teacher-made tests should be criterion-referenced because the teacher should develop them to measure the achievement of predetermined outcomes for the course. If teachers have properly prepared lessons based on the outcomes, and if students have mastered the outcomes, then scores should be high. This type of test may be called noncompetitive because students are not in competition with each other for a high score, and there is no limit to the number of students who can score well. Some commercially developed tests are criterion-referenced; however, the majority is norm-referenced.

The purpose of a *norm-referenced test* is to provide a way to compare the performance of groups of students. This type of test may be called competitive because a limited number of students can score well. A plot of large numbers of NRT scores will resemble a bell-shaped curve, with most scores clustering around the center and a few scores at each end. The midpoint is an average of data; therefore, by definition, half of the population will score above average and half below average.

The bell-shaped curve was developed as a mathematical description of the results of tossing coins. As such, it represents the chance or normal distribution of skills, knowledge, or events across the general population. A survey of the height of sixth-grade boys will result in an average height, with half the boys above average and half below. There will be a very small number with heights way above average and a very small number with heights way below average, with most heights clustering around the average.

NRT scores are usually reported in percentile scores (not to be confused with percentages), which indicate the percent of the population whose scores fall at or below the score. For example, a group score at the 80th percentile means that the group scored as well as or better than 80 percent of the students who took the test. A student with a score at the 50th percentile has an average score.

Percentile scores rank students from highest to lowest. By themselves, percentile scores do not indicate how well the student has mastered the content objectives. Raw scores indicate how many questions the student answered correctly and are, therefore, useful in computing the percentage of questions a student answered correctly.

A national test for biology is designed to include objectives for the widest possible biology curriculum, for the broadest use of the test. Normed scores are reported so that schools can compare the performance of the students with the performance of students who the test developers used as its norm group. The test will likely include more objectives than are included in a particular school's curriculum; therefore, that school's students may score low in comparison to the norm group. Teachers must be very careful in selecting a norm-referenced test, and should look for a test that includes objectives which are the most congruent with the school's curriculum.

Schools must also consider the reliability of a test, or whether the instrument will give consistent results when the measurement is repeated. A reliable bathroom scale, for example, will give identical weights for the same person measured three times in a morning. An unreliable scale, however, may give weights that differ by six pounds. Teachers evaluate test reliability over time when they give the same, or almost the same, test to different groups of students. Because there are many factors which affect reliability, teachers must be careful in evaluating this factor.

Schools must also be careful to assess the validity of a test, or whether the test actually measures what it is supposed to measure. If students score low on a test because they couldn't understand the questions, then the test is not valid because it measures reading ability instead of content knowledge. If students score low because the test covered material which was not taught, the test is not valid for that situation. A teacher assesses the validity of his or her own tests by examining the questions to see if they measure what was planned and taught in his or her classroom.

A test must be reliable before it can be valid. However, measurements can be consistent without being valid. A scale can indicate identical weights for three weigh-ins of the same person during one morning, but actually be 15 pounds in error. A history test may produce similar results each time it is given, but not be a valid measure of what was taught and learned. Tests should be both reliable and valid. If the test doesn't measure consistently, then it can't be accurate. If it doesn't measure what it's supposed to measure, then its reliability doesn't matter. Commercial test producers perform various statistical measures of the reliability and validity of their tests and provide the results in the test administrator's booklet.

Performance-Based Assessment

Some states and districts are moving toward performance-based testing, which means that students are assessed on how well they perform certain tasks. This allows students to use higher-level thinking skills to apply, analyze, synthesize, and evaluate ideas and data. For example, a biology performance-based assessment may require students to read a problem, design and carry out a laboratory experiment, then write a summary of his or her findings. They would be evaluated on both the process used and the output they produced. A history performance-based assessment may require students to research a specific topic over a period of several days, make presentations of their findings to the rest of the class, then write a response which uses what the students have learned from their own research and that of their classmates. The students are then evaluated on the process and the product of their research. An English performance-based test may require students to read a selection of literature, then write a critical analysis. A mathematics performance-based test may state a general problem to be solved, then require the student to invent one or more methods of solving the problem, use one of the methods to arrive at a solution, then write the solution and an explanation of the processes he or she used.

Performance-based assessment allows students to be creative in solutions to problems or questions, and it requires them to use higher-level skills. This type of assessment can be time-consuming; however, students are working on content-related problems, using skills that are useful in a variety of contexts. This type of assessment also requires multiple resources, which can be expensive. It also requires teachers to be trained in how to use this type of assessment. Nonetheless, many schools consider performance-based testing to be a more authentic measure of student achievement than traditional tests.

Classroom Tests

There are fundamental professional and technical factors that must be taken into account to construct effective classroom tests. One of the first factors to recognize is that test construction is as creative, challenging, and important as any aspect of teaching. The planning and background that contribute to effective teaching are incomplete unless evaluation of student performance provides accurate feedback to the teacher and the student about the learning process. Good tests are the product of careful planning, creative thinking, hard work, and technical knowledge about the different methods of measuring student knowledge and performance. Classroom tests that accomplish their purpose are the result of the development of a pool of items and refinement of those items based on feedback and constant revision. It is through this process that evaluation of students becomes valid and reliable.

Tests serve as a valuable instructional aid because they help determine pupil progress and also provide feedback to teachers regarding their own effectiveness. Student misunderstandings and problems as revealed on tests help the teacher understand areas of special concern in providing instruction. This information also becomes the basis for remediation of students and revision of teaching procedures. For these reasons, the construction, administration, and proper scoring of classroom tests are the most important activities in teaching.

Principles of Test Construction

The discussion in this chapter is based on the following principles of test construction:

1. *Tests should be constructed according to a blueprint that reflects the objectives of the content to be learned.*

2. *Tests should reflect the knowledge and skills intended for students to acquire in proportion to the emphasis given to the various objectives in the unit of learning being tested.*

3. *The type of test items provided for students to answer should be chosen according to the best testing procedures for the particular knowledge or skill the student is expected to acquire.*

When a given unit or theme of instruction is prepared, the effective teacher identifies learning objectives for students. The content is then organized, and materials and methods for instruction are planned that will help students achieve those objectives. Prior to the administering of tests, the teacher will have a general idea of how the class is progressing in achieving those objectives, and he or she can usually identify those students who seem to be learning better than others. But, the classroom also has a limited number of students performing at any one time, and the teacher is only sampling the performance of the students in that class. In a testing situation, the teacher has an opportunity to include every student in a common activity that has the potential to assess all students on a common task.

Test Blueprints

In order to optimize this opportunity, the classroom test must be carefully constructed by using a plan that reflects objectives and measures student learning. It is the responsibility of the teacher to identify, select, and construct test items that appropriately assess attainment of objectives. This can be accomplished by starting with a test blueprint and then preparing test items according to the blueprint. A test blueprint is a plan for the teacher to assess the relative importance of the objectives to be tested, and to identify the type of items or activities to test for those objectives. The following discussion explains how to develop and utilize a test blueprint.

Objectives

If a unit of instruction contains several objectives, it is most likely that some objectives require more emphasis than others. The teacher should make a judgment about the degree of emphasis given to each objective so the test will reflect this proportional emphasis. This judgment is the first step in preparing a test blueprint. For example, a unit with four objectives might include the following distribution:

Objectives

I	II	III	IV
20%	30%	15%	35%

This allocation of percentages to the different objectives is the foundation on which the remainder of the blueprint will be developed. After determining the relative importance of each objective, the teacher should allot class time, provide instruction, and evaluate students according to the proportional importance of each objective. This entire process should be viewed as a cooperative effort between the teacher and the students in which they work in much the same manner as a coach does to make his or her team the best it can be. As the planning for instruction occurs, and as the instruction is provided, the teacher should concurrently prepare test questions that coincide with the planning and instruction. While preparing a lesson, the teacher should make notes about test items that evaluate the intended learning of the students. By preparing test items while planning lessons, the teacher can make the instruction appropriate and increase the validity of the test at the same time. Another excellent time to prepare test items is immediately after completing the daily instruction. At this time, the learning that took place is fresh in the mind of the teacher, and any special events or discussions that should be reinforced through a test more easily can be recalled.

Test Items

The test items used in an examination will vary according to the content that is being taught. The teacher must choose the type of items that will be most effective for evaluating students according to the content they have learned. Multiple-choice items may be useful to test a wide range of objectives, and an essay question may be a better choice to test for knowledge about a single event. The length and type of tests will also be influenced by factors such as time and frequency for testing. Tests will vary if they are weekly quizzes or semester examinations. Tests that have essay questions require more time than items that call for simple recognition. These are factors that must be taken into account when the test is actually assembled. However, at the time the test questions are being drafted, the most important criterion is to develop test questions that are most appropriate for the content. The question types most commonly prepared are: true/false, essay, multiple-choice, listing, matching, sentence completion, and recall.

As instruction progresses and as test items are constructed, the learning of the students and the development of the test by the teacher coincide. When the instruction and learning of the unit are nearly ended and the teacher prepares to test the students, it is time to complete the test blueprint.

For the next step in preparing the blueprint, the teacher should list the number of test items prepared under each objective according to the type of item. This step in making the blueprint is illustrated with the following example:

Objectives

Question Type	I	II	III	IV
	20%	30%	15%	35%
true/false	6	8	4	11
multiple-choice	3	7	2	9
matching	0	1	0	2
essay	1	1	0	1
recall	4	6	2	8
Totals	14	23	8	31

This blueprint contains 76 test questions and includes five types of questions. Thus, a pool of items has been developed from which the teacher can prepare the test. The teacher must also take into account the relative difficulty and comparative weight of the different questions. Essay questions are more difficult than true/false questions and should carry different weight or value. The items available for the test will limit the number of items that can be included on the examination. The resolution of these issues will determine the final length and selection of items for the test. For example, if the examination period is the length of a typical class period, the final allocation of items for the test could be as follows:

	Objectives				
	I	II	III	IV	Total
Question Type	20%	30%	15%	35%	100%
true/false	3	4	2	2	11
multiple-choice	3	2	3	4	12
matching	1	2	0	0	3
essay	0	0	0	1	1
recall	2	4	2	2	10
Totals	9	12	7	9	37
% of points	20	30	14	36	100

The final test prepared in this example contains 37 of the original 76 items. It includes 11 true/false items, 12 multiple-choice items, three matching items, one essay, and 10 recall items. The weight or value of each item must next be determined to make certain the value given to each objective is proportionally tested on the examination. In this case, the point value assigned to each type of item may be as follows: true/false = one point; multiple choice = two points; matching = five points; essay = 20 points; recall = three points. With these assigned values to each item, the number of points possible on this test is 100. The points to be earned for each objective are as follows: I = 20 points; II = 30 points; III = 14 points; IV = 36 points. Thus, the test reflects the emphasis given to the objectives and includes a variety of test items whose value varies with their difficulty.

Only 37 of the original 76 items were used for this test. The remaining 39 items are still valuable items and should be kept for future use. These additional items can be used to create another form of this test, which will also increase test security. Some of the items on the selected test may prove to be faulty and, therefore, they will need to be replaced by items from those placed in reserve. A filing system or a computerized schedule can be established in which each item can be analyzed and recorded. A history of that item will enable the teacher to refine the pool of items available for future testing of the objectives in each unit of instruction. The next section in this chapter explains recognized criteria for the construction of test items.

Constructing Test Questions

The most common items teachers construct for testing include essay, true/false, multiple-choice, recall or short answer, and matching. Each of these should be written according to standards that increase the chances of the test being valid, reliable, fair, and serving the unique purpose of that particular test. A brief discussion of the major considerations in constructing these test questions follows.

Constructing Essay Questions

Essay questions are asked to produce a student narrative about an event or to write an explanation that cannot be provided in a better form. Essay items require more time for student responses than other types of items, and the number of essay questions on a test will depend partly on the amount of testing time available and the nature of the questions. Essay questions should be stated clearly, and they should not be overly complex. The teacher should know what an "ideal" answer is, and should write a response after the question has been formulated to identify with the question and the student who will be responding. By writing a correct response, the teacher also establishes a standard for grading the student papers. After writing the preferred response, the teacher should evaluate whether the question is the most effective stimulus to obtain the answer that will evaluate the objective under consideration. If the teacher determines that a correct answer is one that contains four facts and the narrative is relatively unimportant, then the test might be revised to ask students to list the four facts and save the time of writing the narrative. If the time required is excessive and unrealistic, the teacher may assign students to write an essay as an assignment in order to determine attainment of the objective.

Constructing True/False Items

True/false items are relatively easy to construct, but certain criteria are essential to avoid errors in their construction. A statement should clearly be either true or false. Statements that are conditionally true, or are true or false most of the time, are confusing and do not reliably measure student knowledge. Statements that contain absolutes provide clues that have little to do with the content. *Never* and *always* are examples of such words. True/false items provide a quick check on student learning and can be used for short quizzes, but their validity is suspect. The chance of guessing correctly is 50 percent and with a little knowledge and a few subtle clues in some of the questions, a student who knows very little may score at the 70 or 80 percent level on a true/false test.

Constructing Multiple-Choice Questions

Multiple-choice items contain an opening statement, which is called the stem, followed by choices, which are called alternatives. The multiple-choice test is popular in standardized testing for a very good reason. A well-constructed, multiple-choice test is the most efficient and most effective way to reliably assess student knowledge.

There are two broad categories of multiple-choice questions. Some multiple-choice questions are based on a short essay or narrative in which an event or situation is described. In these cases, several questions usually are asked about the narrative and alternatives are provided for students to select the correct answer. A single episode may provide information from which four or five test items can be written. Another more common multiple-choice item is free standing and contains all the information necessary within the single item. These are usually items with a brief stem of one or two statements followed by alternatives. In either case, the stem must be written clearly, contain no ambiguities, and direct the student with sufficient information to select the correct response. The stem must avoid clues that are unrelated to the content. For example, an item in which the stem ends with the word "an" should have alternatives that all begin with a vowel so grammatical clues do not point to the correct answer. It is also necessary to be aware of avoiding information in one question that will help a student respond correctly to another question in the test. Another error to avoid is creating a sequence of multiple-choice questions in which the answer to one question is dependent on a correct answer to another question.

Alternatives for Multiple-Choice Questions

The test developer must make a decision about how many alternatives to provide for each multiple-choice item. On a given test, the number of alternatives should be the same for each item. Otherwise, the different items would vary in difficulty for the wrong reasons. The preferred number of alternatives is four, and the rationale for this recommendation is based on a balance of limiting the chance of guessing the correct answer and the difficulty of writing plausible alternatives.

If only two alternatives are provided in a multiple-choice item, the guessing factor is the same as in a true/false item (50 percent) and the weaknesses in true/false items exist in this case. However, two plausible alternatives are usually not too difficult to write. If three alternatives are provided, the guessing factor is reduced from 50 percent to 33 percent, which is a gain of 17 percent, but still allows considerable chance or luck to enter into the score. Again, three alternatives can usually be constructed without excessive difficulty. When four alternatives are used, the guessing factor is reduced by another 8 percent and it is usually possible to construct four plausible alternatives, but this number becomes difficult at times. If five alternatives are written instead of four, the guessing factor is only reduced by 5 percent and it is extremely difficult to construct five plausible alternatives for every item. Thus, the guessing factor and the difficulty of constructing plausible alternatives work in tandem to recommend four alternatives as the preferred number. It is also recommended that each alternative should stand alone and avoid those alternatives that say "all of the above," "none of the above," "two of the above," and so forth. The format for the items and the instructions should make it easy for the students to respond. Answer sheets for blackening in correct answers may be chosen if the age of the students and the nature of the test make this feasible. Usually, the teacher will ask students to mark on the test and circle correct answers or write in a space provided.

Constructing Recall Items

Multiple-choice items call for students to recognize the correct answer and are "recognition" items. When the student must remember the correct answer to a question, then the item is a "recall" item. Short-answer questions are recall questions and they are usually written in language similar to classroom discussions. Recall items are typically constructed as direct questions or as a "fill in the blank" format. In either case, the student must supply the information rather than recognize it from a list of alternatives. Questions of this type can be difficult to score when students provide answers that are similar to the correct answer but not exactly what the teacher had in mind. Furthermore, some questions can be answered correctly although they do not answer the question. Faulty questions will encourage faulty answers. For example, the following item might be on a test, "Abe Lincoln had a reputation for being very _____." The answer the teacher had in mind is "honest." But the student who writes "tall" can make a strong case for giving a correct response. A list of responses from which the student must choose will eliminate this problem, but it also makes the item a recognition item, even if the list of choices exceeds the number of questions by a large margin. Questions that call for longer answers, such as a sentence or two, also create similar grading problems for the teacher. Careful wording of recall questions and making certain a single question is raised will strengthen the quality of recall questions.

Constructing Matching Items

The final type of question discussed here is the matching item. Matching items contain two lists, and the student is expected to match items on one list with items on another list. For example, a matching item might be the names of states in one list and the names of state capitals in the second list. The student would be asked to match the number of one state, perhaps Indiana, with the capital, Indianapolis, which would be in the second list. These questions should avoid lengthy lists of more than six or eight items. Also, the second list should be longer than the first so that the last answer does not automatically align with the final response. If the matches the teacher wants on the test are lengthy, several items can be constructed. If the capitals of all 50 states were to be matched with their respective state, this might be tested by creating six or seven matching questions to minimize reading time and optimize testing time.

Grading matching items poses special factors. One student may match all of the items correctly while another may miss only one. Does the second student miss the entire question or receive partial credit? What constitutes a wrong answer, and is it possible to be partially correct? Most objective items are either right or wrong, but matching items pose a different situation because there are several questions to answer within the item. The teacher must make the grading decision in advance and inform the students how the matching items will be graded.

Scoring the Test

After the test has been constructed, administered, and scored, criteria or standards of performance will be applied. With the exception of tests for total mastery, standards will include some degree of subjectivity. Custom has established a general grading scale that varies slightly in different school districts, but, typically, letter grades are attached to results on a percentage scale. That scale often looks something like this:

A = 90–100

B = 80–89

C = 70–79

D = 60–69

F = below 60.

The teacher needs to exercise professional judgment about the difficulty of the test and must make the necessary adjustments when assigning student grades. If the highest score on the test is a 95, then some recommend that all scores be raised by five points. This adjustment is based on the belief that the best student in the class deserves a score at the top of the scale and other scores should be adjusted accordingly. Under this plan, a student with a score of 58 would not fail, but would receive a 63 which would be a D.

Another grading plan is pass or fail. In this case, the student either does or does not perform the task successfully. In a swimming class, if the requirement is to swim 25 yards, then students could be graded as pass or fail. The purpose of this test may not be to see who can swim the fastest, but to make sure everyone learns to swim at least 25 yards. This latter standard is called criterion testing, and can be applied in academic and skill areas of learning. It is most important that the teacher establish acceptable standards, that tests assess student acquisition of the knowledge or skills that meet these standards, and that the evaluation of the test can be done as objectively as possible.

This next section addresses procedures for evaluating and revising tests on the basis of content validity, reliability, and student response.

Evaluating and Revising Tests

After the test has been administered and scored, the teacher has a wealth of information available for analysis. This discussion will focus on a few of the most useful techniques and procedures for evaluating the test and determining how to improve it. The most obvious analysis is to determine the range and the arithmetic average of the scores of the students. Judgments about this information depend on the purpose of the test and the level of difficulty expected. If the test is designed to assess mastery, then student attainment of high scores is desirable. If the test is designed to discriminate among students according to who knows the most, then a wider distribution of scores should be expected.

Mastery

Mastery is a desirable expectation when certain fundamental knowledge must be learned perfectly to assure correct future learning. Tests of spelling or multiplication facts are examples where perfect scores should be expected. Students who make errors in these fundamental skills will be unable to learn more advanced topics, and testing for 100 percent mastery is desirable. Mastery may be defined operationally as less than 100 percent if the knowledge contains some optional areas in which a student's failure to understand perfectly or perform exactly is still acceptable. Advanced knowledge in the sciences, subtle interpretations in literature, or performance of a skill at less than a perfect level (making seven out of ten basketball free throws) are instances in which mastery may be defined as less than 100 percent. In order to define "mastery" in this context, a standard or criterion is set as a minimum below which student performance is unacceptable.

Analysis of Tests

When a test is designed to sort students according to their relative knowledge or skill, a different analysis of the test is followed. A test that discriminates students from one another along a knowledge continuum should separate those students who are most knowledgeable from those who are least knowledgeable about the content of the test. There are two kinds of analysis that help determine if the test has succeeded in doing this. One analysis requires a tally of the percent of students who answer each item on the test correctly. Any item that is missed by everyone or is answered correctly by everyone does not distinguish one student from another. If any item is answered both correctly or incorrectly by everyone, then the test has determined what students know, or don't know, but it has not helped sort students according to their knowledge. Such items should be reviewed by the teacher and remain if their purpose is either to test for mastery or provide a psychological climate of success while taking the test. Items that are answered correctly or incorrectly by at least some of the students are items that have some discriminatory power. It is almost certain that on a comprehensive test most students will miss some of the questions. The analysis described next helps determine if the test has ranked or sorted students correctly.

This second analysis is undertaken by dividing the students according to the half of the class that obtained the highest scores and the half that obtained the lowest scores. The percent that answered each question correctly in each half of the class should be compared. This comparison is done to see if any items were answered correctly by more students in the lower half of the distribution than in the upper half. Any item that has a lower percent correct by the best performing students should be reviewed and examined for grammatical or other obvious errors. A slight discrepancy should not be considered an error in the test. If 30 students take a test and the students with the 15 worst scores exceed the percent right on an item by the 15 best students by a small margin, the item is not necessarily faulty. However, a large discrepancy of 15 to 20 percentage points is a good basis for further analysis. The item may be acceptable, but it also may be ambiguous or it may punish some students for "knowing too much." By making this comparison, specific items on the test are identified that may not properly examine students and can be revised according to the weakness in the item. Some items found may be so faulty that they should not even count on the test and may be discarded in order to assign a fair final score. Weaknesses may be in the format, content, or structure. Most test items can be analyzed on this basis, and the problem with the few items that discriminate in the reverse direction are usually not difficult to detect. However, the multiple-choice question is a special case that can be analyzed more thoroughly and refined on the basis of objective data. A discussion of this further analysis of multiple-choice items is provided next.

Analyzing Multiple-Choice Questions

For the purpose of this discussion, we will assume there are four alternatives in each multiple-choice question from which students will make their selection. We will also assume that each item has been compared according to students who have the highest scores with those who have the lowest scores. The item analysis that is described next calls for a more detailed but rather easy way to evaluate multiple-choice items.

Every alternative should function and be chosen by at least someone who takes the test. In a typical class of 30 students, if each alternative is chosen by at least one student, then the item will be answered correctly by no more than 90 percent of the students. This will be true because at least three students would need to provide an incorrect answer for each alternative to be chosen. Such an item meets the standard of less than 100 percent correct and all the alternatives in the item contribute to the purpose of the item. If any alternative is not selected by the students, that item should be rewritten to include either plausible alternatives in each case or to ask for that information with a different kind of question.

In addition to the systematic analysis of test items, all student responses should be read to identify mistaken thought processes, lack of knowledge, inadequate skill, or misunderstandings the students have revealed in their responses. These errors in student thinking can be deduced from an inspection of their responses.

Preparation for Testing

Preparation for testing includes responsibilities for the teacher and consideration for the student. The teacher's responsibility for testing begins prior to the actual testing situation. During the time when instruction and learning take place, the teacher should make certain the class understands what knowledge is especially important for it to learn. It is the responsibility of the teacher to focus on the critical elements of the content to be learned, and to examine students on their acquisition of this critical knowledge. Tests should not be used to "trick" students by testing for obscure information. The relationship between teaching and testing should be congruent and fair.

When tests are given to students, the teacher must pay attention to the logistics and details of administering the test. The test material should be prepared sufficiently in advance to make certain it is clearly printed, and void of spelling or grammatical errors. There must be enough copies for every student and some extras in case a faulty test is given out. The best possible room environment should be provided, which includes proper lighting, ventilation, temperature, and reduction of noise. The test should be scheduled to avoid conflicts with events such as fire drills or public address announcements. Confer with the principal to avoid conflicts with school activities that may interfere with a desirable testing environment. Bring extra supplies of paper and pencils for those who forget them or break their pencils during the test. Place a notice on the door that notifies others that "testing is in progress—do not disturb." Such a notice should prevent interruptions, except for emergencies. The seating in the room should allow each student to work independently and provide for adequate proctoring. These logistical matters are not entirely in control of the teacher, but any of these procedures that can be followed should be completed to assure the fairest possible test administration.

Prior to the administration of the test, the teacher should orient the students to the testing situation. The teacher should also provide assurances to the students with positive remarks that encourage them to do their best. The purpose of the test should be explained, including information about how the test results will be used and how the results are relevant to them personally. Students should be informed about when the results of the test will be reported to them and how this feedback will be provided. In some cases it is appropriate for an entire class to discuss the test results, and in other cases it is best to keep test results personal and confidential. Students should know how the results will be reported to ease their minds about this procedure, and to give them one less factor that may contribute to their test anxiety.

If the test contains any special considerations about taking the test or scoring procedures, the students should be told what they are. For example, if a test includes essay questions, they should be given reasonable parameters to help them pace their time. A single essay question can consume their entire time; if there are several questions, the students might be told to limit their writing time on each question to assure coverage of the entire examination. If certain types of questions carry more weight than others, the students should be told the point value of the different questions. True/false items might be worth one point and multiple-choice items might be worth two points. The test itself should also contain directions. The time allotted for the test should be sufficient to enable all students who are reasonably well-prepared to be able to demonstrate their knowledge.

Test Administration

Students should be kept informed about the time remaining as they progress through the examination. If a clock is in the room in a conspicuous location, this may be sufficient. It may be helpful to provide information about the time remaining by writing it on the board. The proctor might write times on the board in minutes such as ten, five, three, and one. As these remaining times arrive, the proctor can draw a line through the appropriate number. Thus, students can tell at a glance how much time is remaining. The proctor might suggest a pace for a long test that is divided into several sections. If students should complete the first section by a certain time, the proctor should announce, "You should have completed section one by now. If you have not done so, move on to section two." Students should be told in advance if the proctor is going to provide this information.

The Proctor

The proctor must be sensitive to the importance of time during a testing situation. The time spent before the actual testing begins should be minimal. Most students come to a testing situation ready to answer questions and do not want a long delay in getting started. In some cases, the pre-test information may even be provided in a previous session, and test materials may already be on student desks in a folder or upside down so everyone can start promptly when told to begin. Delays by the teacher prior to the testing reduce the time available for students to respond and increase test anxiety. The time provided for the test itself should be the same for everyone. Everyone should be expected to "run the same race" in order to determine the comparative knowledge each student has on the content being tested.

Proctoring the examination calls for close attention to students without "hovering" over the class in a way that may be a distraction. The proctor should not be preoccupied with other tasks during the test. Students should be instructed to remove all materials from their desks and to have an extra supply of pencils and paper. Students whose pencils break during an examination should not be allowed to go to a pencil sharpener and disturb others. The proctor can quietly supply a pencil after receiving a signal from the student. Proctors should not engage in conversation with any student during the examination. Some students may request information, such as the definition of a word. If the proctor responds, it may appear to other students that the proctor is providing unfair assistance. If all the preliminary details have been provided, if the test contains the required information, and if every student has listened and has come prepared, no student should have any questions during the examination.

The proctor must ensure that all students do their own work. Crib notes, conversation between students, and signals that students may have created to help each other should all be monitored. In most cases, if the proctor is in the back of the room, the temptation for students to cheat is minimized. When students cannot see where the proctor is looking, they tend to keep their own eyes from wandering. If the room is small and desks are close, making it easy for students to look on other desks, it may be necessary to create different forms of the same test. This can be done by reversing the order of the questions or any other reorganization of the test that will protect its integrity.

Formative Feedback

After the test has been completed and collected, the teacher should score the test and give feedback to students as promptly as possible. In a discussion of the test results, it is essential to identify correct responses and express approval to the students for doing well on those items. It is important to provide overall information, such as the range of scores, the average, and the grade distribution. It is helpful to identify common errors made by students and to take time to explain the correct responses. Students may challenge answers, and a discussion of these inquiries should be provided without getting into arguments. The teacher and the students can both benefit from a discussion of items over which there is a difference of opinion.

Recording Student and Class Progress

Grade Books

The most traditional method of student records, the grade book, is also considered to be the official document of class progress. Grade books contain information such as:

- Date of assignment;

- Type of assignment (test, open-ended assignment, essay, homework);

- Student grade for assignment;

- Total grade points possible for assignment;

- Class participation; and

- Comments/notes.

In addition to storing information, the grade book should be organized to reflect the system that will be used to calculate grades. Will tests count more than homework assignments? Will any assignments be merely for credit rather than a grade? Similarly, use of the grade book should be flexible, to account for additions and retractions from the teaching schedule. Grade books should be updated frequently to accurately track the growth of the class.

Examination of an organized grade book should provide the teacher with a look at the status of any particular student in a given area at any time. The information stored in a grade book can then be placed into a graph or a chart for an easy visual representation of class progress.

Checklists and Scales

To follow student development in a particular subject area, teachers can also work with checklists. The skills and concepts being taught in a particular content area can be listed for each student, and then checked off when the student has reached mastery. Notes can be written next to a skill if a student is experiencing difficulty or ease with a specific skill or concept. The teacher can then assess the strengths and weaknesses of the class in each skill area, and plan lessons accordingly.

Similar to checklists, teachers can also use a rating scale to record the level of ability that a student demonstrates in a particular area.

Portfolios

Teachers can also record a student's overall growth in a particular area or over the whole syllabus by using portfolio assessments. Portfolios are folders that contain various samples of a student's work that are date-stamped and then archived. Portfolios can show the scope of what a student has studied and the growth that has occurred as a result, while providing a very special and personalized look at the child. Additionally, the portfolio gives the teacher an overview of a student's abilities so that the teacher can determine an appropriate level of instruction. Portfolio assessment is flexible, and any combination of the methods described here can be used. It is important to note, however, that portfolios should only be used to assess each student individually, or to evaluate the work of the teacher. They should not be used to compare one student to another.

All types of work can be contained in a folder, and there can be folders for different topic areas, such as distinct portfolios for math, reading, and science. Teachers may select the pieces to include in the portfolio, or teachers can ask the students what they would like to include. Examples of work samples that can be kept in a portfolio include creative writing samples, artwork, journal writings, science reports, and math problems. Students or the teacher can include record logs that detail such facts as books read, math concepts mastered, or science experiments completed. Each sample placed in the student's portfolio can contain a description of the assignment, and what the student and teacher felt about the finished product, in addition to the date. Personal notes from students, teachers, and parents may be included as well.

At any point in the year, the student and teacher will have a rich resource from which to review. When examining a portfolio, the teacher should be looking for student strengths, weaknesses, abilities, and achievements. The teacher may wish to review the portfolio, and both student and teacher can discuss what they think about the samples, and determine what they both wish to accomplish in the future. Portfolios can also be used in parent conferences to provide insight into the student's growth in the class.

Teachers may also develop class portfolios containing samples from all of the students in the class for a similar type of review of the classroom and its experiences as a whole.

Anecdotal Records

Even with all these methods of recordkeeping, there may still be other information that the teacher would like to record. Anecdotal records are information comments, about either the class in its entirety or about individuals, that are dated and maintained in one place. Remarks about behavior, social development and skills, attitudes about school, learning styles, or any other important thoughts or day-to-day observations should be noted in the anecdotal record. Anecdotal records may also contain information about parent phone calls and conferences by including the date, time, and topic of discussion.

These tools should provide a teacher with the methods to integrate a complete system for evaluating student and class progress and achievement.

Reporting Student and Class Progress

Report Cards

The information that a teacher has recorded about students and their progress is reported to parents and school administration, generally in the form of a report card. Most report cards reflect the grade-point averages for each subject of study, student attendance, and student tardiness. Some report cards provide an area for comments about student behavior and attitudes. Report cards are valued by parents because they are similar to what parents themselves received when in school, and because they convey a student's academic standing in an easy-to-understand manner.

Parent-Teacher Conferences

Parent-teacher conferences are another means of communicating student progress to parents. Typically, a school will have formal, school-wide parent-teacher conferences over a specific period of time. Conferences may also be initiated at any time of the year if the teacher or if the parents feel(s) they are necessary. These meetings provide the teacher and the parents (or guardians) with an opportunity to discuss his/her/their view(s) of the student's feelings toward learning. Specific work samples, such as in a portfolio, may be reviewed, and future goals and expectations for the student should be discussed. The parents and the teachers can also determine a plan for how the parents can become actively involved in the student's education. Any concerns from either side can be addressed. At times, the students themselves may be involved in the conference.

Narrative Reports

If a parent is unable to attend a conference due to scheduling difficulties, the teacher can provide a narrative report, which is a written assessment detailing the student's strengths, weaknesses, and future goals. Narrative reports can also be used if a student is experiencing an unusual situation that is making his/her grades inconsistent or inaccurate. The narrative report is a more informal but more detailed record than a report card.

Maintaining Permanent Student Records

Schools consistently maintain records for students throughout their academic experience. The permanent school record is overseen by the school administration and minimally contains the following information:

- ✔ **Personal:**

    - • **Parents'/guardians' names and contact information;**

    - • **Attendance/tardiness;**

- ✔ **Immunization records;**

- ✔ **Pertinent health information and health needs;**

- ✔ **Academic;**

- ✔ **Past teachers;**

- ✔ **Grade-point averages/transcripts;**

- ✔ **Standardized test scores; and**

- ✔ **Any other specialized test results.**

Additionally, the record contains any narrative comments from school professionals about the child's progress, physical and mental well-being, and behavior. Any other information that is important to the history and to the understanding of the child or the child's particular situation is also maintained in the permanent student record. When necessary, information relating to the custody of children with divorced parents is also noted. These data are strictly confidential, and should only be discussed with the parents, school administration, and relevant teachers.

The permanent student records are filed in a locked, fireproof location and cannot be removed unless they are signed out by a teacher or administrator; at this point, the records—which are the responsibility of that person—are considered legal documents.

Attendance, grade, and health information are generally updated annually. Any other important data are updated as they occur. The current teacher is also responsible for updating any anecdotal information or specialized testing results that are deemed necessary to record. Just as the record is updated by each new teacher, the student record will follow the student to the new school if the student leaves the current one.

Understanding the Importance of Student Records

Teachers frequently review the student records of incoming students at the beginning of a school year. Therefore, it is important to keep in mind that what is included in a student record can influence the opinions of a student's future instructors and administrators. The teacher's comments should be as objective and informative as possible, avoiding any potentially harmful remarks. The responsibility of the student record should not be taken lightly; teachers must take care to focus only on professional, rather than personal, opinions of the student's strengths and weaknesses.

Just as the permanent school record is a confidential and legal document, teachers should similarly be cautious with other student records. Student's grades, progress, tests, homework, and information about personal situations should only be discussed with the student, the student's parents, and the school administration.

Summary

An acceptable testing environment requires teachers to: (1) prepare students by emphasizing the critical knowledge for students to learn; (2) establish a setting with clear instructions and fair tests for students to complete; and (3) give feedback that praises correct responses, and corrects errors and misunderstandings.

References

Further reading of these references may enhance understanding of the chapter and may also increase performance on the examination.

"Measurement, Statistics, and Evaluation for Teachers," Chapter 12, pages 165-179 in *Reading Instruction Essentials* by Anita Price Davis (Third Edition) Boston, Massachusetts: American Press, 2004.

Technology in the Classroom

Overview

The teacher uses computers in education.

Educational Technology in the Primary Classroom

Technology is an important part of the world and, therefore, must be an important part of the educational environment.

Students should be exposed as early as possible to computer literacy so that they will be prepared for a technologically advanced society. Appropriate software can be used to meet content standards and curriculum goals. Teachers must be able to integrate their existing curriculum to meet these standards. Students must be versed in computer curriculum to be prepared for their future.

Classroom Management

There are a variety of classroom settings that can be utilized with regard to computers. Some classrooms may have only one computer, while others may have a computer lab. The majority of teachers and students has access to at least one computer in the classroom.

The teacher must use a variety of innovative methods to allow the students to have quality computer time whenever possible. The computer can be used as an audiovisual tool, with new lessons presented by the teacher to the students, by using the computer as an electronic blackboard. It can also be used as a technology center, where students can research subjects, take tutorial lessons, and learn word processing skills. The students can also use the computer for visual and oral presentations when multimedia projects are presented to the class.

Because of limited computer time, most work has to be completed before working at the computer. The school version of most software includes excellent ideas for setting up a station and provides seatwork activities for that specific program. Students can print out the graphics and keep them in a folder to be used while working at their desk. They can prepare their entire project before working at the computer.

If a teacher is working with a bank of computers (three or more), assigning the students to work in small groups is the best method of classroom management. Many primary classrooms already use centers and small group activities as part of the classroom management system. The computer center can be used as one of these learning centers. For example, computers can be used for the students to research science topics. Reference books, multimedia encyclopedias, and posters can be placed in the center. The students can then exhibit their work on a bulletin board that is part of the computer center. Name checklists can be used so the students are aware of their turn to work at the computer. While a group of students is at the computer, the other students are also at work at other workstations in the class. Students can then rotate with the rest of the class after a certain time allotment.

In some schools, a media center is used so that there is a place for teachers, as well as students, to access computers. In most cases teachers bring their classes into the center at a scheduled time every week. Some administrators prefer this type of arrangement because every student is assured computer time, and it is less costly than supplying computers in every classroom. Each child is given a disk on which to save his or her work. The disk is then placed in a specific classroom file so that the child has easy access to his or her disk each time he or she enters the center. Usually a computer technician or computer teacher, an assistant, and the classroom teacher are in the center. When the child needs assistance, one suggestion is for the student to place a red cube on top of the computer. The teacher can then scan the room for those children requiring aid. Children can use a green cube to indicate that they have completed their project and are now ready to explore selected computer programs on their own.

Chapter 9

Integrating Computers in Instruction

In any classroom environment, one of the major teaching problems is student motivation. Students have a natural motivation to use computers. The more they are exposed to computers, the more they want to learn. A teacher must also exhibit a sense of excitement toward computers. Computers in the class offer a direct integration with classroom curriculum.

Planning for a computer-based lesson is similar to planning for a traditional lesson. The traditional format generally includes: topic, materials, goals and objectives, procedures, and assessment. Once a topic and objective are chosen, then it is necessary to find the materials and resources available to help meet these objectives. Technology is not always the best resource. Sometimes the traditional book, pencil, and paper is the best mode. Many times a marriage of the two (tradition and technology) is needed.

Educational Technology in the Secondary Classroom

Computer Software Tools

There are several software tools which are extremely useful for teachers and students. Word processing allows teachers and students to write, edit, and polish assignments and reports. Most programs have a spelling-checker or even a grammar-checker to enhance written products. Students can use word processors to write term papers or reports of their research for all subject areas. Many word processors allow writers to put the text into columns so that students can produce newsletters with headlines of varying sizes. For example, an English class could write a series of reviews of Shakespeare's plays or sonnets, add information about Shakespeare and his times, then assemble everything into a newsletter as a class project. There are also desktop publishing programs which allow text and graphics to be integrated to produce publications, such as a class newsletter, school newspapers, and yearbooks.

Databases are like electronic file cards; they allow students to input data, then retrieve it in various ways and arrangements. History students can input data about various countries, e.g., population, population growth rate, infant mortality rate, average income, and average education levels. They then manipulate the database to call out information in a variety of ways. The most important step in learning about databases is dealing with huge quantities of information. Students need to learn how to analyze and interpret the data they see in order to discover connections between isolated facts and figures, and how to eliminate inappropriate information.

On-line databases are essential tools for research. Students can access databases related to English, history, science—any number of subject areas. Most programs allow electronic mail (e-mail) so that students can communicate over the computer with people from around the world. There are also massive bibliographic databases which help students and teachers to find the resources they need. Many of the print materials can then be borrowed through interlibrary loan. The use of electronic systems can increase the amount of materials available to students.

Spreadsheets are similar to teacher grade books. Rows and columns of numbers can be linked to produce totals and averages. Formulas can connect information in one cell (the intersection of a row and column) to another cell. Teachers often keep grade books on a spreadsheet because of the ease in updating information. Once formulas are in place, teachers can enter grades and have completely up-to-date averages for all students. Students can use spreadsheets to collect and analyze numerical data which can be sorted in various orders. Some spreadsheet programs also include a chart function so that teachers can display class averages on a bar chart to provide a visual comparison of class performance. Students can enter population figures from various countries, then draw various types of graphs, bars, columns, scatters, histograms, and pies to convey information. This type of graphic information can also be used in multimedia presentations. There are also various stand-alone graph and chart software packages.

Graphics or paint programs allow users to draw freehand to produce any type of picture or use tools to produce boxes, circles, or other shapes. These programs can illustrate classroom presentations or individual research projects. Many word processing programs have some graphic elements.

Computer-Assisted Instruction

Many early uses of computers tended to be drill-and-practice, in which students practiced simple skills such as mathematics operations. Many elaborate systems of practice and testing were developed with management systems so that teachers could keep track of how well the students were achieving. This type of software is useful for skills that students need to practice. An advantage is immediate feedback so students know if they chose the correct answer. Many of these programs have a game format to make the practice more interesting. A disadvantage is their generally low-level nature.

Tutorials are a step above drill-and-practice programs because they also include explanations and information. A student is asked to make a response, then the program branches to the most appropriate section based on the student's answer. Tutorials are often used for remedial work, but are also useful for instruction in English as a second language. Improved graphics and sound allow nonspeakers of English to listen to correct pronunciation while viewing pictures of words. Tutorials are used to supplement, not supplant, teacher instruction.

Simulations or problem-solving programs provide opportunities for students to have experiences which would take too long to experience in real-time, would be too costly or difficult to experience, or would be impossible to experience. For example, one of the most popular early simulations allowed students to see if they could survive the Oregon Trail. Users made several choices about food, ammunition, and supplies, then the computer moved them along the trail until they reached their goal or died along the way. There are several simulations which allow students to "dissect" animals. This saves time and materials, is less messy, and allows students who might be reluctant to dissect real animals to learn about them. Other software might explore the effects of weightlessness on plant growth, a situation which would be impossible to set up in the classroom lab. There are several social studies simulations which allow students to do things like invent a country, then see the effects of their political and economic decisions on the country.

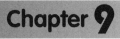

Selection and Evaluation Criteria

The effective teacher uses criteria to evaluate audiovisual, multimedia, and computer resources. The first thing to look for is congruence with lesson goals. If the software doesn't reinforce student outcomes, then it shouldn't be used, no matter how flashy or well-done it is. A checklist for instructional computer software could include appropriate sequence of instruction, meaningful student interaction with the software, learner control of screens and pacing, and motivation. Other factors that should be considered include the ability to control sound and save progress, effective use of color, clarity of text and graphics on the screen, and potential as an individual or group assignment.

In addition to congruence with curriculum goals, the teacher should consider his/her students' strengths and needs, their learning styles or preferred modalities, and their interests. Students' needs can be determined through formal or informal assessment. Most standardized tests include an indication of which objectives the student did not master. Mastering these objectives can be assisted with computer or multimedia aids.

Learning styles may be assessed with a variety of instruments and models, including those developed by Rita Dunn and Anthony Gregorc. Students with highly visual learning modes will benefit from audiovisuals. Student interests may be revealed by a questionnaire, either purchased or developed by the district or teacher. A knowledge of student interests will help the teacher provide resources to suit individual needs. The effective teacher can design activity choices that relate to class goals and also to student interests.

Evaluation of resources should be accomplished in advance by the teacher, before purchase whenever possible. Evaluation is also conducted during student use of materials. Assessment after student use may be done by considering the achievement level of the students and/or by using surveys which ask for students' responses.

Copyright Laws for Computer Programs

Computer technology is becoming a larger focus of the classroom. In addition to being part of the curriculum, computers are frequently used by educators as aids in storing information and developing lesson materials.

Computer software programs fall under the domain of copyright law. Computer programs, such as a word processing program or a graphic design program, are defined as "a set of statements or instructions to be used directly in a computer in order to bring about a certain result" (P.L. 96-517, Section 117).

Backups, or copies of a computer program, are frequently created in case the original disk containing the computer program becomes damaged. Such copies are not considered infringements of the copyright law as long as the following is true:

a. *The new copy or adaptation must be created in order to be able to use the program in conjunction with the machine, and is used in no other manner.*

b. *The new copy or adaptation must be for archival purpose only, and all archival copies must be destroyed in the event that continued possession of the computer program should cease to be rightful.*

c. *Any copies prepared or adapted may not be leased, sold, or otherwise transferred without the authorization of the copyright owner.*

Copies of a computer program cannot be shared or borrowed. The same original disk should not be used to install a program on more than one machine unless the owner has a license to do so from the computer software company. If unsure about the licensing status of a computer program, the teacher can check with the media specialist or school administrator.

Teachers are role models for their community; it is important that all educators be aware of these laws and be in complete compliance.

References

Further reading of these references may enhance understanding of the chapter and may also increase performance on the examination.

"Individual Differences and How to Accommodate Them" Chapter 14, 149-163. *Reading Instruction Essentials* by Anita Price Davis (Third Edition) Boston, Massachusetts: American Press, 2004.

Integrating Educational Technology into Teaching by M.D. Roblyer and Jack Edwards. Columbus, Ohio: Merrill, 2004.

Content Category 3: Communication Techniques

Chapters 10-11

Student Participation, Feedback, and Review

Overview

A teacher relates to his or her students' verbal communications in a manner that promotes student participation and is still able to retain academic focus.

The teacher uses feedback procedures that give information to students about the appropriateness of their responses.

The teacher conducts reviews of the subject matter.

Sandra Morris has spent several weeks teaching a Native American unit in her seventh-grade social studies class. She begins each class meeting with, "Yesterday we talked about ..." or "What did we discuss yesterday?" Ms. Morris knows that this summary of previous material is an essential step in creating transitions between units or lessons. Students need specific reminders of what had been covered previously in class in order to better understand the present material.

Giving students background to new material is a way to help them add meaning to text and ideas. For example, an instructor who teaches the elements of a short story over a period of time takes time at the introduction of each new short story to review and rehearse ones that were studied earlier. Integrating new material with material presented previously in class helps students make sense of new material and view learning as a series of building blocks, not skills in isolation.

Ms. Morris says to her literature class, "Yesterday we studied the significance of authorial tone and style in Poe's *Tell-Tale Heart*, and today we're looking at characterization. Can you give me an example of how Poe uses tone to describe a character? How would you define tone?" Here the instructor requires students to mesh what they studied previously with the current story element. Each time they receive a new mental image, they have an opportunity to place it into a meaningful context.

It also helps students to review previous material in order to remember it better and for a longer period of time. They take notes and learn items, not just to put them away and look at them only at test time, but in order to remind themselves on a daily basis what has been learned before. Without such review, students tend to ignore and certainly forget material until the test, and do not appreciate the importance of careful rehearsal.

Reviews can go beyond oral discussion. Students may write index card summaries of previous material, lists of ideas learned, and outlines of key concepts, and submit these to the instructor, who determines if material is being recalled and understood. Students can act as surrogate teachers, taking the lead role in conducting a five-minute review at the beginning of each class, quizzing one another on central concepts and major ideas from former lessons.

Taking time to review material teaches students an important lesson about learning—that it is imperative to master old ideas before tackling new ones. Teachers who rush to cover content or students who hurry to process it, lose sight of the need to have deep understandings about each piece of information as it appears in the course. Delving into the previous lesson helps students gain insights into the material at hand. A student can ask him- or herself, "What have we already learned that applies in this case? and "How do old scenarios fit the ones at hand?"

Every discipline lends itself to review of certain procedures and knowledge. Summarizing ideas helps students to practice convergent thinking and synthesis, requiring them to place their learning into a meaningful context. If the class has just studied the causes of the Civil War, the teacher takes time to ask the class to recount those causes before moving to effects of the war. If the class has just learned binary equations, the instructor takes time to practice with the class before moving to other problems.

The individual members of the class must be involved and engaged in the summary of previous material; the instructor should not just spoon-feed the class a recap of the material. Students learn to take responsibility for their own learning as they move from one piece of the educational puzzle to another. Each step reinforces knowledge given before, and the rehearsal, whether oral or written, assists students in better remembering at test time.

Effective Use of Language

Effective use of language is one of the major components of learning in classrooms. New visual aids and technology have broadened the range of possibilities for instruction, but without words and their proper use, the potential for learning is severely limited. Discourse has many dimensions, including verbal, non-verbal, and paralingual features. The verbal part of discourse contains the content; the non-verbal includes body language, posture, facial expressions, etc.; and the paralingual features are found in the choices of words, inflections, and subtleties of speech that portray characteristics of speakers, such as arrogance or humility. All three components communicate to students and contribute to the total message that is received.

Relationship Between Teachers and Students

Underlying the discourse that occurs in classrooms is the relationship between the teacher and students. The best relationship is one that creates a trusting confidence in each other and an environment in which opinions, information, and dialogue can be exchanged in a non-threatening classroom setting. Productive relationships with students can be built by recognizing that interactions occur within three different schemata: open relationships, closed relationships, and transitional relationships. Open relationships emerge when both participants are honest, accepting, tactful, emphatic, and active listeners. Closed relationships develop when neither participant engages in discourse that can be trusted because it is dishonest, secretive, or tactless. Transitional relationships exist when one participant is open and the other is not. Transitional relationships may become open or closed depending on how each reacts to the other over time. The teacher who behaves toward his or her students as a person does in an open relationship has the potential to establish a classroom in which honesty, trust, acceptance, empathy, and active listening become the norm. It is in such a classroom that learning through effective two-way communication is most likely to occur. Thus, the behavior of the teacher can promote the atmosphere that is most conducive to a healthy learning environment for students. If the teacher does not verbalize openly and effectively, it is not possible for the students and teacher to establish the open relationship that will be most effective in the promotion of learning. In addition to a healthy psychological classroom climate, there are technical aspects of communication that make a significant difference in learning. These aspects will be addressed next.

Knowledge about, and application of, communication principles enable a teacher to engage in successful classroom interactions with students. Successful interactions occur when learning is optimized through a partnership in learning with students. It is this positive environment that provides the best hope for teachers to a) show acceptance of and value student responses; and b) ignore or redirect digressions without devaluing student responses.

Feedback

When teachers respond to student responses, they are providing feedback. Feedback can be embodied in various dimensions, and the following four possibilities provide a framework in which teacher responses can be classified. These four types of responses are defined by recognizing that feedback may be positive or negative, and that it may also be responsible or irresponsible. Thus feedback may be:

I.   **Positive and responsible**

II. **Negative and responsible**

III. **Positive and irresponsible**

IV. **Negative and irresponsible**

These four categories help clarify how the teacher can show acceptance of and value for student response, and also how he/she can redirect digressions. Responses in Category I include praise for acceptable student comments, which should be provided specifically, immediately, and sincerely. Responses in Category II include teacher comments that correct student errors, describe faulty logic or misinformation, and other student errors that might occur in classroom discussions. Teacher criticism in Category II should be given tactfully and be the basis for improving student learning. Category III responses are exemplified by the teacher who tolerates student errors and even gives praise for sub-standard comments by lowering standards or allowing inaccurate responses to stand without correction. Category IV responses are negative reactions by teachers to students, and are delivered in a harsh and derogatory manner. Sarcasm and insults are included in Category IV responses. The two types of responsible categories (I and II) will support student responses that are acceptable, and also maintain reasonable standards by correcting student responses that are not acceptable. The teacher who accepts and values student comments uses language that is responsible and maintains a relationship in which tolerance for positive and negative remarks is based on optimal student learning and mutual respect. The two types of irresponsible categories (III and IV) will either sugarcoat wrong answers and lower standards listed above, or create tension and hostility by using tactless sarcasm or insults to criticize student work. The teacher who fails to correct student errors by accepting sub-standard student responses dilutes the quality of learning, and risks the loss of respect from students and colleagues who recognize such behavior. The teacher who corrects with sarcasm or other demeaning behavior, creates tension and fear in students. A tense classroom atmosphere will reduce student cooperation, ingenuity, creativity, and the quality of classroom discussions.

Digressions

One of the difficult challenges teachers face is how to ignore or redirect digressions without devaluing student responses. The best approach to this problem is to make preparations that eliminate or minimize this behavior. The teacher behaviors that promote student attentiveness and reduce digressions include a) connected discourse; b) single questions; c) marker expressions and techniques; d) emphasis; e) task attraction and challenge. Teacher behaviors that do not promote student attentiveness include a) scrambled discourse; b) vagueness; and c) question overload.

Connected Discourse

Connected discourse is discussion based on a given topic or theme, in which the information that is exchanged leads to one or more conclusions or major points. The teacher's role includes clarification of the theme or topic to make certain students know the central focus of the discussion. It is also necessary to structure questions and activities that will enable the class to reach closure on the topic under consideration.

Single questions avoid question overload, give focus for student responses, and provide students with an unambiguous task. Single questions can either stimulate higher-order thinking or ask for simple recall. When they are properly stated they are not confusing. Complex topics can be broken into smaller parts through the use of single questioning and can be developed gradually, which will ensure that the topic will be understood better; it is best to avoid trying to do too much at once.

Marker Expressions

Marker expressions are the equivalent of italics, underlining, or color-highlighting passages in written documents. They are points of emphasis the teacher uses to help students focus on or retain the most salient information in a discussion. They can be used to give appropriate praise to students by linking a previous remark by a particular student to the emphasis at that time. For example, "You remember that yesterday John noticed how the presence of a river was a factor in the location of cities. Today, we see another example of that factor in the establishment of St. Louis."

Emphasis is a technique to help students identify and retain significant information. Teachers can prepare students for essential topics by stating, "This next topic is crucial; I want you to work extra hard at it. Ask questions about anything you do not understand." Other forms of emphasis include repetition, summary, and application of the knowledge. All of these methods should be utilized by actively engaging students in classroom activities.

Task Attraction and Challenge

Task attraction and challenge are methods to motivate students, and they include teacher enthusiasm for the task at hand. Teachers engage in this behavior by showing their own excitement for the learning that is about to take place. Often, teachers can alert students to the difficulty of a task and challenge them by saying that something will be hard for them to do. When properly presented, a challenge becomes the motivation for students to prove their ability.

Scrambled Discourse, Vagueness, and Question Overload

Scrambled discourse, vagueness, and question overload are teacher behaviors that make it difficult for students to stay on task. Scrambled discourse is disconnected to the theme or topic under discussion, and often includes garbled verbal behavior. Vagueness is evident by the excessive use of indeterminate language (e.g., *something*, *a little*, *some*, *much*, *few*, *things*, *you see*, *perhaps*, or *actually*). Question overload causes confusion because multiple questions or long and involved questions are asked, and the student is uncertain about what is expected.

Provide Clear Feedback to Students

One of a teacher's important functions is to respond clearly to student responses so that the student knows whether a response was correct or incorrect. In order to advance in learning the subject matter, the student requires clear guidance from the authority—the teacher. If the teacher's response is ambiguous or fuzzy, the student may be left confused, or even worse, in error.

Of course, not every question to which students respond in class has a clearly right or wrong answer. Many times, students will be asked, and should be asked, to express their judgments, opinions, values, and conclusions on topics that have many valid perspectives.

Nevertheless, teachers must frequently test, both orally and in writing, their students' knowledge of facts and objective knowledge that leaves little room for judgments or opinions. In doing so, teachers should leave no doubt in the student's mind whether his or her response was right or wrong.

It is through classroom recitations and discussions that the teacher most often responds directly to a student's answer. Here is one example of a question/student answer/teacher response sequence in which the teacher gives clear, unequivocal feedback to the student (and to the rest of the class):

Ms. Jackson: Who was the first president of the United States? Shannon?

Shannon: Benjamin Franklin?

Ms. Jackson: No, Benjamin Franklin was an important leader but he never became president. Lindsey? Who was our first president?

Lindsey: George Washington.

Ms. Jackson: That's right. George Washington was the first president of the United States.

Notice that Ms. Jackson gives a clear "no" to Shannon's answer, while at the same time reminding the class that Benjamin Franklin *is* an important figure in United States history.

Notice also that when the correct answer is given, the teacher repeats the correct answer to the entire class. This repetition helps pupils learn the name of the first president and ensures that anyone in the class who did not hear Lindsey's response now hears the correct answer.

Although the teacher's response in the above example may seem so natural and obvious that it should need no commentary, even experienced teachers might sometimes handle their response less effectively than Ms. Jackson did.

Consider the following question/student answer/teacher response sequence that begins with the same question as in the sequence above:

Mr. Lopez: Who was the first president of the United States? Roberto?

Roberto: Abraham Lincoln.

Mr. Lopez: Well, that's an interesting answer, Roberto. Many people do think that Abraham Lincoln was the greatest president we have ever had, and so in that sense he is sometimes considered "Number 1." But was he the very first president chronologically, timewise? Stacey?

Stacey: George Washington was the first president.

Mr. Lopez: So, in a sense, both Roberto and Stacey could be right. Lincoln and Washington were both great presidents. Some people think that Lincoln was the greatest; others say Washington was the greatest. But Washington was the first, at least in order of time.

Here Mr. Lopez, perhaps wishing to avoid embarrassing Roberto by saying flatly that his answer is wrong, fails to give a clear-cut, unambiguous response to an answer that is clearly wrong. Instead, he needlessly complicates the question by allowing a different meaning to the word "first"—a meaning which, most likely, neither Roberto nor anyone else in the class had entertained. What had been a simple question requiring a simple answer has become somewhat confusing. The idea of greatness—a matter of judgment—has been introduced into a matter of historical fact.

If Mr. Lopez wishes to lead the discussion in the direction of the relative greatness of presidents, he should settle clearly and decisively the question he first raised: George Washington was the first president. Once that is made clear to everyone, he could go on to take up the question of greatness.

Notice that even at the end of the exchange Mr. Lopez still does not say unequivocally that Stacey was correct when she answered that George Washington was the first president. Instead, he qualifies his statement with the phrase "at least in order of time," a qualification likely to leave some doubt or perplexity in the minds of some of this pupils.

In considering a fact so familiar to adult Americans—that George Washington was the first president—it is good for teachers, especially teachers of the lower elementary grades, to keep in mind that many such facts may *not* be familiar and obvious to some pupils. The teacher's responsibility is to communicate such information clearly and unambiguously, as Ms. Jackson did. The teacher should not unnecessarily confuse a child, as Mr. Lopez did, by introducing a sophisticated interpretation of his own question.

Another area in which it is crucial to give clear, unambiguous feedback to the student is in making written marks and comments on papers and tests. Before returning a set of papers or tests to the class, the teacher should explain clearly any features of his or her marking system that may not be self-evident. For example, the teacher should explain that a circle around a word indicates that the word is misspelled, or that a curlicue through a word or punctuation mark means that it should be deleted.

In marking objective items on a test, the teacher should clearly indicate (with an X, for example) that an answer is wrong. If the teacher puts a question mark beside an answer, the student will be left in doubt as to what the question mark means. Does it mean that the answer is possibly correct but the teacher is unsure? Does it mean that the answer is illegible? If so, is it wrong, or does the student have the opportunity of explaining to the teacher what was written? Some students will ask a teacher for clarification of a question mark, but others are more likely to ignore what they do not understand, and so they will learn nothing from their response or from the teacher's question mark.

When an objective answer on a test is wrong, or a word is misspelled or inappropriate, should the teacher write on the paper the correct answer or word? One's answer to this question may vary according to the grade level, the subject matter, and the individual student. In teaching the early elementary grades, it is especially important that the child be given the correct answer so that he or she would be able to compare that with his or her own answer. In later years, the teacher can shift more responsibility to the child to find out and write down the correct answers. The teacher can review the correct answers orally with the whole class and instruct the students to correct their errors. If the subject matter is relatively easy and the student can readily find the right answer or spelling in a book, then it may be best to let him or her do so. If the matter is difficult, however, and the student is unlikely to discover the correct answer without great effort, then it might be best to provide it for him or her.

Make Specific Statements About Students' Responses

While it is crucial for the teacher to indicate clearly whether a response is correct or incorrect, it is also important to encourage students' participation by praising them for intelligent, reasonable answers. In the previous section, Mr. Lopez erred by not indicating clearly that Roberto's answer was incorrect. We may assume, however, that he erred with a noble motive—the wish to find some merit in his student's response and so to reward the student for his effort. The fact that he did so in an instance in which the student's answer was clearly incorrect shows that it is not always possible or appropriate to find something praiseworthy in a student's response—beyond the mere fact that the student did give a serious, pertinent response.

Very frequently, however, teachers rightly pose questions that have no clearly correct or incorrect answers. They ask questions that require students to make value judgments, see implications, interpret events that are both fictional and historical, express aesthetic preferences, and estimate probabilities.

In such cases, it is not only possible but highly desirable for the teacher to point out to the responding student and to the rest of the class the merits of the response. To do so is much more difficult than simply indicating that a response is correct or incorrect. It requires the teacher to listen carefully to the student's response, to ask for clarification if necessary, and to see quickly what it is about the response that deserves notice and praise.

The following example of a classroom exchange illustrates this principle. Mr. Pizzo's eighth-grade geography class is discussing the reasons why cities and towns are often founded on the banks of rivers.

Mr. Pizzo: Why do you suppose that Cairo, Rome, London, and Paris were all founded on major rivers? Jeffrey?

Jeffrey: Because the people needed to fish to eat?

Mr. Pizzo: Yes, good, that's true—the readily available food sources were certainly a prime consideration to early societies. But are fish the only benefit of rivers? What else do rivers offer people? Ilsa?

Ilsa: Transportation? Didn't they need to get up and down the rivers, and out to the oceans?

Mr. Pizzo: They certainly did. In order to trade with faraway places, it was a great advantage to be located on a navigable river. Can anyone think of another benefit?

Here Mr. Pizzo responds well to Jeffrey's answer by explaining why it is partially correct. Even though Mr. Pizzo was not "looking for" this answer, he recognizes its validity. If an answer is unexpected but at least partially correct, the teacher should give the student credit for it. If the teacher had said, "Well, that's not what I was thinking of," students might get the impression that responding to questions in class is just a matter of trying to guess what is in the teacher's mind.

While recognizing the worth of Jeffrey's answer, though, Mr. Pizzo also moves beyond it by asking for further, probably more important reasons for river settlements. By doing so, he keeps the discussion going and keeps the students trying to think of reasons why so many large cities were founded on rivers.

Methods of Correcting Students' Errors

As mentioned earlier, a student's progress in learning depends in part on the effectiveness of the teacher's response to the student's error. The teacher should have a repertoire of effective ways to respond to errors and be able to select the most appropriate response for a given situation. Four productive ways of responding are to:

✔ **simply give the correction;**

✔ **explain the error;**

✔ **provide the student with information to enable him/ her to correct the error; and**

✔ **ask the student questions to enable him/her to correct the error.**

Simply Give the Correction

Under what circumstances might it be best simply to correct the student? In classroom discussions or question-and-answer sessions, it is often preferable to provide a correction in a matter-of-fact way when the error is simple (e.g., grammar, pronunciation, word choice). In such cases, to provide explanations or ask questions in order to elicit the correction would unnecessarily slow the momentum of discussion, and distract the class from the issue at hand. If the teacher provides the correction simply and quickly, the student and the rest of the class are made aware of the right response without losing the thread of the conversation.

Consider the following situation, for example. In a history class, you are discussing the concept of laissez-faire capitalism, and one of the students mispronounces "laissez" as "layzees." It is much more efficient and less distracting from the topic simply to say the word correctly than to explain to him that "laissez" is a French word and that in "ez" endings the "z" is not pronounced. Asking the student whether he/she is sure he/she is pronouncing that correctly and whether he/she would like to reconsider the pronunciation would embarrass the student and derail the conversation.

In addition, when responding to students' papers, it is sometimes preferable to write in a correction rather than merely point out that something is amiss in what the student has written. If you judge that the student will not be able to understand the nature of the error and will not be able to correct it on his own, then it is better to write in the correction. For example, a student writes in a paper the words "embarrassed of her braces." If the teacher were only to underline or circle the word "of," the student would probably be unable to detect what is wrong with that word. It is a matter of idiom that we say "embarrassed by" rather than "embarrassed of," and since the student has the idiom wrong, the child is unlikely to provide the correction. It is more efficient and effective for the teacher to underline or cross out "of," and write "by" above it or in the margin.

Explain the Error

Sometimes, though, it is not enough for the teacher to correct an error; he/she should provide an explanation of the error. It is especially important to do so in situations in which the error occurs in the very matter that is being taught at the time. In such cases, a mere correction might not help the students understand why the given response was incorrect.

Imagine the following situation. Mr. Bielski is teaching his class how to convert improper fractions to mixed numbers. After explaining that one divides the numerator by the denominator, which results in a whole number and a fraction whose numerator is the remainder of the division operation, he gives some examples. Then, he asks the class to change the improper fraction $^7/_3$ to a mixed number. After a moment, one student offers the answer $4\ ^1/_3$. Instead of just dismissing the answer as wrong, Mr. Bielski sees that the student, instead of dividing the numerator by the denominator, has subtracted the denominator from the numerator, resulting in the number 4. Mr. Bielski explains what the student has done and repeats his explanation of the correct procedure.

In writing comments on students' written work, it is sometimes necessary to explain an error or inadequacy so that the student will understand why the teacher has marked the paper. Because explanations can be very time consuming, teachers often use a system of abbreviations. An English teacher, for example, may use marginal abbreviations such as *agr* for subject-verb agreement, *frag* for sentence fragment, and so on. In doing so, the teacher must make sure, however, that all students understand the abbreviations and the principles they represent.

Provide the Student with Information

Rather than telling the student why a response is wrong, it is sometimes better to lead the student to the correct response. This technique has the advantages of prompting the student to think through the problem and of boosting his or her confidence when the student arrives at the right answer on his or her own. The only drawback is that it can be time consuming, and to use it too frequently might unduly slow the pace of the class.

Imagine that you are teaching a unit on the American civil rights movement in the 1950s and 1960s. You have just asked the class what the leaders of the movement were protesting for or against, and one student answers, "Better jobs." While this answer may be partly correct, you want the class to understand that African Americans were motivated by many more grievances than the quality of jobs. Instead of providing the further answer of "segregation in the schools, public restaurants and restrooms, and the right to vote," you might lead the student toward the answer by reminding him/her that in the 1950s and early 1960s, blacks were denied some of the social and political freedoms they enjoy today.

Ask the Student Questions

This is called the Socratic method, for Socrates practices it frequently in Plato's *Dialogues* to lead his pupils toward a deeper understanding of the truth and a rejection of their previous, uncritical responses. Few teachers are as adept as Socrates in the art of questioning, but every teacher should be able, on occasion, to ask a question or two that will help the student see the error and make the correction.

A fairly common classroom occurrence when this technique is useful is a student's misuse of a word. A student may say, for example, "This is an illusion to Shakespeare," when he means "allusion." In response, the teacher might ask the student, "Isn't an illusion a deception, something that seems real but is not? That's not what you mean here, is it?" At this point the student may be reminded that a subtle reference is called an "allusion"; if not, the teacher may have to explain the distinction between the two words.

Questioning the student is most effective, however, when the error is not just in the use of a word or in a matter of fact but in the student's thinking or reasoning. In such cases, a good teacher can help the student see a flaw in his or her perception of the world and correct it. If in a discussion of French cuisine, for example, a student remarked, "French waiters are rude," the teacher might respond by asking the student why he or she says that. When the student says that he or she has eaten at two different French restaurants in town, and both times the waiter was very rude, the teacher could ask if the student thinks that two instances of rudeness are enough to make a generalization about French waiters. Isn't it possible that these two are exceptions to the rule, and that most French waiters are quite courteous? Isn't it even possible that one, or even both, of the waiters he or she encountered are usually polite but happened to be in a bad mood for some reason? Would it be fair for a Frenchman to judge Americans as loud and obnoxious after seeing two such Americans in Paris? Such a line of questioning should help the student realize that he or she was prematurely generalizing about French waiters.

The teacher should be familiar with all four ways of responding to student errors and practice using them in appropriate situations.

Chapter 10

Recapping Significant Points

Just as it is essential to review previous lessons, recapping significant points of a discussion before moving to a new aspect or problem is equally important. As varying perspectives are given in discussions, students may lose sight of the key points. Asking students to summarize what they have just heard is an excellent way to determine if ideas are being understood. Students may have missed the major concept or tenet, and multiple interpretations become evident in oral sharing.

Here are some questions that can be utilized to recap points in a discussion before moving on, depending on the discipline or subject:

1. *Do the author's ideas make sense? Why or why not?*

2. *If you had to put the main idea into one sentence, what would you say?*

3. *Where do you note the difference between fact and opinion here?*

4. *How can you relate this reading or exercise to your own experiences?*

5. *What information have you gained that will help you perform a new task?*

6. What questions does this article raise?

7. Can you find the supporting details for the main argument here?

8. Based on what you know so far, what can you predict about what will happen next?

9. How would you describe the major events of this historical period thus far?

10. What relationships do you find between early information and present information?

11. Can you give examples of the main points discussed here?

12. Who might disagree with the major ideas here, and why?

Asking students to list in writing what they have learned so far, then orally reviewing it is a quick and effective way to determine if ideas are being understood. Students need time to process and integrate information, when instructors emphasize depth over coverage.

Thesis, Antithesis, and Synthesis

Thesis, antithesis, and synthesis are effective ways to recap class discussion and material. Thesis refers to the central message, claim, or point, which students can be directed to find. Antithesis addresses the opposing claims and arguments to the central message. Synthesis is a blend of these two ideas that convergent thinking used to find a common ground between thesis and antithesis. How can we bridge the gap between these oppositional viewpoints? Pointing out conflicts and gaps in concepts help students to reconcile ideas, and commit to a perspective of their own.

Recapping Discussion and Reviewing Subject Matter

Recapping discussion and reviewing subject matter help to reinforce retention of ideas and concepts. Students may not realize the importance of stopping to reflect on what they are learning until the skill is taught to them. The desire to cover content often overshadows the importance of mastering major points one at a time. Each piece of information must be placed in perspective, with the instructor's assistance, and related to the material before and after it.

Instructors who help students to recap major points of a discussion may promote these skills:

1. Use examples and illustrations to support ideas

2. Use oral sharing to gain information, explain ideas or experiences, and seek answers

3. Demonstrate proficiency in constructing meaning from text

4. Relate materials to individual background and interests

5. Organize and group related ideas

6. Evaluate the validity of information

7. Recognize persuasive text

8. Sequence information

9. Read for information to use for performing a task

10. Read to confirm predictions about text

11. Identify personal preferences when espousing ideas and opinions

12. Participate in group discussions about central and opposing ideas

13. Check for wholeness or clarity of ideas

14. Describe, analyze, and generalize a wide variety of concepts

15. *Identify patterns in logic and arguments*

16. *Make inferences based on available information*

17. *Collect, organize, and interpret data in midstream*

18. *Analyze the likelihood of events occurring*

19. *Apply major points to real-world problems*

20. *Make decisions on how to proceed*

Recapping and reviewing give students an opportunity to self-correct, retell, question, and predict, based on the information available.

End-of-the-Lesson Recap

Equally essential to student review of main points during discussions is the end-of-lesson recap, or summary of subject matter. Closure should be brought to each lesson as it concludes and before another is initiated. Putting a frame on the picture is an important part of learning; recalling key concepts and filling in any gaps of information are vital. Instruments such as self-quizzes may help students to discover how much they have remembered and understand what they have learned.

At the end of the lesson, the teacher or the students can develop ten questions related to the material. If students cannot answer these questions, they know that more study and time are required. Questions can be used as a way to discuss and rehearse the material as well. Misunderstandings and misinterpretations become apparent in classroom oral sharing.

Journal Writing

Journal writing is another way for students to review material at the end of a lesson or unit. Students can respond to questions such as: "What is the most important or meaningful idea learned here? What is the author's central purpose?" Journal writing can be shared among class members for responses and read aloud for discussion. This kind of writing helps students to focus on key ideas, while reflecting in prose narrative style on a summary of the lesson.

Cooperative Learning

Cooperative learning can play an integral role in providing review opportunities: each team member can be assigned a portion of the material on which to give his/her group a review. By taking different parts of a chapter or dividing the unit into themes, group members are responsible for listing the key points. The entire cooperative group creates a list for the class, and lists are compared across groups for the one that most effectively covers the material. The class draws conclusions concerning the ideas based on cooperative efforts.

Some other skills that can be built by students through careful end-of-lesson review include:

1. Developing an understanding of terms and definitions

2. Examining individual viewpoints in relation to the material

3. Developing the skills and understandings needed to perform tasks related to the material

4. Suggesting changes and improvements in ideas and concepts

5. Defending ideas with specific examples and statistics

6. Explaining ways in which the material might relate to a real-world context

7. Summarizing the philosophical positions inherent in the material

8. Evaluating ways ideas relate to other disciplines or subjects

9. Exploring models and applications of the material

10. Relating concepts and issues to the surrounding cultural, historical, philosophical, and political circumstances

11. Comparing and contrasting major ideas

12. Communicating effectively about interpretations of issues

13. Predicting how variables and events will interact, and

make projections based on current evidence

14. Researching case studies as examples of available information

15. Considering the consequences of studied events and behaviors

16. Examining patterns of thoughts

17. Developing questions based on the material that lead to new understandings

18. Determining the difference between theory and fact

19. Analyzing written statements for validity

20. Looking for discrepancies and conflicting points of view

Weekly and Monthly Reviews

To ensure retention of material, students should also be engaged in weekly and monthly reviews of subject matter. Similar to end-of-lesson summaries, weekly reviews must address key points and organize concepts.

For example, if an instructor has taught students about technology terms for a week, before introducing new terms, time should be taken to ensure understanding of the current vocabulary. Similar techniques, such as self-quizzes, graded quizzes given by the instructor, journal writing, cooperative learning activities, and oral review of the material can be used.

A technology instructor might conduct a review by stating, "We have covered several computer terms this week. In the next ten minutes, I want you to write as many of these terms as you recall from memory, with their definition beside each one." Students can then compare their results with class notes, and discuss any questions related to material with the instructor and peers. Without such a review, neither instructors nor students would have an opportunity to synthesize knowledge or discover gaps in learning.

Weekly reviews help instructors determine if students are making responsible use of information and knowledge. Can students place isolated facts into a meaningful context? Can they relate them to real-world problems and applications? Are all terms and definitions clear? It is essential that students have clear understandings and mastery of current material, before they move on to any new ideas.

Along with weekly reviews of subject matter, effective instructors spend time at the end of each month to look back at what has been learned and accomplished. This monthly review reinforces concepts and gives students assistance in retaining material. Monthly reviews must cover the scope and sequence of all major ideas, and give students an overview and sense of completeness. Are there any issues or topics not understood by the class as a whole? Where is understanding weak? The review reveals such gaps in the knowledge base.

Students should take an active role in the monthly summary, bringing all applicable notes and materials. Instructors can ask students to list three or four major themes or concepts they discover in their notes. Emphasis should be placed on unifying concepts: Students should ask themselves which ideas stand at the center of the information, which are central to developing others, and which are missing or unclear?

Another approach to monthly reviews is to require students to write possible test questions that cover the material. Students examine the material in terms of what is fundamental or key. Test questions can be shared with members of the class, who can attempt to answer them in writing; then their responses can be discussed. Writing test questions helps students to sort out and prioritize information, as well as to synthesize and analyze ideas. The teacher, the textbook, and experts in the discipline must be brought together at this point to provide an effective overview of material.

Summary

Effective teachers establish an open and trusting atmosphere that supports interaction with students. Praise is provided immediately and specifically when warranted, and constructive criticism promotes learning. Teachers help students achieve their goals by using connected discourse, single questions, marker expressions and techniques, emphasis, and task attraction and challenge.

Does any of the new knowledge make other information obsolete? Do any new facts replace previous ones? Reviews provide an opportunity for field testing the worthiness of ideas. Extensive understanding of concepts may not occur until the learner places knowledge in an overview—that is, in an overall perspective. Coherence and interrelatedness of ideas become apparent when one focuses on the process of knowing how to arrive at different forms of knowledge.

Overall, in conducting reviews of subject matter, instructors must pay close attention to a summary of the previous lesson at the beginning of the new one; a recap of the significant points of discussion before moving on to a new topic; and a weekly or monthly review of lessons to ensure long-term retention. In going over what has been learned, teachers need to ensure that knowledge is placed into a meaningful context.

Reviews can be oral, written, and even completed by technological means. Students may use e-mail to answer teacher questions about material, to form study groups around organizing questions, and to communicate about the central point of each lesson. It is the educator's responsibility to reinforce the idea that each concept and skill should be mastered before a new one is integrated into the learning experience.

What is the student's responsibility in review of material? A central obligation of the student is to bring all necessary notes, text, and materials to the review session, and stay up to date with topics and issues introduced in the course. Through the review experience, students can discover gaps and discrepancies in their comprehension and absorption of ideas, themes, and facts.

Oral and written summaries of what has been learned give shape to the course design, and help students differentiate the end from the beginning. They visualize the overall course concept and achieve a global view through synthesis and convergence of major themes. The summary brings a wholeness to the material, taking seemingly isolated bits of information and tying them together with a common thread. What are the similarities and differences in these concepts? How does this issue contrast with that one? Review brings a unity and coherence to the scope and range of ideas presented in the class.

Review also reinforces the notion of organization and sequence, by placing ideas into a meaningful time frame and order. As each part of a lesson is introduced during the week or month, students do not always see how the parts make up the whole or fit together. In summarizing items from the course, the learner amasses the wealth of facts and opinions learned, and makes sense of them by fitting them into a useful pattern.

From class goals to objectives to assessment, each instructor has certain aims for each course. If time is not given to focusing on main concepts before new ones are introduced, students do not have an opportunity to process and inculcate what they have learned. Learning is looking back as well as looking ahead. Students who rush through material or attempt to process it too quickly miss the dual experiences of reflection and introspection. Material must apply to their real-world, ill-defined problems in such a way that it guides them in effective decision-making.

Involving students in effective review of material is fundamental to learning, comprehension, and retention of ideas.

References

Further reading of these references may enhance understanding of the chapter and may also increase performance on the examination.

"Clarifying Expectations with Students," pages 87-90. *Opportunities and Options in Classroom Management* by Patricia B. Kyle and Lawrence R. Rogien. Boston: Pearson, 2004.

"Assigning a Variety of Assessment Activities," page 65. *Opportunities and Options in Classroom Management* by Patricia B. Kyle and Lawrence R. Rogien. Boston: Pearson, 2004.

"Encouragement and Effective Praise," pages 241-246. *Opportunities and Options in Classroom Management* by Patricia B. Kyle and Lawrence R. Rogien. Boston: Pearson, 2004.

"Individual Differences and How to Accommodate Them" Chapter 14, 149-163. *Reading Instruction Essentials* by Anita Price Davis (Third Edition) Boston, Massachusetts: American Press, 2004.

No Child Left Behind Act
http://www.ed.gov/nclb/landing.jhtml

Communication in the Classroom

Overview

A teacher effectively communicates both verbally and nonverbally.

A teacher creates and preserves academic focus by using verbal, nonverbal, and media communication.

Principles of Verbal Communication

There are several principles that apply to written and oral messages in the classroom. The message must be accurate. As Mark Twain said, "The difference between the right word and the almost right word is the difference between lightning and the lightning bug." Teachers in particular must be careful to use very specific words that carry the appropriate denotation (literal meaning) as well as connotation (feelings, associations, and emotions associated with the word). Content teachers must carefully teach vocabulary related to the subject area.

It is possible to be completely accurate, however, without being clear. At times a teacher may use an excessive amount of jargon from his or her subject area. While students must learn vocabulary related to the subject area, the teacher must ensure that he or she teaches the words and then reviews them so the students have practice using them. At other times a teacher may assume that students understand difficult words. Many students are hesitant to ask what a word means; teachers must be alert to nonverbal signs that demonstrate that students don't understand a word (confused looks, pauses in writing a word down, failure to answer a question containing the word, etc.). Taking a couple of seconds to ask students to define a word will help them understand the larger content area concepts.

Words should also be specific or concrete. The more abstract a word, the more ambiguous it will be. For example, "physical activity" is very general; "Little League baseball" is much more specific. Although students need to learn abstract words, explaining them in a concrete manner will increase their understanding. Saying that a war causes economic difficulties is general; being more specific would be to say that it reduces the amount of tax money available to cities because of money spent on munitions.

A teacher's communications must also be organized. Students will not be able to follow directions that are given in jumbled order, interrupted with, "Oh, I forgot to tell you." Effective teachers plan their directions carefully, writing them down for the students or making notes for themselves so they will give directions or explain concepts in appropriate order.

Other communication strategies include monitoring the effects of a message, or making sure that the audience actually received and understood the message. A teacher may encourage students to be active and reflective listeners by having each student summarize what another has said before making his or her own contribution.

Voice

The way a teacher uses his/her voice conveys prejudices, feelings, and emotions. When a teacher's words convey one meaning and his or her tone of voice conveys another, the students will believe the tone rather than the meaning. Students immediately know the difference between "That's a great idea" said in a low voice with a shrug, and "That's a great idea!" said with energy and a smile. A teacher's tone of voice can tell a student, "I'm asking you, but I don't think you can answer this." Messages can be modified by varying the loudness or softness, by varying the tone, by using high or low pitch, and by changing the quality of speech.

Nonverbal Communication

Even when the verbal or written message is accurate, clear, specific, and organized, nonverbal communication can confuse the message. Sometimes the nonverbal aspect of communication can carry more weight than the verbal. Nonverbal messages can be sent by the way teachers dress and the way they use their facial expressions. Experienced educators realize that students respond better when teachers dress professionally. Most people find it easier to take seriously someone dressed in neat, clean clothes than someone in wrinkled, ill-fitting clothing. Also, students behave better when they themselves are dressed better.

Eye Contact

Facial expressions communicate a world of emotions and ideas. Teachers use many voluntary facial expressions. All students have seen "the look" from a teacher, usually when a student does something out of order. A frown or raised eyebrow can also be very effective. Although positive involuntary expressions such as smiles and laughter are appropriate, teachers should guard against involuntary negative facial expressions that convey contempt, anger, or dislike to a student.

Eye contact can be used to control interactions. Teachers often look directly at students to encourage them to speak, or look away to discourage them from speaking. "The stare" can be part of "the look" which teachers use for discipline reasons. Making eye contact with students is important when the teacher is giving instructions, sharing information, or answering questions. Many people make a habit of scanning the room with their eyes and pausing briefly to meet the gaze of many members of an audience. However, eye contact should last about four seconds to assure the person in the audience (or classroom) that the speaker has actually made contact.

Students also use their eyes, making contact with the teacher when they want to answer a question, but often looking at the floor or ceiling when they want to avoid being called on. However, teachers must be careful when making assumptions about eye contact. Research has revealed that students who are visually oriented tend to look upward while they are thinking about a response; kinesthetic learners tend to look down while they are thinking; auditory learners may look to the side. The teacher who says to a student, "The answer's not written on the floor!" may not understand the student's mode of thinking. Effective teachers who are encouraging higher-level thinking may find a classroom filled with eyes that look in various directions.

Cultural factors may also contribute to confusion about eye contact. Many cultures teach children that it is very disrespectful to look an adult in the eye; therefore, these students may stand or sit with downcast eyes as a gesture of respect. Forcing the issue only makes the students and teacher uncomfortable, and actually hinders communication.

Body Language

Body language can also convey feelings and emotions to students. A teacher can emphasize points and generalizations by gesturing or tapping something on the chalkboard. If a teacher gestures too often or too wildly, students find it difficult to determine what the teacher is trying to emphasize. Too many gestures can also cause the students to watch the gestures instead of attending to the information.

Beginning teachers especially need to convey a relaxed but formal body posture, which denotes strength, openness, and friendliness. Hiding behind the desk or crossing the arms indicates timidity or even fear. A teacher who meets students at the door with a smile and even a handshake shows students he or she is confident and in control.

Media Communication

Media communication has become a vital part of the classroom process. Effective teachers use a variety of audio-visuals in every class, including posters, graphs, overhead transparencies, films, videos, CD-ROMs, and laser disks.

Summary

A teacher's expectations for student behavior can be revealed through a combination of verbal and nonverbal communication. Jere Brophy and others have researched the relationship between teacher expectations and student behavior. This research shows that teachers often communicate differently when dealing with high-achievers and low-achievers. This behavior is not always deliberate or conscious on the part of the teacher, but it can communicate negative expectations. When dealing with high-achievers, as opposed to low-achievers, teachers tend to listen more carefully, give them more time to answer, prompt or assist them more, call on them more often, give more feedback, and look more interested. The effective communicator will be careful not to differentiate communication based on a student's achievement level.

Planning Processes

Madeline Hunter describes a planning model which requires teacher decisions about content, teacher behavior, and student behavior. The three parts of this model overlap and are related to each other; a decision in one category influences a decision in another. Decisions about content are often made at the state or district level. Teachers use frameworks from the state, curriculum documents developed by the district, and materials from district-chosen textbooks as bases for planning lessons.

A teacher using this model would make decisions about content, including goals and objectives for a lesson or unit, length of lesson or unit, emphasis of lesson, textbooks, and additional resource materials. Decisions about his or her own behavior include teaching strategies, accommodations for various learning styles, types of activities, sizes of groups, uses of technology and other resources, and room arrangements. Decisions about students' behavior include individual or group responses, format of responses, ways students will demonstrate learning, and products of activities.

Robert Gagné outlines nine external events which are important in planning an appropriate sequence of instruction. They are: gaining attention; informing students of the lesson objectives; stimulating recall of previous learning; presenting stimuli with distinctive features; guiding learning; eliciting student performance; providing informative feedback; assessing student performance; and enhancing the retention and transfer of learning.

The term "lesson cycle" has been applied to processes of lesson planning developed by a variety of people because the process repeats itself continually. These planning processes usually include the development of objectives and a focus for attention, a design for instructional input, constant monitoring of student understanding, provision for rehearsal and practice of knowledge, and opportunities for enrichment or follow-up.

Teachers choose objectives for a lesson from a curriculum guide, or develop their own from their knowledge of their subject area and the needs of students. These objectives are clearly communicated to the students in terms of what they will learn (not activities they will do) during the lesson. In a deductive lesson, these objectives are explained to students at the beginning; in an inductive lesson, objectives are clarified at the end of the lesson. Teachers develop a focus or introduction to the lesson (called an anticipatory set by Hunter) which should hook the students' interest and focus attention toward the upcoming activities. Instruction may take a variety of forms. The teacher provides instructional activities which will produce the desired outcomes from the students. A wide variety of instructional methods may be used for input, from mastery lectures or labs to cooperative learning or several different types of inductive strategies. The teacher is constantly monitoring student behavior, checking for understanding, and modifying the instruction as necessary.

After or during instructional input, the students rehearse or apply what they've learned. In guided practice, the teacher watches carefully to make sure students have grasped the material correctly. Because the teacher is on hand to assess student responses, he or she is able to provide correction or additional input if necessary. During independent practice, students work independently. At the end of each lesson (or at the end of the class), the teacher or students summarize or review what has been learned. An additional feature is enrichment, which should be for all students, not only the faster ones. Enrichment means that students either delve deeper into a subject they've been studying, or broaden their understanding of the general topic. For example, students who have been studying the stock market could research the history of its development, or they could study the market in other countries.

Lesson cycles are repeated for additional blocks of content. A lesson may last anywhere from a few minutes to several days; it isn't limited by the period or the bell.

Self-Directed Learning

Effective teachers not only set goals for their students, but also teach students to set and accomplish their own goals, both individually and in groups. Students need to learn how to plan for their individual learning as well as for learning with a group of students. If students are unaccustomed to setting goals, the effective teacher begins by modeling the process. The teacher explains how he or she develops goals and objectives for the class. One way of encouraging students to set goals is to ask students to set a performance standard for themselves with regard to time needed to complete a project. For example, students might determine they will need 15 minutes to answer five questions, writing one paragraph of at least five sentences for each question. In order to accomplish this goal, the students must focus their attention very carefully and limit themselves to about three minutes per question. The teacher should then ask questions to help students determine whether the goal was realistic, and if not, what adjustments they need to make.

Other steps could be to ask students to develop their own questions about material to be learned or to plan activities to accomplish the goals of the lesson. The highest level is to have students determine the goals for their own learning. For example, a science teacher might introduce the topic of earthquakes, then help students determine what they need to know about earthquakes, and the activities and resources which will help them learn. Students also need to develop plans for products that will show that they have met their goals.

Another way to encourage self-directed thinking and learning is to use higher-level questioning strategies, and to teach students to use them as well.

References

Further reading of these references may enhance understanding of the chapter and may also increase performance on the examination.

"Clear Communication" Chapter 3, pages 26-38. *Opportunities and Options in Classroom Management* by Patricia B. Kyle and Lawrence R. Rogien. Boston: Pearson, 2004.

"Individual Differences and How to Accommodate Them" Chapter 14, 149-163. *Reading Instruction Essentials* by Anita Price Davis (Third Edition) Boston, Massachusetts: American Press, 2004.

Content Category 4: Teacher Professionalism

Chapters 12–14

Goal-Setting

Overview

The teacher identifies long-range goals for subject areas that are appropriate to student needs.

The teacher constructs and sequences related short-range goals for a given subject area.

All successful teachers begin the term with a clear idea of what they expect students to learn in a given course. Establishing long-range goals for a course—goals that are age-appropriate and reflect student ability and needs—help to clarify the knowledge and skills that teachers and students will work toward during the school year.

Long-range goals can be established for the classroom by the Board of Education, by knowledgeable curriculum specialists, or by a single teacher or group of teachers. Stated in clear, concise language, these goals define the knowledge that students will achieve or the skills that they will acquire through specific instructional activities. For example, a language arts instructor might state the following long-range goals for high school students:

> ✔ **The student is able to identify major American poets and authors of the twentieth century;**
>
> ✔ **The student is able to write narrative, informative, and persuasive essays;**
>
> ✔ **The student is able to properly cite research references;**
>
> ✔ **The student is able to identify important themes in literature;**
>
> ✔ **The student is able to identify with multicultural perspectives on the American experience.**

After developing a list of potential goals for a course, it is necessary to evaluate those goals against the following criteria:

Importance: The resulting learning must be significant and relevant enough for students to aim for.

Instruction: Appropriate classroom activities must be able to support the learning of the stated goal.

Evaluation: Students must be able to demonstrate the achievement of the goal.

Suitability: The goal must be challenging, as well as reachable, for all students.

Importance

There are many ways to evaluate the importance of selected goals. Teachers can judge goals on the basis of whether the stated outcome is necessary to gain advanced knowledge of a particular field of study, as in the following goal: Students will memorize the letters of the alphabet or master the use of punctuation. Goals can be evaluated on the basis of whether or not their achievement will lead students to become better citizens, such as: Students will apply their knowledge of the Constitution to judge a contemporary court case. Goals can also be judged on the basis of whether or not their achievement will lead students to become well-adapted members of society or competitive in the workforce, as in the following: Students will be able to demonstrate their ability to use the Internet to locate information. Finally, goals can be selected on the basis of whether or not their achievement will help prepare students for college admissions standards.

Instruction

In order to ensure that students achieve the stated goal, appropriate classroom activities must be chosen to support its learning. When students have completed these activities, they should be able to successfully demonstrate the knowledge or skills that they have achieved.

Evaluation

Through the successful completion of writing assignments, tests, projects, or activities, students must be able to demonstrate that they have achieved the stated long-range goals.

Suitability

All goals for a given course must be achievable for the entire class, while leaving room to challenge students to master new skills. In order to determine if long-range goals are appropriate, teachers can refer to a number of resources, including student files that may include the results of basic skills tests and reading level evaluations, as well as writing samples.

Identify Knowledge, Skills, and Attitudes

After identifying long-range goals for a given subject, it is necessary to recognize the short-range goals that are essential to achieving the larger objective. In order to do this, teachers must be aware of the underlying skills needed to successfully achieve the stated long-range objective. For example, in order to write an essay, a language arts teacher must ensure that students are able to compose complete sentences and paragraphs, develop a coherent outline of ideas, create a thesis, write an introduction, advance the stated thesis through supporting ideas in the body paragraphs, and form a logical conclusion. If students are unable to master these basic skills, they will be unable to achieve the long-range goals of producing an essay.

Likewise, a biology teacher, whose long-range goal is for students to understand the process of photosynthesis, will identify another list of necessary skills. For example, students must know basic elements like hydrogen, oxygen, and carbon, and students must understand how these elements combine to form water (H_2O) and carbon dioxide (CO_2). Moreover, a geometry teacher would know that in order for students to find the area of a triangle or the circumference of a circle, they must know how to compose and solve basic geometric problems.

Construct or Adapt Short-Range Objectives

Short-range objectives should be stated in simple terms, and should outline identifiable behaviors and skills. When constructing short-range objectives for a course of study, teachers must make certain that each objective leads to the realization of a long-range goal, and that the skill or knowledge is easily observable. For example:

✔ **Students will be able to demonstrate an understanding of Shakespearean language;**

✔ **Students will be able to list the pros and cons of various forms of energy, including nuclear energy, natural gas, solar energy, dams, and coal;**

✔ **Students will be able to solve advanced word problems involving multiplication and division;**

✔ **Students will be able to complete a diagram outlining the processes involved in digestion; or**

✔ **Students will be able to recite a poem by a well-known twentieth-century poet.**

When short-range objectives have been supplied by the Board of Education or the local school system, teachers must be able to interpret and adapt them, making certain that they are appropriate to the age and ability of their own students. For example, a high school senior might be able not only to list the positive and negative implications of nuclear fusion as an energy source, but also to write a persuasive essay, arguing for or against nuclear energy. While an elementary school student might find reciting a poem from memory to be a formidable task, he or she might be appropriately challenged by the assignment of selecting a poem and reading it aloud to the class.

Organize and Sequence Short-Range Objectives

As learning is achieved by moving from basic skills and knowledge to the understanding of complex ideas and functions, it is important for teachers to sequence short-range objectives according to their appropriate place in the development of higher-order thinking. For example, a history student might first be introduced to the life and achievements of Einstein through a documentary film, and later study his most famous equation for the production of energy ($E=mc^2$). Following this, the student might be introduced to the top-secret Manhattan Project that involved hundreds of physicists in the race to turn Einstein's equation for energy into an atomic weapon. Still later, the disastrous results of the atomic bomb in Hiroshima and Nagasaki might be introduced through first-hand accounts from survivors. Finally, he or she might be required to study current treaties surrounding the control of nuclear proliferation. The students might conclude their course of study with a class debate on nuclear proliferation, and how it promotes or threatens chances for global peace. From the study of historical events like the Manhattan Project and basic terms like nuclear proliferation, to the application of this knowledge in a classroom debate, the short-range goals that guide the activities of this history class have been sequentially ordered to allow students the opportunity to gradually develop and demonstrate higher-order thinking skills.

Other examples of the sequencing of short-range objectives that build upon knowledge can be found in the very clear development of skills outlined in the study of mathematics. From the simple memorization of numbers beginning in the first grade, to the mastery of addition, subtraction, multiplication, and division studied throughout elementary school, to the more complicated functions in middle school like algebra and the application of these skills in advanced word problems, to the study of geometry, trigonometry, and calculus in high school—mathematical studies are clearly delineated to build upon previously acquired skills. Without knowledge of multiplication, the idea of division would be impossible to master. Without an understanding of division, fractions would be beyond the reach of students. Since no decent math teacher would consider asking students to give the area of a triangle without first ensuring that the students know basic algebra, all teachers must be aware of the basic skills necessary to achieve higher-order skills, and must arrange classroom activities and short-range goals in the order that best promotes learning.

References

Further reading of these references may enhance understanding of the chapter and may also increase performance on the examination.

"Expectations," pages 40-42. *Opportunities and Options in Classroom Management* by Patricia B. Kyle and Lawrence R. Rogien. Boston: Pearson, 2004.

"Clarifying Expectations with Students," pages 87-90. *Opportunities and Options in Classroom Management* by Patricia B. Kyle and Lawrence R. Rogien. Boston: Pearson, 2004.

"Execution of the Lesson (Objectives)," pages 51-52. *Opportunities and Options in Classroom Management* by Patricia B. Kyle and Lawrence R. Rogien. Boston: Pearson, 2004.

"Individual Differences and How to Accommodate Them," Chapter 14, 149-163. *Reading Instruction Essentials* by Anita Price Davis (Third Edition) Boston, Massachusetts: American Press, 2004.

National Goals (2000)
    http://www.negp.gov/

No Child Left Behind Act
    http://www.ed.gov/nclb/landing.jhtml

Materials, Activities, Managing Time

Overview

A teacher chooses, adapts, and develops materials for a given set of educational objectives, and for the learning needs of his or her students.

The effective teacher continually seeks materials that help instigate and enhance student learning. In some instances, the teacher may select instructional materials from those readily available based on the appropriate age level for his or her students. In other instances, he or she will need to adapt available materials to better serve individual needs and learning styles. And in yet other instances, the teacher will need to design and develop materials specifically suited to his or her learning objectives and the needs of the students. The acquisition, adaption, or creation of materials primarily will be done prior to the beginning of the school year. However, some of it will need to occur while the school year is in progress, as particular learning challenges arise and as individual student needs are discovered. A considerable proportion of the time invested in locating and shaping these materials will bear dividends, since materials which prove to be well-suited to a particular unit are eligible for repeated use.

A teacher chooses, develops, and sequences learning activities that are suitable to instructional objectives and student needs.

One of the most challenging and important synthesizing activities of the teaching professional is determining how to match what needs to be taught with the specifications of those who need to learn it. The successful teacher spends considerable time becoming familiar with required instructional objectives, curriculum, and texts. This should be done well in advance of the start of the school year. General knowledge about the intellectual and social developmental levels of students, the particular needs which characterize any specific group of students, including their individual learning styles, are more apparent to the teacher after the first few days and weeks of school. The effective teacher must then be organized enough to choose and sequence learning activities before the school year begins, but flexible enough to adapt these activities after becoming acquainted with the special needs and learning styles of specific students.

A teacher manages his or her time in the classroom efficiently.

Educational Resources

The teacher uses a variety of educational resources (including people and technology) to enhance both individual and group learning. The effective teacher includes resources of all types in the curriculum planning process. He or she should be very familiar with the school library, city/county library, education service center resources, and the library of any college or university in the area. The teacher should have a list of all audiovisual aids that may be borrowed: for example, kits, films, filmstrips, videos, laser disks, and computer software. All audiovisual aids should be related to curricular objectives. Many librarians have keyed their resources to objectives in related subject areas so the teacher can incorporate them with ease into the lessons. However, resources should never be used with a class unless they have been previewed and approved by the teacher. The list of resources to be used in a lesson or unit should be included in the curriculum guide or the lesson plan for ease of use.

Planning for Resources

The effective teacher determines the appropriate place in the lesson for audiovisual aids. If the material is especially interesting and thought-provoking, he or she may use it to introduce a unit. For example, a travel video on coral reefs or snorkeling might be an excellent introduction to the study of tropical fish and plants. The same video could be used at the end of the study to see how many fish and plants the students can recognize and name. Computer software that "dissects" frogs or worms may be used after a discussion of what students already know about the animals and how their internal organs compare with those of humans. A video of a Shakespearean play could be intermixed with discussion and class reading of scenes from the play.

Videos, films, and filmstrips may be stopped for discussion. Research reveals that students comprehend better and remember longer if the teacher introduces a video or film appropriately, then stops it frequently to discuss what the students have just seen and heard. This method also helps keep students' attention focused and assists them in learning note-taking skills.

Print Resources

The most common print material is the textbook, which has been selected by teachers on the campus from a list of books approved by the state. Textbooks are readily available, economical, and written to match state curriculum requirements. However, the adoption process is a long one, and textbooks (particularly science and history) can become out-of-date quickly; therefore, the teacher must use additional resources with recent dates.

Local, state, and national newspapers and magazines should not be overlooked. Some newspapers and magazines have special programs to help teachers use their products in the classroom for reading and writing opportunities as well as for sources of information. Local newspapers may be willing to send specialists to work with students or act as special resource persons.

A limitation of textbooks is their tendency to provide sketchy or minimal treatment of topics, partly because publishers are required to include such a broad range of topics. An ineffective teacher may use the "chapter a week" theory of "covering" a textbook. This method pays no consideration to the importance of information in each chapter or its relevance to the overall district curriculum. Nor does it promote critical thinking on the part of the teacher or the student. Students tend to believe the textbook is something to be endured and not employed as a tool for learning. The effective teacher chooses sections from the textbook that are relevant to his or her learning goals and omits the rest. He or she also supplements the sketchy treatments by using an abundance of other resources.

Visual Materials

The most available visual tools in classrooms are the chalkboard and the overhead projector. There are several principles that apply to both. The teacher must write clearly and in large letters. Overhead transparencies should never be typed on a regular typewriter because the print is too small. Computers allow type sizes of at least 18 points, which is the minimum readable size. Also, both boards and transparencies should be free of clutter. Old information should be removed before new information is added. These tools work more effectively if the teacher plans ahead of time what he or she will write or draw on them. Using different colors will emphasize relationships or differences.

Posters and charts can complement lessons, but the walls should not be so cluttered that students are unable to focus on what's important for the current lesson. Posters and charts can be displayed on a rotating basis. Filmstrips, films, and videos are appealing to students because they are surrounded by visual images on television, computers, and video games. Films and filmstrips have the advantage of being projected on a large screen so all students can see clearly. Videos and computers can be connected to large displays or projected on large screens, but these projection devices are rather expensive. If the available screen is too small for large-group viewing, then the teacher might break the class into groups and have several different projects for them to do on a rotating basis.

Some of the best graphic aids will be those developed by individual students or by groups of students. Along with learning about subject area concepts, students will be learning about design and presentation of information. Students can take pictures of their products to put in a portfolio or scrapbook.

Videodisc and Interactive Video

Videodiscs provide a sturdy, compact system of storage for pictures and sound. They can store more than 50,000 separate frames of still images, up to 50 hours of digitized stereo music, or about 325 minutes of motion pictures with sound. An advantage of videodisc over videotape is that each frame can be accessed separately and quickly. The simplest level of use involves commands to play, pause, forward, or reverse. Individual frames can be accessed by inputting their number.

These programs can become interactive by linking them to a computer. The teacher can then individually access, sequence, and pace the information from the interactive system. An art teacher with a collection of pictures of the world's art treasures can choose which pictures to use and the order in which to show them, then design custom-made lessons which can be used repeatedly or easily revised. He or she might decide to develop a program on landscapes as portrayed in art during a certain period of time. By using the videodisc's reference guide, the teacher determines which pictures to use and the length of time he or she wants each displayed. He or she can develop numerous lessons from one videodisc.

More comprehensive interactive programs can use the computer to present information, access a videodisc to illustrate main points, then ask for responses from the student. A multimedia production run by the computer can include images, text, and sound from a videodisc, CD-ROM, graphics software, word processing software, and a sound effects program. Teachers can develop classroom presentations, but students can also develop learning units as part of a research or inquiry project.

The cost of a multimedia system remains relatively high, but students can use it to develop high-level thought processes, collaborative work and research skills, as well as content knowledge and understanding.

Human Resources

Parents and other members of the community can be excellent local experts from which students can learn about any subject—mathematics from bankers, art and music from artists, English from journalists, history from club or church historians or librarians, business from owners of companies. The list can be endless. Effective teachers make sure that any guest who is invited to speak or perform understands the purpose of the visit and the goals or objectives the teacher is trying to accomplish. Preparation can make the class period more focused and meaningful.

Field trips are excellent sources of information, especially about careers and current issues such as pollution control. One field trip can yield assignments in mathematics, history, science, and English, and often art, architecture, music, or health. Teachers can collaborate with each other to produce thematic assignments for the field trip or simply to coordinate the students' assignments. Often a history report can serve as an English paper as well. Data can be analyzed in math classes and presented with the aid of computers.

Procedures for Learning Success

There are several steps the teacher should follow to ensure success for student learning: a) know and start at the proper level of the students; b) share with students learning objectives and the processes chosen to attain them; c) prepare for the successive steps in the learning process—from instruction, through guidance and support, to feedback; d) choose relatively small steps in which to progress, and include regular assessments of these progressions; e) distinguish between the learning a student can do independently and that which is best facilitated and monitored by the teacher, and choose methods appropriate to content and skills; and f) include a variety of activities and methods that appeal to the full range of student learning styles and preferences.

Organizing Activities

Instructional objectives necessitate that the skill or knowledge to be taught should be valuable on its own, or should clearly lead to something else which is valuable. When the class begins, these long-range objectives should be shared with students as part of the teacher's planned "idea scaffolding," to acknowledge learning as a mutual enterprise. Sharing these objectives is the first important learning activity because this serves as the basis for the communal task of "making sense" of the learning in progress.

Since teachers are expected to be professionally prepared to recognize the cognitive and social levels of students, a simple review of the generally accepted theories of Piaget, Erikson, and other research theorists may be necessary to recall specific characteristics appropriate to various developmental levels. Familiarity with the learning objectives, the material to be mastered, and the level of the students, enable the teacher to choose and develop a wide range of appropriate activities, and tentatively to sequence them in ways that facilitate learning.

A high school language arts teacher, for example, who wishes to convey to his or her students the excitement and value of closely reading literary texts will, at the start of the year, address this learning objective with them. The teacher may also include a personal experience of close reading that is inspiring and revealing. He or she can then plan a series of short-term goals, such as "Students will be able to read carefully enough to gather important details of plot" and "Students will be able to read sensitively enough to notice the connotative dimensions of words and appreciate the nuances suggested by cumulative connotation." Naturally, recognizing denotative details will precede appreciating connotative dimensions. Both will precede the students' ability to identify and appreciate the author's choice of point of view.

Careful, incremental goal-setting allows for considerable flexibility in pace and methods, and leads to further valuable sequencing of strategies. For example, a variety of activities may be used to enhance close reading: the teacher may model close reading of a very short story; the teacher may assign small group work with close reading of paragraphs in which one student identifies an important detail, and another student suggests its relevance to the details; the teacher can show the class an overhead color-marking of important descriptive words from one page of a short story or poem; students can work on individual in-class color-marking for the next page, which can be followed by a group discussion of student results; the teacher can assign homework assignments to color-mark a short story or poem; and students can work on group assignments that require them to graph elements of literary text.

Such preliminary planning is enhanced for any specific group of students by a perceptive teacher's growing awareness of individual student learning styles. Since students do not fall precisely into theoretical stages, activities must be designed for a range of developmental levels and learning styles. This includes concrete as well as abstract dimensions, opportunities for instruction by the teacher, and exploration and discovery by individual students and groups.

Once the learning enterprise is launched, the teacher's continued instruction, support, regular assessment, and feedback help maximize the potential of learning opportunities.

Outcome-Oriented Learning

Effective teachers plan carefully so that outcome-oriented activities will produce students who are self-directed learners, in group or individual environments. The teacher should know how to plan so that the curriculum guides, lesson plans, actual lessons, tests, and assessments are correlated. Effective teachers plan in advance, explain the unit's goals and objectives to the students, then choose activities which will help the class reach the desired outcomes.

In outcome-oriented learning, teachers define outcomes, or what they want students to know, do, and be when they complete a required course of study. The teachers set high but realistic goals and objectives for their students, then plan instructional activities which will assist students in achieving these goals.

The key to effective outcome-oriented planning is to consider what outcomes must be achieved, then determine which teacher and student behaviors will ensure that students will achieve the outcomes.

Outcome-based planning starts with the end product— what must be learned or accomplished in a particular course or grade level. For example, an algebra teacher may decide that the final outcome of his or her algebra course would be that students use quadratic equations to solve problems. He or she then works "backwards" to determine prerequisite knowledge and skills students need to have in order to accomplish this outcome. By continuing to ask these questions about each set of prerequisites, the teacher finds a starting point for the subject or course, then develops goals and objectives. The outcomes should be important enough to be required of all students.

An outcome-oriented system means that students are given sufficient time and practice to acquire the knowledge and skills. It also means that teachers take into account students' various learning styles, time required for learning, and make adaptations by providing a variety of educational opportunities.

Planning and Performance of the Classroom Teacher

The amount of time in which effective learning and instruction occur depends on a number of variables, but the planning and performance of the classroom teacher are major factors. The time available for instruction can be determined by calculating the amount of allocated time in the schedule. For example, a class that meets five times a week from 10:00 A.M. to 10:50 A.M. has an allocation of 250 minutes per week for that subject. Students will not interact academically with their teacher and/or the content of the subject 100 percent of that time. There are time "leaks" that reduce the allocated time. However, the most effective teachers have learned how to minimize those leaks, and maximize the amount of time spent by students on academic learning tasks.

A major difference between effective and ineffective teachers is the amount of time they arrange for their students to engage in productive "on task" learning. Effective teachers also recognize the difference between successful and unsuccessful engagement in academic learning. Time spent on learning does not provide any assurance that learning will take place unless student comprehension also takes place. Optimum learning occurs when students experience a high success rate during the time they are engaged with the content. Thus, productive "on task" student behavior requires the additional dimension of high comprehension that accompanies student interaction with content.

This section provides a discussion of the teacher behaviors that increase the efficient use of time, which leads to higher achievement through increased student engagement in learning.

Beginning Classwork Promptly

Effective teachers are skilled in beginning classwork promptly. Prompt beginnings are brought about by teacher planning that provides rules and norms for students that clarify their expected classroom behavior. These rules include basic requirements about where students should be when the class period begins. Effective teachers are also punctual and begin classwork promptly. Depending on the subject of study, classroom rules may call for students to be in their seats, at their computers, at a learning station, with a team of students, at a laboratory station, lined up in rows, and so forth. Clear directions and enforcement regarding student responsibility for the beginning of each class set the tone for the entire class period and help to avoid distracting delays.

Student Activity

A second element that teachers must provide is student activity that initiates the learning experiences planned for that class period. Merely requiring students to be at a certain physical location in the learning environment, without a concurrent activity to initiate their learning, is inadequate to promote efficient use of class time. The burden for initiating classroom learning should be shared between students and their teacher. However, the teacher must assume responsibility by taking the following actions:

1. *Have materials prepared and organized for students.*

2. *Check attendance efficiently as students enter the room or by some other expeditious method.*

3. *Maintain eye contact instead of organizing other materials, or being diverted to other activities at his/her desk or on the bulletin board.*

4. *Provide opening prompts or directions to students to help them get started with their responsibilities.*

It is the responsibility of the teacher to see that the focus of teacher and student talk is on academic subject matter. The daily objectives of each class session require that learning activities, teacher presentations, class discussions, and seatwork must be related directly or indirectly to the content or skills to be learned in that session. Distracting activities, especially discussion by either the teacher or the student that strays significantly from the topic, must be minimized or eliminated. Teachers can tactfully refocus students who are off task without demeaning student participation. Teachers must recognize when a diversion is too intrusive and develop in advance ways to suggest how another time or topic might be a more appropriate way to inject the activity or remark. When diversions have no productive value and waste learning time, they must be tactfully eliminated. Such elimination may be handled by a direct response to the students, or it may be handled in a private conversation if the diversions are repeated by particular students. The teacher must also be careful to avoid unproductive digressions. The classroom does provide an opportunity for teachers and students to express anecdotes, experiences, and opinions, but they should relate to the content of the lesson by serving as examples, clarification, or contextual materials.

As each class period unfolds, events usually flow from one topic or activity to another. The effective teacher manages these transitions in a systematic, academically oriented way. The variety of events that occurs and poses the threat of a disruption to learning include a) shifting from one activity to another; b) wait time when some students finish before others; c) interruptions that result from tardiness or from students who failed to bring their supplies; d) routine housekeeping tasks; e) setting up equipment; and f) significant changes in the topic under discussion or study.

Transitions

The effective teacher is aware of transitional interruptions and prepares solutions for them in advance. Each transition calls for methods that will minimize the loss of learning time. When shifting from one activity to another, it is crucial to reach closure on the first activity and to make it clear to students that a new activity is underway. This means that any materials or issues that related to the initial activity are shelved, even if temporarily, to give complete attention to the new activity. The teacher can help with this transition by stating that the class will engage in a new activity, and then he/she will provide instruction, materials, and any other element needed to help students focus on the new activity.

When students are given time to complete an assignment in class, some students will finish first. Unless plans are made for a productive activity for these students, valuable time for these students will be wasted. When an assignment for class work is made, the teacher should provide an attractive activity for those who finish early. The activity might be an opportunity to work on a homework assignment, thereby reducing the time the student will spend at home that night on schoolwork. It might be an extra credit task or it may be study time for another subject. In any event, the teacher should avoid asking students who have completed their assignments to wait until everyone is finished.

Tardy students or students who forget books or materials should not disrupt classroom learning. Regular procedures should be established for these common events. For example, it could be a rule that tardy students who bring a tardy slip from the office should enter the room, give the teacher the slip without comment, go to their seat, and the nearest student will quietly show them where the class is in the lesson. Such a policy simplifies an occurrence that has the potential to interrupt the flow of the classroom.

Equipment for the classroom should always be set up in advance and tested to make certain that it works. Valuable time can be lost replacing a burned-out bulb, hunting for an extension cord, or setting up a screen on a tripod that suddenly broke.

Routine classroom events include passing out papers, getting books, writing on the board, distributing materials, and taking attendance. Pre-planning enables the teacher to expedite each of these activities and preserve valuable learning time. Papers can be pre-sorted by rows and given to the first person in each row to hand back to other students. Distributing books might be accomplished by delegating this task to one student in each group (row, team). Information can be written on the board ahead of time and covered with newsprint until it is used. Possibly the information could be put on a transparency and presented with an overhead projector. Some classrooms may have computers on a network, and, therefore, the board or transparency may not be needed.

One of the more difficult transitions to make is to know when to shift from one topic to another. This may be difficult because any topic may reach a boring stage if it continues too long, but if it ends too soon, it may leave some students frustrated. Teacher judgment based on professional observation must determine when to continue or cease a discussion. However, teachers must be sensitive to student interests and respect their needs in making a transition to a new topic. When flowing into another topic, the teacher can offer to meet with students at another time if they have more to say, or the topic might be included at another appropriate time. The purpose of the classroom activity is to meet specific goals, and once those goals are met, it is best to move on to achieve additional goals rather than linger and lose valuable time.

Summary

The efficient use of time requires teacher leadership and student behavior that maximizes the use of time, and optimizes learning. This can be accomplished by a punctual and effective beginning to each class, a focus on academic subject matter, and provision for smooth transitions and minimal effect from interruptions.

References

Further reading of these references may enhance understanding of the chapter and may also increase performance on the examination.

Reading Instruction Essentials by Anita Price Davis (Third Edition) Boston, Massachusetts: American Press, 2004.

Time Management
http://teacher.scholastic.com/professional/futureteachers/time_management.htm

14

Methods & Implementation

Overview

A teacher displays forms of knowledge such as ideas, rules, principles, and values.

The teacher implements directions for carrying out instructional activity.

Just as students have learning styles, teachers also have learning styles as well as teaching styles. Since teachers, naturally, prefer their own learning style (a learning style is a set of preferences), they may teach according to their personal way of learning. Many teachers end up teaching the way they were taught when they were students—whether or not their own teachers were using effective methods!

When a teacher becomes aware of his or her own learning and teaching styles, then the teacher has the freedom of choice. The teacher can choose the most effective methods to reach all the students in class. Thus, it is worthwhile for each teacher to learn more about his or her learning and teaching styles.

This chapter focuses on giving directions so that students can complete instructional activities. Directions are an important part of the information that teachers dispense to their students, and it is important to develop strategies and techniques for giving good directions.

Deductive Strategies

Methods can be divided into two categories: deductive and inductive. Deductive methods are those in which teachers present material through mastery lecture, or students teach each other through presentations. In deductive lessons, the generalizations or rules are taught from the beginning, then examples and elaboration are developed which support the generalizations or rules. Deductive thinking often requires students to make assessments based on specific criteria which they or others develop.

Inductive methods are those in which teachers encourage students to study, research, and analyze data they collect, then develop generalizations and rules based on their findings. During inductive lessons, a hypothesis or concept is introduced at the beginning, but generalizations are developed later in the lesson and are based on inferences from data.

The lecture is a deductive method, whereby information is presented to students by the teacher. New teachers are especially attuned to lecture because that is the usual mode of instruction in college classes. An advantage of lecture is that large amounts of information can be presented in an efficient manner; however, effective teachers avoid dumping loads of information through lectures. Mastery lectures should be short, usually no more than 10 or 15 minutes at a time, and constantly interrupted with questions to and from students. Questions during a lecture tend to be lower-level ones, where the teacher is building a foundation of knowledge for students to use in later activities. The effective teacher, however, uses higher-level questions even during lectures.

Information sessions must also be supplemented with an array of visual materials that will appeal to visual learners as well as auditory ones. Putting words or outlines on the board or a transparency is very helpful; however, this is still basically a verbal strategy. Drawings, diagrams, cartoons, pictures, caricatures, and graphs are visual aids for lectures. Teacher drawings need not be highly artistic, merely memorable. Often a rough or humorous sketch will be more firmly etched in students' minds than elaborate drawings. Using a very simple sketch provides a better means of teaching the critical attributes than a complicated one. The major points stand out in a simple sketch; details can be added once students understand the basic concepts. For example, a very simple sketch of the shapes of the snouts of alligators and crocodiles can fix the difference in students' memory; identification from pictures then becomes easier.

Teachers should also be careful to include instruction on how to take notes while listening to a speaker, a skill that will be useful during every student's career, whether listening to instructions from a supervisor or a speaker at meetings and conferences. One way a teacher can teach this is to show students notes or an outline from the mini-lecture he or she is about to present, or to write notes or an outline on the board or overhead while the teacher is presenting the information. This activity requires careful planning by the teacher and will result in a more organized lecture. This type of structure is especially helpful for sequential learners, those who like organization. It will also help random learners develop organizational skills. A web, map, or cluster is a more right-brained method of connecting important points in a lecture or a chapter. The effective teacher will use both systems and teach both to students, so they have a choice of strategies.

Inductive Strategies

Inquiry or discovery lessons are inductive in nature. Inquiry lessons start with a thought-provoking question for which students are interested in finding an explanation. The question can be followed by brainstorming a list of what the students already know about the topic, then categorizing the information. The categories can then be used as topics for group or individual research. Deductive presentations by students of their research can follow.

Some advantages of inductive lessons are that they generally require higher-level thinking by both teacher and students, and they usually result in higher student motivation, interest, and retention. They can be more interesting to the teacher, who deals with the same concepts year after year. Disadvantages include the need for additional preparation by the teacher, the need for access to a large number of resources, and additional time for students to research the concepts. The teacher spends a great amount of time in planning the lessons, then acts as facilitator during classes.

Generally, the greater the amount of planning and prediction by the teacher, the greater the success of the students. This does not mean that the activity must be tightly structured or set in concrete, but the effective teacher tries to predict student responses and his or her reactions to them. The need for purchasing additional resources has been moderated by computerized bibliographic services, interlibrary loan, and CD-ROMs with all types of information. Because inductive, research-oriented units require more class time, subject-area teachers must work together to determine what concepts are essential for students to understand; other nonessential concepts are omitted.

An English teacher wishing to introduce an inductive study of *Julius Caesar* might ask students what would happen if a group of United States senators and representatives banded together to kill the current president and take control of the government. After brainstorming ideas about causes and effects of the assassination, students could categorize the ideas (political, irrational, economic, etc.), then work in cooperative groups to develop their predictions about each area. Groups could also research the assassinations of Lincoln, McKinley, and Kennedy, then study *Julius Caesar* for comparison of motives and effects. A culminating activity could be to write a scenario of what might happen in an assassination of the current president. English and history teachers who want to team-teach could develop this project together.

A computer science teacher planning an inductive study could ask students if they think there will ever be a computer that's smarter than a human being. This would lead to a definition of terms, investigation into human intelligence, artificial intelligence, computer languages, and films such as *2001: A Space Odyssey*, along with demonstrations of computer programs related to artificial intelligence.

Books such as *The Timetables of History* or *The People's Chronology* can be used as a reference for history, English, science, business, and the arts. Students can analyze ten-year periods to discover what was happening in Western Europe and the Americas, then look for connections. Is literature connected to political events? Do art and music reflect current events? What effects do scientific discoveries have on economics? Does the U.S. "Black Friday" of October 28, 1929, have any relationship to the "Black Friday" in Germany in 1927? What predictions does William Beveridge make in his 1942 "Report on Social Security"? A major class project could be to extend a section of the timetables to include African and Asian events. Over a period of several years, this could become a valuable resource for the school.

A science teacher has numerous opportunities for inductive approaches; in fact, he or she could develop his or her complete curriculum around problems to solve. He or she could ask students to brainstorm a list of everything they can think of that runs by electrical power, then to predict what the world might be like today if electricity had not yet been discovered, or if it hadn't been discovered until 1950. Would there have been any world wars? Atomic weapons? Movies? Pollution? Their study could include effects on the people in the time it was discovered (including violent reactions), resulting devices which use electricity, ecological issues, possible future uses of electrical power, etc.

Science teachers could also lead a discussion of ethical issues in science during a study of cell biology. What would happen if biochemists discover how to clone people (suddenly not such a far-fetched idea), and a dangerous criminal steals the formula and clones himself or warlike leaders of nations? What effects might this have on law and order, peace and war? Should there be laws to stop scientific experiments of certain types?

Teachers of mathematics could integrate inductive strategies by introducing a lesson on place value or number systems by asking students how mathematics might be different if people had eight or twelve fingers instead of ten. Students could then investigate number systems and even invent one of their own.

Art or music teachers could show a selection of paintings or play several recordings and ask students in what decade they were created. Students must explain their reasons for giving a particular date. Research could lead to discussion on what paintings or music of a particular decade had in common, their countries of origin, the influence of religion on art or music, and whether political events influence art and music. They could also be asked to predict what art will look like or how music will sound in the year 2050. Students could do projects based on how someone in the year 2050 might write about current art or music. Content area teachers can team with an art teacher to discuss mathematics in art and music, the influence of historical events on the arts, poems, or plays related to the art or music world, or the science of sound. Art or music students could develop original projects as part of subject-area class assignments.

Business teachers could conduct an inductive lesson by asking students what kind of business they would like to own if money were no object. Students would need to explain their reasons, then research the business they chose. The class could brainstorm questions for study, then categorize them to determine general areas of research. Students who choose the same business could work together; resource people from the business community could visit the class to explain business concepts, answer questions, and predict what business will be like in 10, 20, or 50 years.

Cooperative Strategies

Cooperative learning lessons may be developed as deductive or inductive. Deductive activities include practice and review of information through games, tournaments, and presentations made by the teacher or by students. Inductive activities include research, analysis, and synthesis of information.

Discussion Strategies

Discussions are often thought of as unstructured talk by students sitting around in a circle, answering the basic question, "What do you think about _____?" However, profitable discussions are carefully planned, with specific objectives leading to understanding of specific concepts.

Discussion lessons may be deductive or inductive, depending on the emphasis. Deductive lessons will be more structured, often with clear answers which the teacher expects and leads the students to provide. Inductive lessons will be less structured, but very well planned. Teachers ask open-ended questions and accept a variety of answers which are well supported by information or inferences from the text. The effective teacher plans a variety of questions, with learner outcomes in mind, and leads the discussion without dominating it. He or she also will make certain that all students participate and have an opportunity to contribute. Students may also plan and lead discussions, with careful assistance from the teacher.

An English teacher may plan a discussion of *Our Town*. All students could write a variety of questions, e.g., based on levels of Bloom's taxonomy. Half the class would discuss among itself the questions presented by the other half of the class; the roles could change for the last half of the period or the next class period. The teacher's main role is to facilitate and make sure students follow the guidelines.

An important advantage, which is also a disadvantage, is the amount of time required for genuine discussion. The advantage is that all students have opportunities to contribute to learning and, therefore, feel a greater sense of ownership; the disadvantage is that productive discussion takes a great deal of time.

Comparison/Contrast

An important higher-order thinking skill is the ability to compare and contrast two things or concepts that are dissimilar on the surface. Thomas Gordon has described a process of synectics whereby students are forced to make an analogy between something that is familiar and something that is new; the concepts seem to be completely different, but through a series of steps, students discover underlying similarities. For example, a biology teacher might plan an analogy between a cell (new concept) and a city government (familiar concept). Although they seem impossibly different, they both have systems for transportation, disposal of unwanted materials, and parts that govern these systems. By comparing something new with something familiar, students have a "hook" for the new information, which will help them remember it as well as better understand it. For example, students trying to remember functions of a cell would be assisted by remembering parts of the city government.

Teaching Styles

A teacher may give some thought to his or her basic approach to teaching. Is the teacher a sympathetic and friendly teacher, or a realistic, pragmatic, and practical teacher? On the other hand, the teacher may be more logical, intellectual, and knowledge-oriented, or curious and imaginative. Out of a teacher's basic approach to teaching comes the teacher's values. For example, Silver and Hanson describe four categories of teachers: a) nurturers who value interaction and collaboration, and tend to stress role-playing, teamwork or team games, group projects, and so forth; b) trainers who value knowledge and skills, and stress drills, observations, demonstrations, and time on task; c) intellectuals who value logic and critical thinking, and who stress inquiry, concept development, problem-solving, and analysis; and d) facilitators who value creative expression and flexibility, and who stress inductive learning, divergent thinking, hypothesis formation, and metaphoric expression. It follows that these different categories of teachers will choose different instructional activities to achieve educational objectives held in common by all teachers.

With regard to giving directions, however, some teachers will choose to be more directive, giving more commands and orders, thereby leaving less room for the student to make choices concerning activities and behaviors, whereas other teachers will choose to be less directive, giving few commands and allowing students to make more choices for themselves. These are differences in teaching style. These differences reflect the different values and priorities of the teachers, and should be considered equally valid; no one style, in general, is superior to another. Nonetheless, there are times when most teachers will find that they must be open to adopting the most effective teaching style for accomplishing the objectives at hand. In other words, sometimes teachers adopt a strategy that is not their natural preference in order to be more effective.

To illustrate this point further, consider the tools a carpenter may have in a toolbox. A hammer is not necessarily a better tool than a saw or a screwdriver. However, there are some tasks that may require a hammer, and neither a saw nor a screwdriver can do the job or perform the task as well as a hammer. Likewise, teachers have natural preferences or styles, but, if they understand the characteristics of their own style, they can select the tools or approaches that will allow them to be most effective.

This information about teaching styles explains the importance of giving directions effectively and efficiently, and meeting the many needs of diverse learners. Even as some teachers may be directive and others less directive or nondirective, so there are some students who demand detailed, step-by-step, precise, and definite directions; that is their learning style. Likewise, there are some students who prefer to make more decisions for themselves, and they need very general directions, preferring to fill in the details for themselves. For example, the teacher may tell the class, "I want you to write a five-paragraph theme about anything you choose." Some students will pick up their pens and begin to write. Other students may ask, "What should we write about?" Those students would benefit by the teacher simply saying, "If I were you, I might write about ..." and providing some suggestions.

Directions

Every teacher knows that some students are more easily motivated than others. Some students receive directions and they busily get to work. Other students resist. Some students ask, "Why are we doing this?" Such a question should not be thought impertinent or obstreperous. Students who ask this question really need to know why. Unless they can see some personal benefit or reasonable justification for the activity, they will resist completing it. Taking the time to explain the nature of the activity, why it is important, and what it will lead to next is well worth the investment if it results in a motivated student performing at his or her best.

Some studies suggest that analytic, left-brain students need step-by-step, sequential directions. They need to begin at the beginning, proceed methodically, step by step through the information, and finally derive the conclusion. On the other hand, global, right-brain learners need to hear the conclusion first; they need to know the goal or outcome before they begin. Instead of progressing step-by-step, global learners work in random, sporadic patterns; analytic types might even call it haphazard. However, the nonlinear approach works for global learners.

An effective teacher will attempt to accommodate the needs of all students in class. This is one reason effective teachers give verbal announcements, send home written reminders, put signs on the wall and in the hall, write messages on the board, and direct students to take notes. The more ways the teacher can find to communicate the information, the more likely the message will get through.

Sometimes the teacher is most effective when starting directions by saying, "This is what we are going to do today in order to ..." and then telling what the objective of the learning activity is. This will satisfy the needs of the global learners. Then, the teacher can say, "Now the way we are going to do this is, first, ..." and then give the steps, one by one. This way the teacher can address the needs of the sequential learners. Teachers who are aware of preferences in teaching and learning styles can give more successful directions.

Objectives

In addition to giving students general directions and specific instructions about academic tasks and instructional activities, teachers need to announce and explain objectives. Teachers also need to announce all formal tests or assessments, giving students and their parents complete and accurate information.

The more information a teacher can provide about a test, the better the student can prepare for and perform on the test. Teachers need to tell students when they will have to take the test. Just announcing the test topic or the chapters to be covered on the test is insufficient. Teachers need to thoroughly describe the test: How many questions will be on the test, how much time will students have to answer the questions, what kind of questions—multiple-choice, fill-in-the-blank, true or false, matching, or essay? All of these questions should be answered so that conscientious students can adequately prepare for each test. The point value of each question or of each section of the test should be made clear.

To help those students who may be more sensitive or prone to test anxiety, the teacher should also be careful in making speculative or prejudicial comments about tests. The teacher who says, "Oh, this test is really going to be hard," may cause some students to panic and suffer increased anxiety about their test performance.

When teaching a lesson, an effective teacher gives clear, complete, and concise instructions, making certain that students understand why they are doing the lesson (the objectives). When preparing students for a test, an effective teacher provides complete and thorough details concerning the test, making sure that students have had an opportunity to acquire the skills or knowledge the test will measure.

Performance Standards

In addition, effective teachers describe performance standards so that there is no mystery about what a student must do in order to be successful. Performance standards are the criteria against which success is measured. For example, if grades are awarded, what makes a paper an "A" paper versus a "B" paper or a "C" paper? What must a student do in order to score 95 percent on the test versus 75 percent? Students should know what constitutes above-average, average, and below-average performance. Criteria should be discussed and explained. The value of every assignment should be discussed at the time it is assigned. At the beginning of the academic year, teachers should thoroughly explain the grading scale.

Students should also have opportunities to learn about their performance and how their performance compares to the established standards. They should be provided with information to help them improve their performance. Students need to know what it is that they must do in order to demonstrate proficiency. Teachers of younger children need to take special care to communicate objectives, assessment information, and information about performance standards to parents who often are eager to work with their children to help them achieve success.

Supplies

Informing students about the materials needed for learning and how to use those materials are also important parts of teaching. At the beginning of the school year, teachers and school districts should provide students and their parents with a list of the routine materials that will be needed: pencils, pens, notebook paper, notebooks, crayons, scissors, and so forth.

If the teacher needs to bring special materials to class, he or she will probably find it helpful to include a list of materials needed on the lesson plan. If students need special materials, in addition to their routine school supplies, the teacher should give them a list to take home to give their parents or send a message to the parents.

Students usually have a great deal on their minds, so they need frequent reminders to bring special supplies to class. If students need a dictionary in order to complete the day's lesson, they must know in advance to bring their dictionaries or they will end up wasting a day of precious instruction and time on task.

When a student uses a tool for the first time (the dictionary, for example), the teacher should spend time carefully introducing the tool and explaining its use. With the dictionary, the effective teacher will talk about how the dictionary is organized (alphabetical order), its standard features (pronunciation keys, etymologies, definitions, sentence examples), and special features (appendices with biographies, geographical information, tables, and so forth).

Most experienced teachers have learned firsthand the costs of assumptions. A teacher should not assume that a student knows how to use a calculator, computer, or a ruler. The teacher, paying attention to details to meet the special needs of all students in the class, should carefully explain whatever tools or materials will be used.

Classroom Assessment

Teachers spend a great deal of their time explaining and giving directions. To some, that seems to be what teaching is all about. But, despite all the effort that teachers expend, and all the expertise they develop in explaining and instructing, some students ignore instructions. Some experts even suggest that some students intentionally skip the directions or avoid instructions because of their learning style. For these reasons, teachers must check to make sure that students do understand the directions and are, in fact, following instructions.

"Does everyone understand?" "Are there any questions?" are probably two of the most misused and unproductive questions that teachers ask. Seldom does the student who doesn't understand ask a question. There are better ways to check comprehension.

The teacher can give the students a chance to get started on the work and then check each student's progress. Sometimes a teacher may want to call on a student to ask a specific question or to "say back" an important piece of information.

Angelo and Cross, authors of *Classroom Assessment Techniques*, recommend classroom assessment techniques as being most effective at checking comprehension. They further recommend that classroom assessment can a) increase students' active involvement in learning; b) promote students' metacognitive development; c) foster student cooperation and a sense of community in the classroom; d) increase student satisfaction with learning; and e) may even improve students' performance.

A simple classroom assessment technique is to ask students to write a summary of the information or instructions given. The teacher can then quickly read the summaries to determine if there have been misunderstandings or incomplete understanding.

The teacher could give the students a feedback form, asking the students questions about the test they took (Did you think it was a fair test? Did you enjoy one part more than another? What kind of test do you prefer? Why?) or a reading they have completed (How well did you read this? How useful was this reading assignment in helping you understand the topic? How well did you understand the reading?). Asking students to do something (write or talk or draw) to demonstrate that they have understood instructions is a much more effective method of checking comprehension than simply asking what has become to many students (and maybe even some teachers) nothing more than a rhetorical question, "Do you understand?"

References

Further reading of these references may enhance understanding of this chapter and may also increase performance on the examination.

Angelo, T. A. and K. P. Cross. *Classroom Assessment Techniques*. San Francisco: Jossey Bass, 1993.

Dunn, R. Presentation on Using Learning Styles Information to Enhance Teaching Effectiveness at Learning Styles Institute, Lubbock, Texas, June 5-9, 1993.

Lawrence, G. *People Types and Tiger Stripes*. Gainesville, Florida: Center for Applications of Psychological Type, 1993.

Silver, H. F. and J. R. Hanson. *Learning Styles and Strategies*. Princeton, New Jersey: The Thoughtful Educational Press, 1980.

Answer Sheet

1–12 are Constructed-Response Items. See sample essays in Detailed Explanations of Answers section.

Practice Test 1	Practice Test 2
Multiple Choice	**Multiple Choice**
13. Ⓐ Ⓑ Ⓒ Ⓓ	13. Ⓐ Ⓑ Ⓒ Ⓓ
14. Ⓐ Ⓑ Ⓒ Ⓓ	14. Ⓐ Ⓑ Ⓒ Ⓓ
15. Ⓐ Ⓑ Ⓒ Ⓓ	15. Ⓐ Ⓑ Ⓒ Ⓓ
16. Ⓐ Ⓑ Ⓒ Ⓓ	16. Ⓐ Ⓑ Ⓒ Ⓓ
17. Ⓐ Ⓑ Ⓒ Ⓓ	17. Ⓐ Ⓑ Ⓒ Ⓓ
18. Ⓐ Ⓑ Ⓒ Ⓓ	18. Ⓐ Ⓑ Ⓒ Ⓓ
19. Ⓐ Ⓑ Ⓒ Ⓓ	19. Ⓐ Ⓑ Ⓒ Ⓓ
20. Ⓐ Ⓑ Ⓒ Ⓓ	20. Ⓐ Ⓑ Ⓒ Ⓓ
21. Ⓐ Ⓑ Ⓒ Ⓓ	21. Ⓐ Ⓑ Ⓒ Ⓓ
22. Ⓐ Ⓑ Ⓒ Ⓓ	22. Ⓐ Ⓑ Ⓒ Ⓓ
23. Ⓐ Ⓑ Ⓒ Ⓓ	23. Ⓐ Ⓑ Ⓒ Ⓓ
24. Ⓐ Ⓑ Ⓒ Ⓓ	24. Ⓐ Ⓑ Ⓒ Ⓓ
25. Ⓐ Ⓑ Ⓒ Ⓓ	25. Ⓐ Ⓑ Ⓒ Ⓓ
26. Ⓐ Ⓑ Ⓒ Ⓓ	26. Ⓐ Ⓑ Ⓒ Ⓓ
27. Ⓐ Ⓑ Ⓒ Ⓓ	27. Ⓐ Ⓑ Ⓒ Ⓓ
28. Ⓐ Ⓑ Ⓒ Ⓓ	28. Ⓐ Ⓑ Ⓒ Ⓓ
29. Ⓐ Ⓑ Ⓒ Ⓓ	29. Ⓐ Ⓑ Ⓒ Ⓓ
30. Ⓐ Ⓑ Ⓒ Ⓓ	30. Ⓐ Ⓑ Ⓒ Ⓓ
31. Ⓐ Ⓑ Ⓒ Ⓓ	31. Ⓐ Ⓑ Ⓒ Ⓓ
32. Ⓐ Ⓑ Ⓒ Ⓓ	32. Ⓐ Ⓑ Ⓒ Ⓓ
33. Ⓐ Ⓑ Ⓒ Ⓓ	33. Ⓐ Ⓑ Ⓒ Ⓓ
34. Ⓐ Ⓑ Ⓒ Ⓓ	34. Ⓐ Ⓑ Ⓒ Ⓓ
35. Ⓐ Ⓑ Ⓒ Ⓓ	35. Ⓐ Ⓑ Ⓒ Ⓓ
36. Ⓐ Ⓑ Ⓒ Ⓓ	36. Ⓐ Ⓑ Ⓒ Ⓓ

PLT Grades 5–9

Practice Test 1

This test is also on CD-ROM in our special interactive PRAXIS™ PLT 5–9 TEST*ware*®. It is highly recommended that you first take this exam on computer. You will then have the additional study features and benefits of enforced timed conditions and instantaneous, accurate scoring. See page 14 for instructions on how to get the most out of REA's TEST*ware*®.

Practice Test 1

Case Study I

Lacie is a first-year teacher. She teaches several classes of biological and physical science every day. Lacie wants her students to perform well academically, to learn the basics of science—both biological and physical, to employ the scientific method of problem solving, and to make science a lifelong learning experience. Lacie is eager to try approaches to teaching her class other than the typical textbook instruction.

Lacie's principal is open to innovative ideas from all of the teachers; she just wants her teachers to let her know ahead of time what they are going to be doing in their classrooms. For this reason, the teachers submit their lesson plans on Friday for the next week; the principal eagerly reviews the plans before the actual teaching of the lessons takes place. After considering the plans, she can discuss any problems with the teachers. She is often able to commend the teachers on innovative ideas and positive inclusions in the lesson plans, and she is also able to find areas that complement instruction in other classrooms on the school campus.

As a new teacher, Lacie is trying to determine how best to teach her class. She is trying to make a decision about how much to lecture, when to lecture, and even if she should lecture. Even though many teachers in her school use lecturing, Lacie is trying to decide if this method is right for her and her students.

Lacie is interested in teaching with an interdisciplinary approach. For example, she wants her students to understand how science impacts the community in which they live. The state curriculum guide and the standards for her grade focuses on scientific methods, such as data collection, organization, and reporting. Lacie wants her program to stress real-life examples of scientific methods used in local businesses.

Lacie, with the approval of her principal, decides to contact businesses in the community and arrange for field experiences for her students. First, she wants each business that she selects to have a person come and talk to her students about science's role in their field. Then she wants to spend several days helping the students do a library and computer database search on the topics introduced by the speaker. Next, she wants her students to use the school science laboratory to practice using the data collection and other scientific procedures employed by the business. Finally, thus prepared, she wants to take her students to see science in action at the work site.

Lacie lists the community businesses that she selects on a sheet of butcher paper that she posts on a bulletin board.

Local Businesses That Use Science

Chemistry	Biology	Physics
Soda pop bottling factory	Hospital Medical Lab	Geotech Architecture, Inc.
ABC Concrete Contractors	Ms. Grant's truck farm	Maria's Auto Shop

During the period of community-involvement field experience, Lacie continually directs her students' attention to the fact that science is a way of solving problems. Following the period of field experiences, Lacie asks her students to identify a problem in their school and to devise a scientific way of studying that problem and solving it. Once they have identified the problem, she reminds them of the steps in the scientific method:

1) developing a hypothesis;

2) deciding on a procedure (deductive reasoning);

3) collecting and analyzing data; and

4) deriving a conclusion. (Lacie reminds her class that a scientist never proves a hypothesis; a scientist confirms or fails to confirm a hypothesis.)

Once they have considered several problems for investigation, Lacie's students must select one for their research. Lacie realizes that the probability that each group would select the same question will be highly unlikely. A majority vote will be the determining factor for the selection.

The problem that Lacie's class selects is the following: It is late spring, and the classroom gets so hot during the afternoon that the majority of the students are uncomfortable. Their research question becomes, "Why is it hotter in our classroom than in the music room, art room, or library? How can we make our classroom cooler?"

Lacie tries to help the students focus on the problem at hand by 1) leading the first classroom discussion with them, 2) allowing the students to brainstorm with her, and 3) using a K-W-L chart. Lacie will complete the chart with the students as they share their own experiences of "What I Know," "What I Want to Know," and—at the end of the unit—"What I Have Learned." After working with the K-W-L chart, the students will be ready to work in groups for two class periods to decide procedure, collect and analyze data, and (finally) derive a conclusion. The students in each group will answer the question, share their findings with the rest of the class, and compare their answers with those of the other groups. Lacie is eager to see how the plan will work.

Constructed-Response Items

1. The case study suggests that Lacie will help the students focus on the problem at hand by using the K-W-L and conducting a class discussion. The ability to lead a good classroom discussion is a fundamental element of any effective teacher's repertoire. Leading an effective discussion, however, is one of the most difficult, unpredictable, and sometimes frustrating experiences that a teacher will face. Write a brief essay that addresses several elements that can contribute to a successful discussion.

2. The case study presents Lacie as a new teacher trying to decide if lecturing is a method right for her class and for her. Critics see lecturing as far too passive of a student activity. Others suggest it promotes student non-participation and inactivity, while others say it is just plain obsolete. Then there are those who claim that lecturing is the most efficient way of communicating. Discuss your philosophy on lecturing and its pedagogical values. What are the ingredients that constitute a good lecture? What alternative methods could take the place of lecturing?

3. Today's educators often use cooperative learning and problem-solving activities in the classroom. After describing both methods, indicate if Lacie's class demonstrated either, both, or neither and why.

Case Study II

Mr. Treskoski is a first-year teacher who has recently moved from another state to a small town in New York State. In his sixth-grade social studies class, Mr. Treskoski has his students read the local newspaper each Monday in order to increase their understanding of and involvement in civic issues at the local and national levels. In addition, he assigns the students to watch the local and national news at home on either Tuesday nights or Wednesday mornings in order to use this information to supplement their understanding of the issues.

For several weeks, the class has been following the upcoming mayoral election. The incumbent mayor, The Honorable Mayor Lucinda Griego, is running for reelection against a political newcomer, Tambra Crumpler.

While Mayor Griego has a strong record of advocating better living conditions for all the citizens of the town, Candidate Crumpler is an attorney who bases her platform upon taking a strong stand in combating the illicit gangs that she says are creeping into the community.

When the class is discussing the candidates' platforms, Molly Winters says, "My dad says that there isn't a gang problem here. He told me that it's just news media hype to sell papers and to get Ms. Crumpler elected. What do you think, Mr. T?"

In unison, the students turn their eyes to Mr. Treskoski.

"That's an interesting thought," says Mr. Treskoski. "Let me think about that and get back to you tomorrow. I'll need to do some research before I decide what I think. But right now, let's talk about what you think."

During his planning time, Mr. Treskoski goes to Mr. Hinohosa, the school librarian, and asks him to recommend sources that his class might use for learning about gangs; he is also eager to find out whether the district has the technological capabilities to link with the nearest university in order to conduct a computer search for information related to gangs. Mr. Treskoski finds that the school does not have the technological capability to link with a university for a computer search but that as a teacher, he can conduct a computer search of Infotrak at the local community college without charge—except for the photocopying of the materials.

The next day, Mr. Treskoski explains to his class about the computer search; he asks the students to keep the idea of a computer search in mind as they examine the school's library materials on gangs and find gaps in the information readily available. On Friday, after all the students are thoroughly acquainted with the library materials, Mr. Treskoski has a "Town Meeting" of the class to decide what they know and what they want to learn; Mr. Treskoski will help his students select topics for their reports on things that they need to learn. Mr. Treskoski agrees to meet with Dr. Harvill at the college to conduct the search of terms that the students have helped him select for other information that they need.

During the following week, the students eagerly wait for all the articles to arrive through Interlibrary Loan at the community college. When the Interlibrary Loan photocopies arrive from the community college, Mr. Treskoski assigns each student to one of six groups of four children each. He gives each group five of the 30 articles to examine for information on gangs and for signs of yellow journalism. Each group will then present a report to the entire class. To each group he assigns one high-, two medium-, and one low-achieving student. The low-achieving student in one group is Lynn Stovall, a student who is involved in the district's full inclusion program for students with developmental disabilities.

After three days, Mr. Treskoski receives a phone call from the mother of Carlita Rivas, the high-achieving student in Lynn's group. Mrs. Rivas is upset because her daughter has been assigned to work in the same group as Lynn. "This boy can do nothing to help with the project," complains Mrs. Rivas. "I'm sure that he is a nice boy, but I don't want my daughter to have to work with such a poor student. What is wrong with him, anyway? Is he retarded, or what?"

Mr. Treskoski has another student with a problem. Maria is a bright and ambitious student who has aspirations of pursuing a college education. However, she procrastinates on the assignments that do not interest her; she has not even begun to prepare her part of the assignment on gangs and yellow journalism. She has indicated that she will turn in her work late, has changed her topic several times, and has not even begun to prepare her final draft. She remains resistant to suggested strategies and techniques for improvement. She worries that her grades will suffer and her choice of prestigious colleges will be either limited or nullified.

Constructed-Response Items

4. What strategy or strategies might Mr. Treskoski employ to help Maria?

5. Independent and group writing projects can be one of the most beneficial ways of conveying information to the students. They are also

a good way of monitoring the students' understanding of theories and themes presented during lecture or readings. List various writing projects that Mr. Treskoski might assign to his students and some of the benefits associated with each.

6. What should Mr. Treskoski do about Mrs. Rivas' complaint?

Case Study III

The school where Mr. Buzz teaches is using an expanding horizon approach to teach social studies. Mr. Buzz has encouraged his students to develop ideas for activities that they might use to advance their knowledge of world geography. A suggestion from Jane, one of the students, to research holidays in South American countries receives no votes when she suggests it; the students remind her that there are some class members who belong to a religious denomination that does not recognize any holidays except those related to their religious beliefs. These students would not be allowed to participate in such a study; this inapplicability for some of the students makes the proposal unacceptable to the majority of the class.

On Class Meeting Day, Elena presents to the sixth-grade class her idea to write to pen pals in South America. The motion carries 14-2.

Dave Botts and Norman Rogers cast the two votes against the motion. Both boys are students who have special needs and who attend the resource room for literacy help and social skills instruction for one hour each day. Before this year, the boys attended a self-contained class for five hours daily. This year, however, the district has implemented an inclusion program, and the boys' IEPs place them in Mr. Buzz's class.

Both boys' IEPs require that they participate in all classroom activities for the time that they are in their inclusion classes and that they receive individual support as necessary in order to ensure that they get an appropriate education.

After the vote, Mr. Buzz assumes leadership of the class. "We are going to be studying South America this semester," he says. "Would you like to go ahead and start our South America unit next week so that we can all learn more about South America before we write letters to our pen pals?" Mr. Buzz then tells each group to discuss this idea and report back. All of the groups respond positively.

"Fine," he says. "Each group will choose one country in South America. Your group will study your chosen country and become our resident experts on it. You may use the Internet and the media center. You may approach this in any way you like. For example, you may want to tell about folkways of the country. You may want to wear clothing or bring food from the country. Perhaps you'd like to make a papier-mâché map of the country or show a short video about it. However your group chooses to approach the project is the right way for you. There is no right or wrong way to do this. Each person in your group might do a different part, or you might choose to work on each part together. Your group will then teach a lesson to the rest of the class about your country."

Mr. Buzz encourages the students to draw information from two of their fellow students who have recently entered the United States from South America; these students have photographs and other memorabilia from their native land. He also mentions that they might invite the relatives of the two South American students to the class to use as resources.

Mr. Buzz asks the school counselor, the resource teacher, the principal and her staff, and the fifth-grade teacher whose students were in music class at that time to attend his students' presentations. Unknown to his students, Mr. Buzz gives each guest a question to ask and requests that they each preface the question with a statement somewhat similar to the following: "I would like to know more about what you said regarding _____ in your presentation. This is a topic of interest to me and about which I would like to learn more." Mr. Buzz is hoping to encourage higher-level thinking skills in his students by having the guests ask the "planted" questions.

The day following the last of the group presentations, Mr. Buzz gives direct instruction to the class in order to fill in any gaps that he thinks are important to the students' understanding of the unit on their South American countries. Then, the next day, he allows the students to work in their cooperative groups on a review for a test scheduled for the following day. The test is an objective, multiple-choice test covering all four countries.

The first five of 25 multiple-choice items are as follows:

1. Which country has Bogotá as its capital?

2. Which country is the most likely to directly affect the climate of the United States?

3. Where would the people be most likely to wear lighter clothing all year round, Southern Columbia or Central Chile?

4. Which country is larger, Columbia or Argentina?

5. Which quality would be expected to overlap the most between Brazil and Argentina? Is it religion, language, or vegetation?

Constructed-Response Items

7. With various students in his class, Mr. Buzz must face multicultural issues. What do you believe are some of the more pressing issues

facing Mr. Buzz with regard to classroom diversity? Explain how you would demonstrate an awareness of and a sensitivity to the issues of gender, culture, religion, ethnicity, and so on.

8. Mr. Buzz is encouraging his students to use the media center, the Internet, and videos. Some feel that technology is the answer to all the financial and intellectual needs of the classroom of the future. Others argue that it is just another tool to augment an instructor's arsenal, and, in fact, teachers place too much emphasis upon its usefulness and importance. Many argue that technology is a detriment to the classroom as it takes agency away from the instructor while simultaneously pacifying a generation already suffering from a technologically induced attention deficit disorder. What role should technology play in Mr. Buzz's classroom and how could it enhance or hinder his teaching?

9. In recent years educators have given much thought to providing for various learning styles and acknowledging multiple intelligences. What is meant by learning styles and by multiple intelligences? What, if anything, has Mr. Buzz done to acknowledge and provide for varying learning styles and multiple intelligences?

Case Study IV

Bill Drayton is a first-year teacher whose teaching field is reading. Bill is an exemplary teacher and is already assuming a leadership role in both the community and within the school district. He has started taking classes at a university in order to earn a Master of Teaching credential.

Bill's brother, on the other hand, changed majors/minors in college after taking a course requiring working in a classroom. He then decided that teaching was not for him; Bill, however, believes that teaching is the profession that is best for him.

Late in the fall semester, Bill arrived home right as a rental moving truck pulled up in front of the house across the street. The "for sale" sign on the house had recently been taken down, and Bill was eager to meet his new neighbors. He walked across the street and introduced himself to the man who stepped out of the truck.

As the introductions were taking place, a van pulled up into the driveway and a woman came around the side of the van in order to help a young girl in a wheelchair exit the van. "Come and meet my wife, Rachel, and our daughter, Myra," said the new neighbor, who had introduced himself as Harry Jacobsen.

"Myra is in fifth-grade," said her mother.

"Then you'll be in one of my classes," said Bill. "We have two fifth-grade classes. Each one spends half the day in Ms. Wade's room, and the other half of the day in mine. I teach language arts and math, while she teaches social studies, science, and art. We have a lot of fun because we teach around themes. For example, Ms. Wade's social studies classes are learning about how New York history was influenced by geography, so in my language arts class, we're reading stories about New York history and discussing how the geography contributed to the things that happened in those stories. We also pretend that we are early New Yorkers and write journals and newspapers about the events that shaped our history as those events relate to geography. In my math classes, we're using math to understand New York geography. We are working problems about lengths of rivers, miles between cities located on the waterways, and so forth."

"One of the activities that I plan to employ in my language arts class during the thematic study of the impact of geographic features on the history of New York is storytelling. Following two days of activities, which will include my storytelling sessions, I plan to tell the children that they are to each write a story to tell to the class. I plan to use some writing prompts to get them started, and we will publish their work in several ways: using the author's chair, publishing the stories with the copy machine, tape recording some of the stories, and sharing our works with the younger children in our wing."

Myra's eyes lit up. "Can I be in his room, Mama?" she asked.

Rachel shook her head. "No, honey, I'm sorry." Then Rachel explained to Bill that Myra had to go to a private school because the local schools were not wheelchair accessible. "Myra can't get through the outer doors, the inner doors, up the stairs to the classroom, the cafeteria, the gym, or anywhere else. In fact, she can't even get into the toilet stalls," she explained. "These changes would take many thousands of dollars, and the district can't spend that kind of money on Myra."

When Bill goes back inside his home, he hears the phone ring. Upon answering the phone, Bill finds it is Jim Bono, the first-year teacher who is teaching science down the hall.

Jim enters into a long account of the problems he is facing with Marilyn Jabeck, a student in his fifth-grade class. Marilyn often speaks out in class without permission. When Jim gave assignments during the past week, she demonstrated rudeness by saying things like, "Who says?" During the last few days when the students begin to work on their class work individually and the room is silent, Marilyn has been getting up without permission and stomping across the floor to sharpen a pencil or to throw a paper away; her actions have been disturbing all the students—and have been particularly distressing to Jim Bono. When another student is talking, Marilyn has not been at all reluctant to interrupt the student and to begin telling a story of her own.

Bill looks at the clock and realizes that he has spent the last two hours of his time off thinking about his job. He does not regret this time spent. Even after a full week on the job Bill still enjoys thinking about the past few days, hearing about the experiences of his colleagues, and planning for the coming week.

Constructed-Response Items

10. Like Jim, every teacher must, at some time or another, deal with an intentionally disruptive student. *Disruptive* might be defined as active or deliberate rebellion, insubordination, contempt, and/or pretentiousness. While each student and situation will be different, there are still certain fundamental approaches to dealing with disruptive students. What are some approaches to dealing with disruptive students, and how would you implement them?

11. Both Bill and his brother had to answer the question, "Why teach?" The question of "Why teach?" has presumably as many answers as there are teachers. Yet, there are certain universal traits that the majority of successful teachers share. What are these traits? That is, what do you feel are the fundamentals that constitute a successful teacher? In essence, why teach?

12. How should Bill respond to the parent about the accessibility of the school to handicapped students?

Multiple-Choice Questions

13. Social isolation, unwarranted nausea, headaches, and irrational fears or obsessions are symptoms of

    (A) nerves.

    (B) nothing.

    (C) tall tales.

    (D) neurotic disorders.

14. When teaching a concept, the teacher should provide

    (A) examples and nonexamples.

    (B) several examples.

    (C) only interesting examples.

    (D) definitions.

15. One use of homework is to

    (A) introduce new concepts.

    (B) provide structure to the classroom.

    (C) develop short-term retention.

    (D) revisit learned skills and concepts.

16. Which of the following are the components of the process approach model?

    (A) Transform and teach

    (B) Sensing and acting

    (C) Reach, touch, and teach

    (D) Reaching and teaching

17. What is one benefit of practice activities?

    (A) The teacher can observe where students need additional instruction.

    (B) The students can develop their creative writing skills.

    (C) Students can revisit previously learned skills.

    (D) Students can learn new concepts.

18. If only one computer is available to a class, students should be able to use the computer

    (A) singly or in small groups.

    (B) if they are familiar with computers.

    (C) only during full class instruction.

    (D) to record class progress.

19. Students start using drugs and alcohol

    (A) due to curiosity, desire for pleasure, peer pressure, and/or problem avoidance.

    (B) to deal with stress from school.

    (C) due to parental influences.

    (D) depending on social groups.

20. When reprimanding a class, which is most effective?

    (A) Loud shouting

    (B) The threat of harsh consequences

    (C) Using a soft voice

    (D) Angry outbursts

21. Effective teachers can build the self-esteem of students by

    (A) posting all failing grades on a bulletin board.

    (B) using negative reinforcement.

    (C) providing successful experiences for each student.

    (D) amplifying responses.

22. Which of the following is a useful way of bringing a daydreaming student back on-task?

    (A) Call on the student.

    (B) Walk over and stand near the student.

    (C) Question the class.

    (D) Stop and stare at the student.

23. The belief that corporal punishment is the best way to respond to student misconduct

    (A) is outdated and obsolete.

    (B) does not have widespread support in the educational community.

    (C) leads to a decrease in school delinquency problems.

    (D) correctly identifies the approach to take with students who misbehave.

24. At random and without announcement, students are required to pass through metal detectors as they enter the school. This procedure is used to

    (A) alert students to the possibility that classmates are carrying weapons to class.

    (B) make sure students are not carrying weapons to class.

    (C) remind students that someone is watching them.

    (D) promote school safety.

25. Student learning is most successful when

    (A) objectives are clearly outlined.

    (B) colorful graphs and maps are used.

    (C) the same examples are used.

    (D) the classroom size is small.

26. Feedback sessions for a test are most effective

    (A) when they are immediate.

    (B) when they are delayed by a day or so.

    (C) when they are delayed for a few weeks.

    (D) when the feedback is written on paper only.

27. If a teacher introduces a concept using examples and nonexamples and asks the class to provide a definition of the concept, the teacher is considered to be teaching

    (A) deductively.

    (B) inductively.

(C) using definitions.

(D) using examples.

28. In attempting to change a student's inappropriate behavior, all of the following would be crucial pieces of information for a teacher to have in order to attempt to change the behavior, EXCEPT

(A) current consequences of the behavior.

(B) what is reinforcing to the student.

(C) strategies attempted by other teachers in the past to change the be-havior.

(D) a very specific description/definition of the inappropriate behavior.

29. Research supports all of the following statements about the use of com-puters in education EXCEPT

(A) computers in the classroom have a motivational effect on many students.

(B) students who use computers to write papers in class write longer papers.

(C) computerized tests cannot measure higher order thinking skills.

(D) when utilizing technology (such as computers), the teacher needs a back-up plan in case the technology fails.

30. Effective praise should be

(A) authentic and low-key.

(B) used sparingly.

(C) comprised of simple, positive responses.

(D) used to encourage high-achieving students.

31. A student portfolio

(A) contains artwork by a student.

(B) is used to compare student work.

(C) is graded on a scale.

(D) contains documents and/or products to show student progress.

32. Teachers ask questions to

    (A) engage the students' attention.

    (B) evaluate students' knowledge.

    (C) invite students to learn.

    (D) All of the above.

33. A teacher ran out of copies of a worksheet before handing them out to the entire class, thus interrupting

    (A) materials.

    (B) class interest.

    (C) instructional momentum.

    (D) passing out the papers.

34. In the middle of a discussion, a student asks to sharpen a pencil in response to an academic question. The teacher should

    (A) see if the pencil needs to be sharpened.

    (B) allow the student to sharpen the pencil.

    (C) signal no, and then ask someone else the question.

    (D) repeat the question to the student.

35. How can a teacher reprimand a student while maintaining the academic focus of a class?

    (A) Respond with a punitive or angry desist.

    (B) Respond with a simple reprimand.

    (C) Ignore the behavior.

    (D) Take the student out of the room.

36. Two weeks after a student writes a poem about a rape, she comes to the teacher and confides that she was the girl in the poem. She tells the teacher that her mother's new boyfriend raped her (the student) and that she is afraid her mother will be mad if she tells her what happened. The teacher should

    (A) tell the student to go ahead and tell her mother what happened.

(B) call the student's mother on the phone and tell her what the student said.

(C) report the student's sexual assault to the appropriate authorities.

(D) tell the student that she needs to talk to a school counselor.

Answer Key

1.	(*)	13.	(D)	25.	(A)
2.	(*)	14.	(A)	26.	(B)
3.	(*)	15.	(D)	27.	(B)
4.	(*)	16.	(C)	28.	(C)
5.	(*)	17.	(A)	29.	(C)
6.	(*)	18.	(A)	30.	(A)
7.	(*)	19.	(A)	31.	(D)
8.	(*)	20.	(C)	32.	(D)
9.	(*)	21.	(C)	33.	(C)
10.	(*)	22.	(B)	34.	(C)
11.	(*)	23.	(B)	35.	(C)
12.	(*)	24.	(D)	36.	(C)

*Constructed-Response Item. See sample essays in Detailed Explanations of Answers section.

Detailed Explanations of Answers

PLT 5-9

PRACTICE TEST 1

Case Study I

Constructed-Response Items

1. **Essay 1**

   While many varying factors contribute to a successful classroom discussion, I will address four components that Lacie should use that will increase the odds of having a successful classroom discussion. The components are instructor's subject knowledge, classroom goals, all inclusive student involvement, and instructor's enthusiasm.

   Initially, Lacie needs to be knowledgeable about the specific material and overall subject matter to be covered. She will require, not just an off handed familiarity of the subject, but a comprehensive understanding, so that she will be ready to answer the broad range of questions that the students are bound to ask.

   Next, Lacie should have a set of goals with regards to the discussion. That is, the discussion should have a larger pedagogical purpose, such as the presentation of a certain style, structure, concept, theory, or issue that she might want her students to consider. Perhaps there is a topic at issue, or a specific dynamic that Lacie wants to address. Thus, the discussion period ought to be a time to achieve both short range and long range educational goals.

Ultimately, a successful discussion will include all the students and not just the talkative or energetic ones. Lacie should involve non-participatory students by calling on them by name, and giving each time to answer in a thoughtful manner. It may even be necessary to assign a short paper or give a brief in-class writing assignment in order to get feedback from all the students, as some are just too uncomfortable to speak-up in class.

Finally, Lacie should be engaged and enthused about the assignment, the material, and the overall subject. It should be something that Lacie can learn from. If the person in charge is not learning, participating and interested, how could one expect the students to be?

Essay 1 Analysis

This essay would receive a score of 2.

This essay is exemplary of the proper response to essay question one because it responds directly to the question at issue with specifically detailed answers. First, the essay has a thesis which is clearly formulated, specific, and focused, "I will address four components that Lacie should use that will increase the odds of having a successful classroom discussion... instructor's subject knowledge, classroom goals, all inclusive student involvement, and instructor's enthusiasm." The essay's language is accurate and articulate without appearing to be overbearing or pretentious. Words are used correctly and there is no attempt to speak beyond the writer's vocabulary.

The essay also demonstrates a clear sense of purpose. That is, the writer defines and accurately employs the central ideas.

Essay 2

How can Lacie lead a good classroom discussion? We all know that good discussions thrive on conflict. That is, argument as inquiry. So the way for Lacie to instigate an effective classroom discussion is to present some open-ended questions along with controversial subject matter. The manifestation of vibrant and meaningful rhetorical discussions will ensue. Once we introduce conflict into the nature of the topic at issue, it will yield thought-provoking and meaningful discussion. Questions that are open-ended and at the same time provocative will lead the students into a meaningful discussion that they can embellish. Certainly there will be students who will take the lead in a conversation, and they will then promote other students to join in. We all know how hard it is to keep silent once an exciting discussion is happening around us. Also, Lacie might want to break the class up into teams or put one side of the room against the other in order to show how one set of ideas will work off the other side. With these types of dynamics working in tandem, it is not difficult to see how a good in class discussion is initiated and maintained.

Essay 2 Analysis

This essay would receive a score of 1.

This essay is not as conceptually strong or structurally sound as the first essay. This is due in part to the erroneous use of terminology as an attempt on the part of the test-taker to sound more scholarly than it actually is. Additionally, the essay repeats itself rather than develops its initial ideas.

This essay is weak in structure and organization. It does not define its central terms clearly. It also lacks opposing viewpoints and the acknowledgment of alternative ideas.

It does not have a well-developed introduction, body, and conclusion. It is unfocused and fragmented throughout. It attempts to develop its thesis (argument thrives on conflict), but it falls short of this goal. That is, it fails to develop and build upon its thesis statement. Rather it simply restates it or loses sight of it altogether.

Essay 3

In order to facilitate a successful classroom discussion Lacie must be familiar with her students and their academic needs. Lacie needs to be prompt in responding to the requirements of her students while at the same time be forgiving enough to understand that her students have a life and family outside the classroom. It might be a sick child, a late assignment, or even a late bill or other financial matter that could cause the student to be distracted from the discussion or other assigned class-work. Of course, all students need to participate and attend class regularly, but sometimes there are extenuating circumstances that are just too demanding or require immediate attention; it is like when your boss calls and says that you have to cover the shift at one o'clock and class starts at one p.m., or when your printer breaks down the night before an assignment is due. That's stressful too. So a good discussion is when the teacher is in charge and lets the students talk a lot about the story or whatever.

Essay 3 Analysis

This essay would receive a score of 0.

This essay is a good example of one of the most common problems in essay writing: not answering the essay question. That is, the essay does not clearly address the assigned topic; it does not answer any part of the question asked.

The essay is designed to be mainly filling paper rather than really saying something. The reader must work to hard too know where the essay is going. Plus, the essay offers no pedagogical evidence to support any of the statements it makes. The result is a convoluted, disjointed, and ultimately unsatisfying paper.

The essay's use of terminology is for effect and not substance. The sentence structure is only adequate, and the verbose use of adjectives detracts from the content.

Additionally, the presumptive use of "we all know" diminishes the authors assertions, e.g. we might not all know, and it is up to this essay to enlighten the reader.

2.   Essay 1

With today's economic climate forcing classroom sizes ever bigger, the need for efficient verbal communication, that is the complete and complex exchange of information and ideas, is more important than ever.

Some might argue that technology is the economic answer. However, the cost in actual learning capacity is too great. While technology certainly has its purpose, it can never fully replace the value of human interplay. It can never respond to a group of people the way a teacher can. A lecture is an academic performance, and as any good dramatist knows, the audience drives the performance. Thus, lecturing, that is a series of academic talks, is the most comprehensive way a teacher has in presenting the amalgamating of course theory and content.

Additionally, the intrinsic value of a lecture is the inherent flexibility it offers. Students are not excluded from an engaging lecture, quite the opposite. Teachers can speed up, slow down, or explore alternative avenues of explanation during an engaging lecture.

Essay 1 Analysis

This essay would receive a score of 2.

This essay is well-structured and well-organized. It addresses the assignment by answering the questions asked of it. It has a thesis that is clearly formulated, precise, specific, and focused. It defines its central terms and uses them accurately. It also addresses opposing viewpoints and acknowledges alternative ideas.

It has a well-developed introduction, body, and conclusion. It remains focused and unified throughout. It attempts to develop its thesis, and it flows logically from one concept to another. That is, it builds upon its thesis statement rather than simply restating it.

The essay's use of diction and terminology is both accurate and clear. It answers the question.

Essay 2

Today's students can't relate to lectures. Lectures are boring. When students make mistakes, they get lectured. It's like scolding. Who wants to come to school and get scolded? No one. Students aren't going to respond well to that. And besides, lectures are long and monotonous to students who are used to the fast paced action of TV shows and video games. You can't expect young people to sit still while someone lectures at them.

Maybe in the old days things were different. Maybe then students were easier to control, maybe their attention spans were more longer, or maybe they just didn't care. Whoever says that lectures are obsolete knew exactly what they were talking about; lectures are antiquated, and they don't involve the students. They just alienate the students.

I wouldn't lecture to my class. I would have them create videos and computer programs, have discussion type groups, hold field trips, and watch the Discovery Channel. There are lots of alternatives, but lecturing to your students is just not a good thing to do anymore.

Essay 2 Analysis

This essay would receive a score of 1.

While this essay has several major flaws, its most pronounced one would have to be in its diction. The essay defines "lecture" as "scolding." Thus from its inception the essay is confused in its use of vocabulary. It further complicates itself by inferring that all lecturing must be monotonous and mundane. Thus, the essay responds in an emotional way to an erroneous assumption. The resulting language and assertions are incorrect. The content is mediocre.

Essay 3

Lecturing is only passive if the teacher is passive. Lecturing can be as energetic and animated as the teacher wants it to be. There is no one saying that lectures have to be dull. I would bring props and dress in costumes to make my lectures entertaining.

I would lecture to my class because that's the way I was taught. I don't think there is anything wrong with lecturing in school. That's what is done in school. I think that lecturing is an important part of school. Besides, what other ways are there to teach certain things? If one wants their students to learn the periodic tables then a lecture on the subject is in order.

The students should be able to follow it. They are pretty smart and capable of understanding information like that. I don't think that there is any other way of dealing with certain topics but to lecture. So that is what I would do.

Essay 3 Analysis

This essay would receive a score of 0.

This essay lacks a thesis. It does not develop or expand an idea. Rather, it simply states several assumptions without drawing a thoughtful conclusion. Because of its lack of structure it fails to address the assignment. Without a thesis that is clearly formulated, precise, specific, and focused, the essay's central terminology cannot be well defined nor are they accurately employed. Additionally, the paper fails to acknowledge and/or address opposing viewpoints and alternative ideas. The essay also includes over-personalization.

Essentially this essay reads as though it was mainly filling paper rather than actually saying something. The lack of a thesis leads to the rambling haphazard nature of the essay. The essay is hard to follow because there is no subject to develop. The insufficient use of details and lack of supporting examples only augment the lack of thesis development.

Ultimately, the essay's thesis is predicated on a false assumption. This, coupled with a lack of supporting evidence, ideas, or examples, simply voids the essay of any viable credibility.

3. Essay 1

Cooperative learning usually involves cross-sectioned grouping. Within the cooperative learning groups, each student is a valued member and participates in the activities. Brainstorming is often a part of cooperative learning; with brainstorming, a component is to accept all ideas without judging their value. Group members often distribute the tasks among the members.

When a group identifies and finds solutions to problems, the term *problem-solving* is currently the term used in education to describe the process. The class in the case study has certainly identified several problems to consider.

Lacie's class uses both cooperative learning and problem-solving. The use of certain terms, such as cross-sectioned grouping, the identification of separate roles for individual students and the groups as a whole, the employment of brainstorming, the acceptance of each group member, and recognition of group accomplishments are all part of cooperative learning. All of the cooperative learning characteristics seem to be present in Lacie's class.

Problem-solving is at the heart of the structure in Lacie's class. Several problems—why the classroom is hotter than others and how to make the classroom cooler—are a part of the problems the class identifies—and eventually solves.

Lacie, then, seems to have included—and included very well—both cooperative learning and problem-solving in her class.

Essay 1 Analysis

This essay would receive a score of 2.

This essay satisfies all the requirements of a good composition. The essay answers the questions asked: it describes both cooperative learning and problem-solving; it indicates if Lacie demonstrated either, both, or neither; and explains why the writer answered as she/he did. The writer has adhered to a logical sequence of presenting the information—all of which is accurate. The answer is above average and very acceptable.

Essay 2

Keeping the students happy is what teaching is all about. If the students are content, teachers have fewer problems. If teachers have fewer problems, they are more likely to keep their jobs.

This type of classroom atmosphere is one that has the students learning on their own. Lacie has less work to do; the students are the ones doing the work. The students should be the ones tired at the end of the day—not the teacher.

Lacie should get good reviews from the students, the parents, and the administration. Keep up the good work!

Essay 2 Analysis

This essay would receive a score of 1.

Though the essay states the writer's points, the questions are not answered. There are no definitions of terms and no relation of the terms to Lacie's class. The writer has just presented a viewpoint. The majority of the content will prevent the essay from receiving the highest score.

Essay 3

Lacie seems not to have included either cooperative learning or problem-solving in her class. Rather the students seem to have taken over the class. My impression of cooperative learning and problem-solving is one of the teacher in charge and the students cooperating with the teacher. Lacie's classroom seems to be mob rule.

Essay 3 Analysis

This essay would receive a score of 0.

This essay is unacceptable. First, the test-taker was to have defined the terms and, next, to have indicated if either method exists in Lacie's class.

The essayist seems, most of all, to have asserted his/her opinion: "the students seem to have taken over the class." Most educators would not view the class as being "mob ruled"! The essay is not well-structured.

Additionally, the writer seems to have a flawed perception of what the processes imply: "the teacher in charge and the students cooperating with him/her."

Though the writing is clear and the spelling good, the content keeps the essay from being of passing quality. The essay would receive poor marks.

Case Study II

Constructed-Response Items

4. **Essay 1**

Maria appears to be a prime candidate for a student-centered learning environment. That is, Mr. Treskoski could delegate more pedagogical responsibilities to Maria. This would give Maria a more direct role in her own education. Mr. Treskoski might, for example, make Maria the leader of a small discussion group. Once the groups have been formed and the materials are collected, Maria might then be responsible for a class presentation; she may head a debate team, or she might lead the class in a discussion group. Maria might also benefit from a group research project. Working with a small group of other students who share her interests, she might coordinate a project that produces a video or other short media presentation. It seems ironic to give a student like Maria more independent freedom and more responsibility for her learning, but it may in fact be exactly what she requires. It is up to Mr. Treskoski to help Maria discover alternative forms of self-generated or collaborative learning that utilize her skills and interests.

Essay 1 Analysis

This essay would receive a score of 2.

This is an example of a well-written essay because it effectively applies contemporary pedagogical strategies to an actual classroom situation.

The essay follows the assignment and answers all parts. That is, it responds to the question thoughtfully. It gives the reader the impression that the writer is going somewhere with the idea. The paper's main ideas are carried forward by a succession of relevant supporting arguments.

The details and examples are appropriate and clearly related to the ideas they support. Each paragraph is finished before moving on to the next paragraph. The essay has a clear order that is easy to follow.

The essay's diction is accurate, clear, and concise, both in word choice and in phrasing. It would receive the highest score.

Essay 2

This is an opportunity for Mr. Treskoski to play upon Maria's concerns regarding her prospects for upper-division education. Mr. Treskoski may explain, for example, how adverse study habits will jeopardize college opportunities. He can use Maria's own concerns to motivate her. Obviously Maria already understands that she is jeopardizing her own academic future, and an astute teacher can turn that anxiety into motivation. At the same time Mr. Treskoski must remain impartial to Maria's situation and allow her to be responsible for the consequences of her actions. If she wants to further her education, she must understand what needs to be done and take the necessary actions. College is for adults who are self-motivated and want to learn.

Essay 2 Analysis

This essay would receive a score of 1.

This essay is not as effective as the first since it demonstrates a lack of pedagogic responsibility. Since Maria is already preoccupied with concerns regarding her educational future, it would be counterproductive for Mr. Treskoski to add additional anxiety. Causing Maria greater anxiety over her academic future would only distract her, rather than give her greater learning opportunity. An astute instructor will turn nearly any classroom situation into a positive learning experience; causing Maria additional stress would be counterproductive to learning.

Otherwise the essay, although brief, is void of major compositional errors.

Essay 3

If Maria has such great potential and shows such genuine concern over her academic future, then Mr. Treskoski must make the grading criteria simpler and more flexible. These changes will help students like Maria achieve her long-range goals. It is up to Mr. Treskoski to help students like Maria get to where they want to be academically.

Of course he can also make the grading criteria more rigid, thereby demonstrating to students like Maria that institutions of higher learning have a zero tolerance level for slackers. If Maria can't keep up, then she does not belong in college. After all, Mr. Treskoski has other students and responsibilities to worry about.

He could have Maria transferred to a class designed for slower students so that she won't have to work so hard. Then Maria will be with people progressing at her own pace.

Essay 3 Analysis

This essay would receive a score of 0.

This is a weak essay because it represents a lack of focus on the part of the author. The writer simply proposes various ideas that are contrary to one another, as well as being counter-productive to learning.

Thus, the essay does not clearly address the assigned topic because it does not answer all parts of the assignment. The essay (or parts of it) seems to be mainly filling paper rather than really saying something. The reader must work to determine where the essay is going. Additionally, the lack of a thesis, examples, and evidence creates a disjointed, subjective, and aimless effect.

5. Essay 1

Mr. Treskoski could assign a research paper. Whether a short or long format, it offers opportunities for either a) an independent project whereby students examine issues outside of course content, or b) papers that explore in greater detail course content (i.e. issues, theories, and central themes). Research format "a" will obviously expand individual horizons with an understanding of new material, while research paper format "b" will offer a more personal, in-depth understanding of materials already covered by the course.

Another form of independent student writing that Mr. Treskoski could assign includes reviews of books, movies, plays, music, newspapers, magazines, and/or journal articles. These writings give students a chance to intercontextualize various forms of media while at the same time offering them an examination of a larger social commentary.

Additionally, and maybe more importantly, the review assignment offers students a chance to apply the theories that they acquired in the classroom to external media representations, giving the student an opportunity to see classroom theory put into actual social practice.

Mr. Treskoski could also have his students keep daily and/or weekly reading journals, where they can keep notes, ask questions and think abstract concepts through without regard for academic form or structure. Mr. Treskoski can then make periodic inspections of the students' journals to know what concepts need elaboration and what concepts make sense.

Essay 1 Analysis

This essay would receive a score of 2.

The content addresses the advantages of each writing project and suggests how that project can be used to benefit not only the students, but the instructor as well.

The essay follows the assignment by answering all parts. It gives the impression that the writer is going somewhere with the idea because they have thought seriously about the topic. The essay's main ideas are propelled by a succession of relevant supporting ideas, details, and examples.

The arguments are appropriate and clearly related to the ideas they support. Important words and ideas get clear emphasis and the word choices are accurate and appropriate to the context in which they are used.

Thus, the instructions have been followed well.

Essay 2

One writing project that Mr. Treskoski would find effective would be to have students assist him in a research project. He could find four volunteers from a local high school who could then help him in researching detailed documentation for his doctoral thesis. When students are exposed to research at a sophisticated level they then would respond accordingly. Thus, I suggest that students be exposed to the independent research project early, thereby elevating their appreciation for higher education, their appreciation for independent study, and their understanding of parallel relationships.

Essay 2 Analysis

This essay would receive a score of 1.

The author draws the reader's attention to the teacher's personal goals instead of demonstrating his or her pedagogical knowledge of various types of independent writing projects. It is an example of one of the most common of writing pitfalls: that of over-personalizing the assignment. While it is advantageous to apply personal experience to academic knowledge, it becomes unnecessary and counterproductive to draw too many personal comparatives and conclusions.

Essay 3

Independent writing is actually writing by oneself. It means that when you write something for class, the best way to do it is independently, that is with no help from the instructor or other students. It means being self-governing, autonomous, self-sufficient, unconventional, and individual. Independence in writing is very important for today's student because if you're going onto college or technical school, then you'll be expected to write by yourself. Of course you'll be needed to write well enough to pass your entrance exams too. You can't ask the teachers for assistance because they have important things to do. They'll need students to write by themselves, or by that I mean, to write independently. Mr. Treskoski should assign his students independent writing projects so that they could get the idea of independent writing, or that is, meaning, writing all by themselves.

Essay 3 Analysis

This essay would receive a score of 0.

This essay contains some of the more common and ironically correctable writing mistakes that authors make. Most of these errors could have been avoided simply by proofreading the essay prior to submission.

The diction is inaccurate, unclear, and confusing. The abundance of repetitions distracts the reader while they add to the careless and disorderly nature of the essay.

The other problem with this essay is not so easily correctable. It involves knowing the material. This author obviously does not have a very clear understanding of what contemporary writing theories are. Yet, the writer makes an attempt to counterfeit his or her way through the question.

6. **Essay 1**

Mr. Treskoski should thank Mrs. Rivas for her interest. He should tell her to expect that throughout the year, he will group students in a variety of ways. Both Carlita's and Lynn's groups will change from time to time. He should indicate that it is a major goal of the class for students to work with others who are very like and very unlike themselves. Mr. Treskoski should mention that he will not be able to answer her questions about Lynn because of the Family Right to Privacy Act (FRPA). It would be both ethically and legally inadvisable for him to answer any questions about Lynn.

Essay 1 Analysis

This essay would receive a score of 2.

The essay provides a polite response from Mr. Treskoski to Mrs. Rivas. He has clearly explained the flexible grouping he encourages and the basis for it. Mr. Treskoski has legal and ethical responsibilities when answering the question about Lynn's problems. The essay is correct in content and the writing. This essay would receive a high score.

Essay 2

Mr. Treskoski should firmly explain that he has to make the instructional decisions about the class. He should advise Mrs. Rivas to tell Carlita that her daughter has a social obligation to help Lynn. Futhermore, he should mention that unless students build community, they will not learn the value of civic virtue, a main goal of social studies education.

Essay 2 Analysis

This essay would receive a score of 1.

While it is a major goal of social studies to instill civic value in students, Mr. Treskoski should not violate the legal and ethical guidelines that protect Lynn's confidentiality regarding his disability. The tone that the essay suggests Mr. Treskoski use with the parent is condescending. The essay does, however, seek to encourage community. This response would receive a satisfactory mark.

Essay 3

Mr. Treskoski should tell Mrs. Rivas that he understands her concern. He should patiently explain to Mrs. Rivas that Lynn has fetal alcohol syndrome and is also mentally retarded. He should tell her that he will send materials on fetal alcohol syndrome home with Carlita. Mrs. Rivas can read the materials and better understand Lynn's problems. He also can ask Mrs. Rivas to share the information with Carlita. Perhaps Carlita can tell her friends about Lynn and help Lynn in the group.

Essay 3 Analysis

This essay would receive a score of 0.

It is a violation of both legal and ethical guidelines to discuss a special education student's handicapping condition with another student's parent. The Family Right to Privacy Act (FRPA) assures the confidentiality of student records. Mr. Treskoski would be committing both ethical and legal violations if he discusses Lynn with Mrs. Rivas and if he encourages her to share the information with Carlita. Because of content, this essay is completely unacceptable.

Case Study III

Constructed-Response Items

7. **Essay 1**

In today's multicultural classroom it is critical for Mr. Buzz to include all students regardless of race, creed, or gender. While conversations pertaining to such issues might be very important to contemporary pedagogy, certain topics are also highly sensitive, emotionally charged, and controversial, and therefore potentially dangerous.

One way to diffuse a potentially volatile situation is for Mr. Buzz to bring it out in the open right from the first day of the class. That is, have each student introduce him or herself and have each talk a bit about their background, heritage, ancestry, culture, etc. Many students will feel relieved to hear such candid comments and to note tolerance and acceptance. It will help Mr. Buzz and his students pronounce names correctly; this may reduce the potential for future embarrassment.

It is also important that Mr. Buzz remain perceptive to his own prejudices. At the same time it is important for Mr. Buzz to be open to multicultural opportunities for learning and respect each student's boundaries with respect to his own personal privacy.

Essay 1 Analysis

This essay would receive a score of 2.

The essay scored well because it demonstrates a balanced, thoughtful understanding on the part of the author regarding the sensitive issues surrounding cultural diversity. That is, it represents a thoughtful balance between the educational potential of the multicultural classroom as well as the potential dangers. The word choices are accurate and appropriate to the context, not too offhand or indifferent and not too pretentious or conformist. That is, the diction is accurate, clear, and concise without being condescending.

The necessary details and examples are appropriate and clearly related to the ideas they support. Each paragraph is finished before the paper goes on to the next paragraph. Overall the essay has a clear thesis and is structured accordingly.

Essay 2

Mr. Buzz's multicultural classroom is the perfect opportunity for him to obtain all the information he can from his students with varying cultural backgrounds. His students can be delegates for cultural awareness and can communicate the necessary information required to dispel many cultural myths and stereotypes. Books like *Huckleberry Finn* offer only a literary glimpse of the history of racial prejudice, but students in the classroom can elaborate on the everyday experience of living with ethnicity. It seems that it would be a valuable opportunity for class participation to incorporate student scenarios into the academic mix. Students could relate their home experiences to the class. This would allow students to see that we are all the same and that there is nothing to fear but fear itself. We are all the same under the skin. Minorities could show us that in the classroom, and then we would all just get along.

Essay 2 Analysis

This essay would receive a score of 1.

This essay received a satisfactory score because it in fact perpetuates the multicultural stereotyping it proposes to eradicate. When the author suggests that each student be a delegate for his or her cultural heritage, the writer is simply reiterating a stereotype that one inherently knows everything about one's culture simply by birthright or osmosis. Thus, the essay's entire thesis is based upon an erroneous and potentially volatile presumption.

The author professes to see the pedagogical opportunities for multicultural classrooms while concurrently missing the mark on sensitivity and social awareness. That is, the writer claims to understand the pedagogical opportunities available in the multicultural classroom while he or she misses the opportunity to deal with his/her own introspective bias. Essentially, then, this essay's content erodes its own assertion.

Essay 3

Ethnic diversity is simply too sensitive a topic to be brought up in the classroom. Although it is socially important, it is just too easy to offend someone; then Mr. Buzz will have a lawsuit on his hands. Then the institution will be sued. A new teacher (such as Mr. Buzz) cannot afford to "make waves"; it is better to remain mute on the subject of multiculturalism than to light a powder keg. So much depends on political correctness today, that the idea of addressing multicultural issues in the classroom is just too scary. Besides, if families want their offspring to learn about cultural heritage, ancestry, etc. they will teach them at home or in church. I just don't think its appropriate to discuss those kinds of issues in an exam question.

Essay 3 Analysis

This essay would receive a score of 0.

This essay scored poorly because it demonstrates reluctance on the part of the writer to deal with provocative, yet unavoidable, classroom issues. Thus, the essay failed to address the assignment. It has no thesis to build upon. It avoids rather than focuses on the issue.

The lack of desire to respond to the question translates into a lack of thoughtfulness on the author's part. It demonstrates unwillingness for open dialogue and as such, the essay, admittedly, has nothing of value to say.

8. ## Essay 1

Obviously, technology is neither the answer to all the problems facing academia, nor is it the root of all evil. It resides somewhere in between. It is a tool that Mr. Buzz can use for educational purposes, and as with any tool, when used properly, and for the right job, it can be an effective time and energy saver. Technological applications range from managerial uses, such as class scheduling, syllabi posting, class information sharing groups, gathering source materials, Webster's and Britannica on-line, and communications with the fellow instructors and fellow students any hour of the day or night. Technology also offers the opportunities for papers, presentations, lectures etc. to be posted and previewed or reviewed by the instructor or colleagues; ongoing course discussion groups can continue long after the scheduled class period is over.

Yes, there is a substantial cost involved, but it is investment cost. Once invested, the cost of upkeep is minimal. Also, there will always be a need for human intervention, so the fear that robots will someday educate us is ridiculous. Technology is a tool. Used properly it will make life easier. Used improperly, it will cause more harm, stress, and strain than need be.

Essay 1 Analysis

This essay would receive a score of 2.

This essay scored well because it was perceptive enough not to place technology at either end of a spectrum, but in the middle. That is, the author does not present classroom technology as a cure-all for all academic woes, nor does it suggest that technology is a modern scourge that has no place in today's classroom. Rather, this essay presents a well-balanced argument based upon sound principles of logic and reason. The author remains objective, while at the same time knowledgeable about the subject matter, and answers the question of technology's role in Mr. Buzz's classroom clearly and astutely. The essay addresses the question by giving the impression that the writer is going somewhere with the idea. The paper has a thesis (main idea; i.e. technology is a tool), which is carried forward by a succession of relevant supporting ideas. The writer shows a thoughtful perspective on the subject by giving details and examples which are both appropriate and clearly related to the ideas they support. The essay has a clear order that is easy to follow.

Essay 2

Technology in the classroom, an idea whose time has come. As we venture ever deeper into the twenty-first century, we become ever aware of the advantages to a life of technological advancement. Many of us today could not live without our computers, microwave ovens, and cellular phones. The student of tomorrow is bound to be even more reliant upon technology than the student of today. They will feel at home on a computer that the use of one will almost seem second nature. It will not be a question of if technology should be in the classroom, but how much, and to what extreme. Ultimately, there will be no need for the expense of campuses because computers will do everything from class scheduling, role taking, and paper grading, to web-based publishing, and transcript distribution. Students will not need to go to a classroom because everything will be done right from their own living room; there will be nothing but virtual classrooms on-line. Ultimately there will be no need for school buildings, no upkeep, nothing but virtual schools and universities. Imagine how economical education will be then.

Essay 2 Analysis

This essay would receive a score of 1.

This essay's weakness is that it takes a long time to address the use of technology in the classroom and when it does address the issue, it does so in such a far-fetched and unrealistic manner as to render its argument mute. There is no thesis so the body of essay is unfocused and lacks development. There is no logical progression between ideas. The paper reads as a mere subjective assertion or description. Thus, the essay seems to be mainly taking up space, rather than really saying something. The reader must trudge through a wordy introduction before knowing where the essay is going. Without an argument and supporting evidence, the paper produces an empty, subjective, and disagreeable effect. The author maintains an overly enthusiastic attitude toward technology, and does not permit the development of counter arguments or alternative points of view.

Essay 3

Technology has always gotten the short end of the stick. When radio came out, they said it would kill the theaters. When TV came out, they said it would kill the movies. Nothing happened. Theaters didn't die! Radio didn't die! Movies and TV didn't die! So why give computers such a bad rap? Robots are not going to take over the world. Computers aren't going to kill us. Look at the Y2K scare. Nothing happened. Technology always is shown in a bad light. Now we take our digital watches and our cable TV's for granted. What if they weren't there? They're technology. They were considered high tech once upon a time. What about word processors? Technology will have a place in the classroom because it is here to stay. They said TV would kill the movies and it didn't. How can technology be so bad for us when it makes our life so easy and much better?

Essay 3 Analysis

> **This essay would receive a score of 0.**

This essay exhibits two common writing problems. The first is a chatty and less scholarly tone. The second major flaw is its redundant questioning. This overwhelms the reader with extraneous information while simultaneously giving the essay a choppy, haphazard feeling. These questions inadvertently induce an additional frustration on the reader's part because the purpose in writing this essay is to answer questions, not to postulate additional, unanswered ones. Of course, the most obvious problem with this essay is that it never addresses the question at issue. The author never tells how to incorporate technology into the classroom. The writer simply rants about technology as a recurring social phenomenon and never addresses the topic. This essay becomes broader in scope as it progresses instead of narrowing its focus and targeting direct issues.

9.   Essay 1

Many educators have written books and created materials on learning styles and multiple intelligences available for use by classroom teachers. Rita Dunn has acknowledged that students may be visual, auditory, and kinesthetic learners. Howard Gardner has recognized eight different intelligences; his recognition of many intelligences replaces the old idea of one intelligent quotient.

Mr. Buzz has ensured that his students have activities that meet their interests, learning styles, and that give them all a chance for success.

Visual learners can use the computer for research. These learners have such options as making models or posters and viewing plays to present their findings. In addition, they can view the posters, models, and plays of others to increase their knowledge.

Auditory learners can write plays and listen to and watch the plays of others to learn more about South America. Auditory learners can work with others as they write their essays.

Kinesthetic learners have ample opportunities to move about as they study and learn. They can write plays; they can use the library and computers for research. They can move about as they write their essays; they are free to work with others. These learners who often find the classroom confining now have the benefit of moving about.

The projects and activities in Mr. Buzz's classroom capitalize on many different intelligences. Gardner proposes eight different intelligences; the projects that Mr. Buzz has suggested appeal to those with special gifts in the area of Linguistic Intelligence and Interpersonal Intelligence. With his interest in and concern for his students, he will be receptive, I am sure, to those who might want to research the scientists of the era (Naturalist Intelligence), the mathematicians of the time (Logical-Mathematical Intelligence), or even the sports and athletes (Bodily-Kinesthetic Intelligence) at the turn of the century.

Mr. Buzz has acknowledged and provided for the various learning styles and multiple intelligences of his students. They should all capitalize on his planning.

Essay 1 Analysis

This essay would receive a score of 2.

Essay 1 does a good job at answering the question. The writer has demonstrated a knowledge of both learning styles and multiple intelligences. Specific examples are provided. Furthermore, the essay relates these topics to the activities in the classroom.

The essay flows logically and will score at the higher end of the holistic scoring chart.

Essay 2

Mr. Buzz has neglected to provide for the learners who learn best in traditional ways. He has neglected the students who have typically done well in classrooms where the students sit in their desks and the teacher teaches. He has failed the good students. In this day of trying to meet the needs of the students who should not even be in school, we have forgotten the ones who are gifted academically—the ones with the high IQ's. Teachers have given their jobs to the students, and the "good" students have suffered for it. This classroom is an example of forgetting about education and making the teacher's job easy.

Essay 2 Analysis

This essay would receive a score of 1.

The writer of this piece has presented a view that is contrary to the classroom plan of Mr. Buzz. In pushing this alternative opinion, however, the writer has failed to comment on the visual, auditory, and kinesthetic styles of learning and has narrow-mindedly considered only one type of intelligence as acceptable: the traditional view of IQ. The essayist has failed to give credit to the planning and the evaluating that has gone into this organization of instruction.

Although the author of the essay has presented a differing opinion clearly, the essay itself will receive a low mark—primarily because of ignoring the questions asked.

Essay 3

Learning styles vary among people. Mr. Buzz himself has a different learning style. He teaches without a desk and board. His students may suffer the consequences if they waste time. He needs to check on them more often. Parents are going to be upset when they see kids wasting time on computers.

Teaching to multiple intelligences is a way to make it easy for the lazy to squeak by. School is for learning, not for playing, which Mr. Buzz has forgotten.

Essay 3 Analysis

This essay would receive a score of 0.

The writer has not structured the writing of this essay. Instead, he/she has taken off on a tangent and has tried to grind several axes. In so doing, he/she has totally ignored the questions: What is meant by learning styles and by multiple intelligences? What, if anything, has Mr. Buzz done to acknowledge and provide for multiple intelligences and varying learning styles? The essay does not give the definitions and information that the question requires. This essay would receive a score at the bottom of the scale.

Case Study IV

Constructed-Response Items

10. Essay 1 ───

It is important to establish ground rules early in the semester. Let students know that disruptive behavior will not be tolerated in the classroom. That way, students will feel more comfortable knowing where the boundaries are. The following are some ways to handle or deter disruptive behavior:

Depending on the infraction, the best response might be to simply ignore certain antagonistic behaviors. If, however, the student persists in exhibiting blatantly aggressive or other hostile behaviors, it may be necessary to take more drastic action. You might have to ask the student to leave the classroom, or, depending on the infraction, use the behavior as a springboard into a class discussion on social etiquette.

Also, other students might intervene instead of waiting for the teacher. They might exert the necessary peer pressure to squelch the situation before it escalates. Some might say that this is not the responsibility of the students but of the teacher. However, the classroom is an environment for learning on a holistic level, so any pedagogical opportunity should be used.

Regardless, disruptive infractions must be curtailed early so that the teacher remains the person in charge and prevents further situations from getting out of hand.

Essay 1 Analysis ───

This essay would receive a score of 2.

This essay does a good job at answering the question. It can be difficult to know how to answer generalized questions where the apparent answer, as this question acknowledges, "depends on the individual situation." In other words, the essay responds to the question. The essay attempts "to really say something." That is, it gives the impression that the writer is thinking seriously about the question and its objective. The essay answered the question asked by exemplifying various responses toward disruptive behavior in the classroom. For that reason, it addresses the assignment well.

Additionally, it has a clearly formulated, precise, specific, and focused thesis. The author defines the central terms well and accurately employs them. The author demonstrates a clear sense of purpose.

Also adding to the essay's sophistication level is the fact that it flows logically and persuasively attempts to address an opposing viewpoint and/or alternative idea.

Essay 2

While there may be one or two students who occasionally disrupt a classroom, it is not understandable why these students should get all the attention when the good students do not. When students are being disruptive, then they are asking for attention; by giving it to them, you are saying that it is all right to be disruptive. So don't give them attention. Then you will have time to give the good students all the attention that they require. The bad students will see that the good students are getting all the attention; then they will want the attention. They will then be good to get the instructor's attention. If you yell and scream, then they will think that they can get your attention, and then other students will, of course, do that, too. They will all become disruptive because the bad students did it, too. Time outs work well. They don't have to be long; just long enough for the student to think about what they have done, and then they won't do it again. Maybe bad students could write an essay or something like that so they could think about what they have done.

Essay 2 Analysis

This essay would receive a score of 1.

The absence of paragraph divisions makes any separate ideas or supporting parts of the essay hard to distinguish from one another and as a result, the essay is difficult to follow.

The thesis development is inconsistent. Certain parts of the paper are more fully developed than others. This leaves certain parts of the essay feeling skimpy or shallow. The overall details, comparisons, and examples are not specific. Overall haphazard organization makes the essay convoluted and hard to follow.

Essay 3

Disruptions in the classroom are disruptive to your class and other classes, too. Teachers should get together and come up with a set of rules that deal with disruptions in the best way that they can. That way, the disruptions don't get out of hand and disrupt the entire school. Maybe the students don't mean to be disruptive, but they can't help it. I feel if teachers knew how they wanted to deal with disruptions, then they would not be so disrupted; the disruptions wouldn't be so out of control and then the students would know what the teachers wanted from them. The students would not know what teachers wanted them to do. If teachers just could get together and decide how they wanted to deal with disruptive students, the students would know, too. I feel if teachers don't know how they would like to run their classroom, students shouldn't get mad at them if they don't know themselves what they want them to do. They are not being disruptive on purpose; they are disruptive by accident and then they don't know they are being disruptive. So it's not their fault.

Essay 3 Analysis

This essay would receive a score of 0.

There are several major problems with this essay.

The first is the essay's overall structure. The sentences are short, fragmented and choppy, or too long and stringy, with parts that are not clearly related to one another. Many word choices are unclear or inaccurate. The reader is distracted by these sentence-level errors, such as fragments, run-ons, comma splices, subject-verb agreement, confused sentence structure, punctuation, and spelling errors.

Also, statements such as "I feel like..." are not only inaccurate but also are too casual for the context. It gives the essay a rudimentary sound and appearance. Instructions have not been followed because the question has not been answered. The paper never tells how the author would deal with a disruptive student. Thus, the essay (or part of it) seems to be mainly filling paper rather than really saying something substantial.

11. Essay 1

The answer to the age-old question of "why teach" begins an exercise in stating the most obvious. We teach because we can make a positive difference in a person's life. We as educators have the power to share our passion for learning with students. We offer students new ways of thinking. We broaden horizons by exposing students to new and exciting worlds, literatures, philosophies, and cultures. We promote tolerance and acceptance by introducing students to new avenues of thinking about cultures, genders, philosophies, religions, and beliefs. We provide new perspectives.

We act as role models. We are the examples of where education and learning can lead a person. We demonstrate positive study habits, "stick-to-itiveness" and the ability to conquer seemingly insurmountable odds in order to achieve our goals. Some educators in today's society even serve as pseudo-surrogate parents.

And while we teachers recognize these and other valuable traits as assets to the fabric of society, maybe the ultimate reason we teach is that we have an infinite and unquenchable desire for learning. A desire for learning that can only be satisfied in a classroom.

Essay 1 Analysis

This essay would receive a score of 2.

This essay is clearly organized and follows the assignment by answering its question. The author attempts to "really say something," rather than simply rambling or filling up space. It gives the impression that the writer is going somewhere with an idea. The essay's main idea (thesis) is propelled forward by a succession of relevant supporting ideas. The writing shows a thoughtful approach toward the subject.

The details and examples are appropriate for the subject and clearly related to the ideas they support (i.e. broadening lives through literature).

The idea in each paragraph is completed before the paper goes on to the next paragraph. Thus, the essay has a clear order, and it is easy to follow. The paragraph divisions clearly indicate changes in topic or ideas. At the same time the sentences are varied in length and structure. Important words and ideas get clear emphasis. Word choices are accurate and appropriate to the context of the paper. Consequently, the essay appears neither too casual, nor too pompous or formal.

The essay answers the questions asked of it, so the instructions have been followed.

Essay 2

What is this field known as education? Where does it come from? Who is the one who first stepped into a classroom and decided that our children need to be taught something other than simple practical everyday chores? No longer woodcutting, hunting, and food gathering for men. No longer baking and cooking and cleaning for girls. Now the days would be filled with reading, writing, and arithmetic. The educational system has arrived and with it, the need for men and women who would mold our young people into the leaders of tomorrow.

Education has come a long way since the advent of the organized classroom. What must have began as a get-together in someone's living room (the first classroom?) has now grown into elementary schools, middle schools, high schools, colleges, and major universities throughout this great land of ours. Where was the first college? Maybe in caves, when our ancestors first turned rocks into tools. Where will it end? What will the schools of the future be?

Why do we teach? Because the educational system needs qualified people who know the value of an education and can instill that value in others. We teach because we have a desire to share our knowledge with others. We teach because it is a field of opportunity that is wide open to dedicated individuals. We teach because we want to share the value of education with others. We teach because we have the energy to share what we have learned with others. We teach because like the mountain climber, it's there and we can.

Essay 2 Analysis

This essay would receive a score of 1.

This essay's introduction is exceedingly long. When it does arrive at the body of the paper, it does not say anything significant. Basically it reiterates the same theme over and over (teaching is sharing) with little of its content having to do with the question asked of it. Essentially then, the essay does not directly address the assigned topic.

Subsequently the paper complicates itself with an introduction of erroneous questions that it then fails to answer. Thus, the essay (or part of it) appears to be mainly filling paper rather than saying something substantial. The reader must wade through a wordy introduction before knowing where the essay is going. Additionally, the lack of supporting ideas, details, examples, and evidence creates a shallow, subjective, and unsatisfying effect.

The paper's development is inconsistent. Parts of the essay seem more fully developed than other parts. The unnecessary "history of the educational system" paragraph ends before its ideas have been completed. The hypotheses and conclusions are naive, thus giving the paper a juvenile tone. Haphazard organization makes the essay appear scattered and hard to follow.

Essay 3

There is really is no way for me to answer this question. Why do we teach is like asking why do we eat or why do we breathe? It's just a natural thing that I want to do. You really can't say this is why. It's like asking why am I hungry? My friends ask, "Why do you want to be a teacher?" I tell them that I just like to teach, and then they tell me that that is a noble profession and I should be proud of the fact that I want to be a teacher. I tell them that I am.

So I guess for me teaching is just in my blood or something. I guess the best way I can describe it would be to say I'm infected with the virus of teaching. Ha ha. No really, I guess that teaching is just something that I love to do. Others who are successful teachers must also like kids and want to be around them and like to do it. Because I love teaching kids so much, I guess I just took to the classroom right from the get-go. I do like kids a lot so being around them all day is not a problem for me as it would be for some other people I know. I guess I'm just one of those people persons who likes kids and I just can't wait to get the opportunity to get into the classroom so I can do something constructive with my afternoons besides watching soap operas. Just kidding.

Essay 3 Analysis

This essay would receive a score of 0.

This paper's major flaw is in its diction. The casual, chatty tone detracts from the content thus diminishing the author's credibility. The diction is neither accurate nor appropriate for this situation. Pragmatic and didactic (clear, concise, and informative) word choice and phrasing would be more effective.

The paper lacks a clearly formulated thesis. Thus, the essay lacks definition. The result is an essay without focus or organizational framework (introduction, body, and conclusion). Because there is no thesis, the essay cannot flow logically.

The resulting essay appears to overwhelm the writer, making the author sound disoriented and apologetic. There is not an attempt to address the pedagogical theories or ideologies asked of it. The essay reads more like a daily journal entry than an appropriate response to an exam question.

12. Essay 1

Bill should begin addressing the issue of the school's inaccessibility by telling the mother that he will ask the principal about it the next day. He should close the conversation by telling Myra that he hopes that they can work together someday.

Because it is illegal for a public school to be inaccessible to handicapped students, Bill should talk first with the principal to be sure that the information the parent gave him is accurate. The parent, of course, has legal recourse if the public schools are not providing an education for Myra.

Bill is wise not to mention "lawsuits" and "legal action" until he is sure that the facts are straight, however; it is difficult to imagine an inaccessible public school building at this time in history.

If, indeed, the school is inaccessible, if the principal is uninterested in helping, and if Myra is unable to use the local neighborhood school, then Bill may want to mention that Myra's mother can talk with the district office/school superintendent about the problems that Myra faces. Federal and state laws ensure that Myra can have the accessibility to the public schools. Myra's mother can easily obtain legal counsel should the schools refuse to comply with her requests for public school education for her daughter.

Essay 1 Analysis

This essay would receive a score of 2.

The content of this essay is good. The teacher does not make any threats or raise legal issues until he finds out what the situation is for himself. It may be that the school has not intentionally failed to comply with the law; it may also be that the school is compliant, but there is some confusion. It may be that the school is eager to comply once they are aware of the noncompliance. Both federal and state laws require that schools be accessible to persons who use wheelchairs. Bill is wise to remain discreet.

The essay is totally acceptable.

Essay 2

Bill should simply ignore the whole situation of whether the school meets Myra's needs. Bill has a duty to support his administration; his job may rest on how he handles the situation. I suggest that he drop the issue. The mother seems to be ready to use another school so he should let the situation stay as it is.

Bill may offer to bring materials home to Myra. This offer should change the subject and enable Bill to quietly exit the scene.

Essay 2 Analysis

This essay would receive a score of 1.

Bill should not ignore the whole situation. He does not have an obligation to support his administration—no matter what. Bill would be selling himself short if he drops the issue. He has an obligation as a teacher of current and future students to check on the accessibility to the handicapped of the school in which he teaches. Merely receiving some materials is not a suitable substitute for attending an accessible school in one's own neighborhood.

Essay 3

Tell Myra's mother to sue. It is time the needs of the handicapped are met. They can be met with legal action. Tell her not to tell Bill said to sue because this could get Bill fired. There is no need to talk to anyone at the school. Go to a law firm. Go now.

Essay 3 Analysis

This essay would receive a score of 0.

This parent is trying to get a good education for Myra. She is not "lawsuit happy." Lawsuits take time; this parent wants Myra's education now. Before going to an attorney, the parent may want to talk with the superintendent and/or the teacher may want to inquire as to whether the principal is aware that a wheelchair-bound student in his school district needs accessibility. The main goal is the education of the students—not a lawsuit.

The student has written a very poor essay. An emphasis on Bill's job above everything, and a predisposition to "sue" make the essay unprofessional and unacceptable.

Multiple-Choice Answers

13. **D**

These are symptoms of a neurotic disorder. A neurotic disorder is an emotional disorder that endangers a child's well-being and that adults should take very seriously. A wise adult does not dismiss the symptoms as nerves (A), nothing (B), or tall tales (C).

14. **A**

It has been found that it is most effective to provide a few examples and nonexamples in teaching a concept. The actual number of examples (B) does not make a difference, nor do the examples all have to be interesting (C). From the examples and nonexamples, students can inductively determine the definition (D) of the concept.

15. **D**

Homework should be used to reinforce the learning done in the classroom (D), rather than to start new lessons (A). This will help to place the skills learned in long-term memory (C). Effective classroom management is needed to form structure in a classroom (B).

16. **C**

The process approach can be used in a variety of fields. It uses a sensing function (reach), a transforming function (touch), and an acting function (teach). Students take in information, abstract and add value to this information, and then act on an alternative that is based upon the information.

17. **A**

Practice activities provide an opportunity for teachers to monitor students to see if additional instruction is needed after a lesson (A). Practice activities are used for any subject matter just featured in the class lesson; therefore, (B) is incorrect. Practice activities reinforce skills that the students have just learned, rather than reviewing old material (C) or introducing new concepts (D).

18.

As long as students are well-informed about procedures ahead of time, it is possible to rotate computer use among single students or small groups so that the class can optimize their experience with computers. Therefore, answers (B), (C), and (D) are not the best choices.

19.

All types of students start using drugs and alcohol out of curiosity, desire for pleasure, pressure from peers, and/or to avoid problems (A).

20.

Studies have shown that reprimands are more effective when they are made in a soft, controlled manner. Loud shouting (A), threats (B), and angry outbursts (D) cause more anxiety in a classroom rather than effectively modifying behavior.

21.

A student's enthusiasm for learning and overall self-esteem will increase if she or he has positive and successful experiences in the classroom. Posting grades (A) is a violation of a student's right to privacy. Using negative reinforcement (B) and amplifying responses (D) are not methods of building a student's self-esteem.

22.

If a teacher notices that a student is daydreaming, walking over to the student or placing a hand on his or her shoulder are ways of bringing the student back on-task without disrupting the flow and the momentum of the lesson. Calling on the student (A), who will probably be unable to answer, or stopping and staring at the student (D) will result in lost momentum. Asking questions of the class (C) may not bring the student back on-task.

23.

In general, educators believe that corporal punishment should be avoided. Unfortunately, there are still those who practice forms of corporal punishment; hence, (A) is an incorrect answer. (C) is a false statement. Although corporal punishment might be effective with some students (D), it is not the approach to take with most students.

24. **D**

At best, this procedure can be said to promote school safety. It cannot be assumed that the procedure is sufficient to accomplish the goal of school safety (B). Answers (A) and (C) are not desirable consequences.

25. **A**

Students are able to learn the most when they are aware of and understand exactly what is expected of them. This overshadows the use of special materials (B), repetition of examples (C), or classroom size (D).

26. **B**

Research has shown that it is favorable to provide feedback in test situations when the feedback is delayed by a day or so, rather than giving immediate feedback (A). Delaying the feedback session for a few weeks is not beneficial to the students because too much time has elapsed (C). A class review of the test has been shown to be more beneficial in clearing up misunderstandings than handwritten notations (D).

27. **B**

In inductive teaching, the students are provided with examples and nonexamples and are expected to derive the definition from this information. In deductive teaching (A), the teacher defines a concept and provides a few examples and nonexamples. Definitions (C) and examples (D) are important parts of inductive and deductive teaching.

28. **C**

This question is based on implementing instructional design and conditions that facilitate learning. All of the choices provide information potentially useful to the teacher interested in modifying a student's behavior. However, answer (C) is the least important of the choices for several reasons. Clearly, appropriate behavior programs can be developed by knowing consequences, (A), and reinforcers (B), as well as having a clear idea of what it is that is to be changed (D). But if any of these areas are not known, it is questionable how effective the behavior-modifying program will be. A successful program can be implemented without knowing what has been attempted in the past. Additionally, unless the teacher is knowledgeable about the rigor with which specific procedures were used in the past, the information is moot as procedures are often applied inappropriately. The answer therefore is (C).

29. **C**

Computerized tests can measure higher order thinking skills. Research has supported that computers are motivational for many students (A), that students write longer papers when they use computers than when they write with pen and paper (B), and that, as wonderful as technology is, sometimes it fails, and teachers must have alternative plans (D).

30. **A**

Praise has been shown to be the most effective when it is authentic and low-key (A). It should be used frequently; therefore, (B) is incorrect. It should consist of complex responses that provide information about the reasons for the quality of the student response (C); therefore, (C) is incorrect. It should be used to provide all students with positive experiences (D); therefore, (D) is incorrect.

31. **D**

A portfolio keeps a collection of dated samples of a student's work over time. There can be a single portfolio for all subjects, or portfolios for specific subjects. The work contained in a portfolio then becomes an accurate representation of a student's progress. It may contain artwork by a student, but is not limited to artwork (A). It is not used to draw comparisons between students (B), nor is the project graded on a scale (C).

32. **D**

Questions can engage the students' attention (A), evaluate students' knowledge (B), and invite students to learn (C). Questions can also be used to help students discover new information and to practice or rehearse information.

33. **C**

To keep students on-task, it is very important to keep any distractions to a minimum, or else the instructional momentum will be lost. Always be sure to have enough copies of materials, and check to see if audio-visual equipment is working properly.

34. **C**

Body language is an effective way of avoiding digressions in class. This answer choice provides the best method of dealing with the disruptive behavior while maintaining the class momentum.

Checking to see if the pencil needs to be sharpened (A) and repeating the question to the students (D) disturb the class momentum. Allowing the student to sharpen the pencil (B) rewards the student's disruptive behavior.

35. **C**

Ignoring the behavior will deny the student the attention that is probably desired and will not interrupt the flow of the classroom. Misbehavior, however, should only be ignored when it is not affecting anyone in the class. Responding with a desist (A), reprimand (B), or taking the student out of the room (D) can interrupt the academic focus.

36. **C**

Although the student should seek counseling (D) and will eventually need to tell her mother what happened (A), the teacher's legal responsibility is to report the assault to the appropriate authorities. It would not be appropriate for the teacher to call the student's mother (B).

PLT Grades 5–9

Practice Test 2

This test is also on CD-ROM in our special interactive PRAXIS™ PLT 5–9 TEST*ware*®. It is highly recommended that you first take this exam on computer. You will then have the additional study features and benefits of enforced timed conditions and instantaneous, accurate scoring. See page 14 for instructions on how to get the most out of REA's TEST*ware*®.

Practice Test 2

Case Study I

Brian Huerta is a first-year teacher in a town of 30,000 in New York State. Brian was one of the top students in the teacher education department of his university. He is highly dedicated to both his students and to the school district where he is employed. Brian makes his instructional decisions based upon sound educational theory and research.

Brian is teaching sixth-grade. He has organized his classroom into a self-governing body that is conceptualized as "The Family." Each student has a "twin" of the same gender who serves as his/her thinking/working partner. Each pair of twins has a second pair of twins (either the same or opposite gender) with whom they make up a sib-group. Dividing "The Family" into sib-groups allows Brian to have stable heterogeneous cooperative groups of four, yet maintain the sense of class unity that the family metaphor provides.

At noon, Brian goes to the cafeteria for lunch. Brian knows that the cafeteria is serving Sloppy Joes today, which Brian does not like very much. He would prefer to spend the break in his room reading and drinking a diet soda, but he nevertheless takes a tray and joins his colleagues at the faculty table.

"How's the Family Man?" asks Tom Reynolds as he motions to the empty seat beside him.

Brian grins. He is growing used to the teasing of the older teachers who do not understand his use of the family metaphor as a classroom organizational framework. "The Family Man is rolling along," he says.

As they eat, Brian tells Melody Wilson, the choir teacher, that he is beginning a unit on South America soon. He asks her whether she might be able to incorporate some South American music into her curriculum during the next month. She tells him that she has several Latin American songs that she usually teaches later in the year, but that she can move them up and accommodate him. Although music is not an interest of his, Brian asks her to tell him what makes Hispanic music sound so different from the traditional American forms of music. Melody enters into a rather complicated discussion of Latin melodic structures. Brian nods and listens carefully.

When Tom Reynolds leaves, he says, "So long, Family Man," and Brian salutes him.

"I think this family thing you do is interesting," Melody tells Brian. "I'd like to know more about it."

On the first Wednesday of the South America unit, Brian loads all the students into a school minivan and drives them to the local library. Brian asks Betty Kelly, the librarian, to take eight of the students to the periodical section to teach them how to use the *Readers' Guide to Periodical Literature*. Brian takes the other eight students and teaches them how to use a computer-based book search. Brian and Betty then exchange students.

At the library, Brian shows the students how to find books and nonprint materials on the South American countries that they've been assigned. He helps his students select 14 books, two laser video discs, one software game that teaches Spanish, and the computer game "Where in the World is Carmen Sandiego?" Betty helps the students select 17 magazine articles about their South American countries.

At the front desk, a well-dressed woman bystander criticizes Brian's decision to allow the students to check out nonprint materials. She introduces herself as a retired English professor from a respected university. "You know, young man, it's no wonder that kids these days can't read. They ought to be checking out books and magazine articles exclusively. Checking out computer games and videos doesn't teach children to read. If we don't get back to the basics of reading and writing, we're going to become a Third World country. Teach the children to read. They have enough time to play at home, when our tax dollars aren't paying for it."

"I have an idea," says Brian to the class on the morning after the library visit. "What do you think about inviting parents to come to school the day that each group gives their presentation?"

The class discusses this idea at length. Although Marianne Griego is a developmentally-advanced, mature child who comes from a supportive, well-educated family, she leads the resistance to inviting the parents. Four other girls of varying degrees of maturity join Marianne's camp, but the majority vote to invite the parents.

Constructed-Response Items

1. Brian realizes that Marianne Griego and four other girls of varying degrees of maturity do not support inviting the parents. The majority of the class, however, votes to invite the parents to the group presentations. What else should Brian do about the situation? Give the steps he should use. Explain why you answered as you did.

2. The well-dressed bystander turns to leave the library, and then she comes back to the checkout desk. "What do you have to say for yourself, young man?" How should Brian answer? Why did you have Brian answer in that way?

3. One of Brian's students has been repeatedly playing practical jokes during the class. He has arranged a parent-teacher conference. During the conference what four objectives are most important for Mr. Huerta to achieve?

Case Study II

Gerene Thompson is a first-year teacher who has accepted a position as a fifth-grade science teacher in an inner-city school. In college, Gerene's teaching field was science. She is eager to begin working with her students. In the last week before school starts, Gerene has much to do in order to get ready for the first day of school.

Gerene is new to this geographic area in which she will be teaching. She has many questions and concerns about her first year of teaching, but she also has many high expectations.

In addition to teaching the students literacy skills, Gerene wants to teach them to enjoy science and mathematics. She particularly wants to teach her students about ways of collecting data, especially on living things; this is a skill required by the curriculum of the state. Gerene also wants to reinforce the notion of data collection by assigning a homework project that will involve the students' families.

Gerene brings in an experiment suggested on a website. She distributes to each student a sandwich bag with a colored dot to indicate its brand, but the class does not know the symbols. Gerene asks the students to fill their bags with their cafeteria lunch: one wrapped sandwich, one wrapped cookie, one orange, and a small bag of popcorn. Then she asks each student to hold the bag by its closed top and shake it vigorously 10 times. The students note on a chart the color of the bags that survive this shaking without tearing. The class can decide the best choice for the cafeteria considering the disposal, the environment, and the cost; they can share the findings with the community through an article in the local newspaper.

A mother of one of Gerene's students is a custodial worker at the school. Gerene mentions her plans to incorporate the families into the work in the classroom. The mother is dubious of how she can contribute to the instructional learning in the class.

The custodian also asks Gerene why she—a young woman with a full life ahead—is planning to work as a teacher of young children. The mother goes on to mention that she thinks some of the traits of good teachers involve a maturity that comes with age, compassion that comes only with having children of one's own, and the knowledge that can only come in later life. Gerene is eager to explain the traits that she thinks are most important to a teacher, but she does not have a chance to do so because the principal pages the custodian to come to the office for a phone call. Gerene continues to think about these characteristics as she unloads some materials from her car.

Gerene plans to use groups for some of the data collection. She plans to have the groups present their findings to the class. Gerene will use the following form to assess the group presentations.

> Did the group demonstrate:
>
> 1. Higher level thinking skills? How?
>
> 2. Ability to use technology? How?
>
> 3. Involvement of all members? How?
>
> 4. Use of in-school resources? Which?
>
> 5. Use of community resources? Which?
>
> 6. Evidence of problem-solving skills? How?
>
> 7. Which of these should I target next time?

Gerene is aware that all the students in her class are not on the same level. If she believes the test results and the grades that she sees in the cumulative folders, some will be unable to read the fifth-grade textbook. Gerene knows that she can expect in her classroom students who perform at various rates, who are on a variety of levels, and who have many learning styles.

In addition to these differences, some of the children do not speak English except as a second language; one child does not speak English at all, and Gerene is concerned about how she can teach this child. Gerene is unsure how she can begin to meet the instructional, social, and emotional needs of these individual students in her class. She plans to talk later with Mrs. Breen about this situation. Mrs. Breen has been a teacher at the school for many years, and Gerene will ask her specifically about how she accommodates the non-English speaking students in her classroom.

Gerene plans to visit in the home of each student—with the permission of the principal and of the family—and talk with the primary caregivers about the strengths and needs of each student. Gerene believes that she will be able to meet the diverse needs of each student better if she has as much information as possible at her disposal. She also hopes that she can improve the relationship between the home and the school with such visits.

Gerene is aware that the school does not group homogeneously. In fact, the predominant practice in the entire district is to use heterogeneous grouping, and Gerene will do her best to meet the needs of all of her students. As a first-year teacher, Gerene has never taught in a school that uses ability grouping. She is not sure of her position on the subject, but she assumes that the school has researched the possible options carefully. She assumes that the parents are pleased with the progress of their students in the heterogeneously-grouped classes, but she will be able to talk with them further about this as she visits with them in their homes or at the parent-teacher conferences.

Constructed-Response Items

4. Many schools group students by ability, feeling that this provides the best environment for bright students to excel and remedial students to gain the skills they need to succeed. Many feel, however, that ability grouping prevents some students from reaching their full potential.

    Assignment: Are you in favor of ability grouping? Explain your position by discussing the positive or negative consequences of ability grouping for students and teachers.

5. What specific characteristics do you think a person must possess in order to be an effective teacher? Fully explain each characteristic and show how the absence of each will reduce effectiveness in the classroom.

6. Gerene does talk with the veteran teacher, Mrs. Breen; Gerene however, is unsure of Mrs. Breen's strategy. To surmount the fact that many students speak English as a second language, Mrs. Breen has decided not to allow any use of a language other than English in the classroom. She has prepared a letter to send home to tell the parents that no language other than English will be used during the day in her class; she also recommends that the family begin to speak only English at home and that the family members begin to exclude parts of their culture that might distinguish them from other people in the community. Mrs. Breen asks you—her fellow teacher—to read the letter and comment on how you think the students and their families might receive this information. She also asks for ways you think she might deal with the problem of multiculturalism in her classes.

Case Study III

Mrs. Doe began planning a two-week unit of study of the Native Americans for her fifth-grade class. She began the unit by placing a K-W-L chart on the board. She allowed the students to share facts that they already knew—or thought that they knew—about Native Americans; as they told the class these facts, Mrs. Doe wrote them on the chart. She then showed them a movie on the twenty-first century Native American. After showing the movie to the class, Mrs. Doe asked the class what they learned from the movie and asked them to correct any information that they had previously listed that might be in error. As Mrs. Doe reflectively listened, she asked key questions to her class.

The following day Mrs. Doe reviewed the use of encyclopedias, indexes, and atlases. She divided the students into groups and took them to the library. Each group was responsible for locating information on their topic. The topics were maps showing the typography of the land; a map showing migration routes, a map showing the general areas where the Native Americans settled; and charts illustrating the climate, plants, and animals.

The class spent days 3 and 4 with each group being involved in library research. They wrote their information on index cards. Each group prepared a presentation that included a written explanation of an assigned topic, a shadow box, a sawdust map, or models of Native American clothing. A pictograph was to be used in the telling of a legend or folk story. The presentation was concluded with a collage depicting the Native American way of life.

On day 8, Mrs. Doe arranged a display of Native American artifacts and crafts in the hallway. Having collaborated with the music teacher at the onset of her planning and arranging for a general assembly of the entire student body, she took her students to the auditorium. The general assembly consisted of Native American poetry read by Fawn Lonewolf with Native American music and dance performed by the school chorus. At the conclusion of the assembly, Mrs. Doe invited the class to view the video *The Trail of Tears.* The students helped serve the Native American refreshments, including fried bread. As the students ate, the reading teacher orally read *Knots on a Counting Rope.* Following the reading, the physical education teacher taught the students several games that Native American children played.

Day 10 of the unit was Field Trip Day. The students had a choice of visiting museums. Whatever the student's choice, he or she was to take notes of what they saw, heard, and experienced. They would share this information with the remainder of the class on the following day.

Mrs. Doe found that one of the newly-formed community museums specializing in Native American culture needed some volunteers because they did not have the funds to pay attendants to work a full day. Because they could not keep the museum open very long, they could not take in admissions to increase the hours of operation; the community museum was facing closing despite the interest by visitors to the community during peak tourist days.

Mrs. Doe has the idea to enlist the help of her students in working at the museum as a community service project. She believes that the students have some of the knowledge necessary to participate in the work at the museum and that they can contribute to the experience of visitors to the facility; furthermore, she believes that the students can gain some knowledge and skills in this work that may help them in their knowledge of Native Americans and in their future employment. Mrs. Doe hopes to allow the students to receive credit toward their course for this work that they do on Saturdays, in the afternoons, and on holidays. She realizes, however, that she must secure the approval of the parents, the principal, and, most importantly, the students themselves.

To further complicate the issue, Mrs. Doe knows that many of the churches are planning pageants for the upcoming religious season. She wonders if she should assign homework of any sort or community service experience for the students in her class because of the season of the year. She also begins to wonder about the difference between the purposes of homework and community service projects. She decides to talk with the principal about these matters. Mrs. Doe believes that the principal knows the parents and the community better than she; after all, she is a newcomer to the area and the principal has served the school for more than ten years. Mrs. Doe hopes that the principal can help her make a good decision on the issue of homework, can advise her on district policy, and can suggest whether she needs the input of parents and students on the matter.

After talking with the principal, Mrs. Doe believes that she was able to make a good decision on the question of whether to assign homework and how much is appropriate.

Constructed-Response Items

7. Mrs. Doe is concerned about homework. Explain your philosophy of homework.

8. Mrs. Doe is initiating a community service project in her class. Many leaders have suggested over the last few years that schools should require all young people to serve the public in some way for a period of time each year that they are in school. The service might be within the school or it might be in the community.

    Assignment: Do you agree or disagree with the idea of community service that Mrs. Doe is considering? Support your opinion with specific examples from history, current events, literature, or personal experience.

9. Mrs. Doe finds that two families are unwilling to have their students go on the field trip for religious reasons. Mrs. Doe must decide how to deal with these two students on the day of the field trip. How can she best provide for them?

Case Study IV

Mr. Juan Pesaro is a new sixth-grade teacher at a local school in a medium-sized town; he has just moved to the western section of the country. Prior to living here, he was a resident of the South and was a product of the public school system in a small Southern town; for the last four years he has lived in the dormitory on the campus of a state university and graduated with a B. A. from the university, where he majored in education. This is his first year teaching and his first year living on his own.

Juan was shopping for groceries early on a Saturday morning when he had several encounters with parents. School had only been in session for three weeks when he met these parents in the aisles of the local market. By the time he left the supermarket, he was beginning to wonder if he should change his shopping place and time of shopping in the future.

First, Mrs. Hammett introduced herself to him as he shopped in the produce department. She emphatically announced to him in a voice loud enough to be heard by all in the vicinity: "You are the worst teacher that my Phillippe has ever had. He has never made such low grades before. I am planning a trip to the superintendent's office to demand that you lose your job. First, however, I intend to visit the principal and make your life miserable. I do not intend for Phillippe to have such low marks on his record, and I do not want him to be taught by such a non-qualified teacher. It is your first year, I hear, and I am sorry for the children in your class. You will not be teaching them long, however, and you certainly will not be teaching my child because I have connections. You can expect to hear more from me in the few days as a teacher that you have left."

Mr. Pesaro had barely taken a breath after his response to her when another woman came up to her and introduced herself. "I am Amy Goodwin. Mrs. Hammett just told me you are a teacher of the sixth-grade class. I hope you are not too upset about her remarks. I know all about Mrs. Hammett and about her son. I am, after all, her next-door neighbor so I know what I am talking about. For one thing, she talks too much, doesn't she? Phillippe has a learning disability. His mother always blames the teacher for any problems. Watch out! She may blame you next!"

What kind of difficulties have you had with Phillippe? What do you think his problem is? I have my own ideas about both him and his mother; I think his mother is to blame for most of the troubles that Phillippe is experiencing both in and out of school. Can you imagine living with that woman?"

"I'll be glad to come over to your office and talk with you and the principal about Mrs. Hammett. I may be able to help you. I know the principal, and I may be able to explain to her about how Mrs. Hammett came up to you and made a scene here in the grocery store."

"Do you live near here? Are you interested in a social life in this new town? If so, I may be able to help you. I am a single parent, but I am never too busy to have a good time. I know some of the best night spots to relax and meet people."

After his reply to Amy Goodwin, Mr. Pesaro was just beginning to think he would be able to get his milk and go to the counter to pay when another adult spoke to him.

"I am Maggie Jones, Margelo's aunt; Margelo is a student in your class. Margelo lives with me now. Her parents separated last year, and Margelo has lived with me ever since her mother left the area for a job in Utah. I want to do what is right by Margelo, but I have never had a child and I am in my late 40s. I hope to help her, and I want her to do her best. I want to keep up with what is going on in school with her. How can I stay abreast of what your class is studying in school? How is she doing? What can I do to help her at home?"

Mr. Pesaro gives an appropriate response to Margelo's aunt and moves quickly to the last counter: the refrigerated counter with the milk and dairy products. He goes from there to the checkout counter. Mr. Pesaro finally manages to pay for his groceries and get to the car without any other adult approaching him.

Constructed-Response Items

10. How should Juan Pesaro respond to 1) Mrs. Hammett's concerns about Phillippe's performance in the classroom and 2) her threats to visit the superintendent and demand that Mr. Pesaro lose his job?

11. How should Mr. Pesaro reply to Mrs. Goodwin's comments about Mrs. Hammett and particularly about Phillippe?

12. What should Mr. Pesaro say to Margelo's aunt about 1) keeping abreast of what the class is studying and 2) helping the student at home?

Multiple-Choice Questions

13. What is the self-fulfilling prophecy?

    (A) Students produce work that matches their personal expectations.

    (B) Teachers can predict student progress.

    (C) Incorrect assumptions or beliefs become true because they are expected.

    (D) Students are unable to understand teacher expectations.

14. How should learning activities be designed?

    (A) They should be selected by the students.

    (B) The activities should be based on specific objectives.

    (C) They should test for knowledge.

    (D) They should be utilized on a daily basis.

15. Canter and Canter's assertive discipline asserts that positive behavior should be

    (A) the standard.

    (B) positively reinforced.

    (C) part of the classroom rules.

    (D) not met with consequences.

16. One benefit of using transition statements is that

    (A) students are oriented to the classroom pace.

    (B) non-performers are being tested.

    (C) it enables high-order questioning.

    (D) it determines if students understand the directions.

17. "I" messages are a means of communicating effectively, especially in situations where confrontation is necessary or conflict is possible. "I" messages

   (A) require eye contact.

   (B) are statements beginning with the word "I" where the speaker states his or her thoughts and feelings.

   (C) are statements beginning with the word "I" where the speaker states his or her goals and expectations.

   (D) are incomplete messages where the speaker states, "I want..." and lets the other party complete the sentence.

18. A teacher asks his students to name great Americans who have made significant contributions to American culture. As students start calling out names of people, the teacher notices that all the names are those of white men. The teacher then

   (A) chastises the students for their bigotry.

   (B) adds the names of some men and women who are minorities to the list.

   (C) asks the students to think of some women and people who are minorities to add to the list.

   (D) asks the students if they have ever heard of Dr. Martin Luther King, Jr.

19. As the teacher distributes a test to the class, the best statement to make is

   (A) "Students, I believe that you all are well-prepared for the test. I am confident that you will do your best."

   (B) "Students, this is the hardest test I've ever given my students, so you must really work hard."

   (C) "The last time I gave this test, no one passed. I'll be surprised if this class can do better."

   (D) "Students, I doubt if anyone will be able to complete this test in the time allowed."

20. In selecting materials for a heterogenous class, the effective teacher will look at

    (A) the ratio of pictures to text.

    (B) the size of the font used.

    (C) if the material can hold the attention of learners of all types.

    (D) the size of the material.

21. Students generally like teachers who

    I.   have a sense of humor.

    II. are perceived as being fair.

    III. are perceived as liking students.

    IV. are perceived as being hard workers.

    (A) I only.   (C) I, II, and III only.

    (B) I, II, III, and IV.   (D) I and IV only.

22. Which of the following situations is the best example of providing a sexually nonbiased curriculum?

    (A) Teacher A always tells the girls in her ninth-grade classroom that they can successfully compete with the boys at any level and they should strive to accomplish anything they want.

    (B) Teacher B faithfully devotes the month of March to Women's History Month and teaches only about women during that time.

    (C) Teacher C has instituted a new unit of study entitled "Uncommon Women" that includes the study of famous women writers, politicians, and athletes.

    (D) Teacher D has changed science textbooks recently, and is now incorporating the contributions of women scientists throughout his lectures and supplemental readings.

23. Which of the following communication behaviors are determined by cultural expectations?

    I.   Eye contact   III. Emphasis on high grades

    II. Silence   IV.   Leadership roles

    (A) I and II only.   (C) I, II, and IV only.

    (B) III and IV only.   (D) I, II, III, and IV.

24. An effective way to check students' understanding of directions or an assignment is to

    (A) ask, "Does everyone understand?"

    (B) ask, "Are there any questions?"

    (C) say, "Student Name, do you know what you're supposed to do?"

    (D) move around the room and check to make sure that everyone has started the assignment and is doing it correctly.

25. Refusing to grant points due to misbehavior in a classroom where the teacher gives students points for positive behavior is a form of

    (A) withholding reinforcement.

    (B) positive reinforcement.

    (C) reinforce-ignore strategy.

    (D) averting control.

26. Which of the following teacher responses is a more specific response to a student who has given the correct answer?

    (A) "Patty, that answer shows that you have been doing your homework. You have mastered the conversion of fractions into percents!"

    (B) "Kelly, what a fantastic answer! Congratulations on your hard work!"

    (C) "That is a most ingenuous response, Alexis. I had never thought of that before."

    (D) "How did you ever come up with that answer, Maria? That's good work!"

27. Working one-to-one with a student at any age is a nearly perfect example of

    (A) instruction.

    (C) motivation.

    (B) strategy.

    (D) guided practice.

28. A student was causing disruptions, but only during the middle of the day. When the teacher changed the student's seat to one closer to the door and away from the window, the disruptions ceased. What could have caused the change?

    (A) The teacher did not appear to be as loud.

    (B) The student grew out of a phase.

    (C) The student was distracted by the recess activities he/she observed outside.

    (D) The student did not like the subject being taught.

29. A teacher has a routine for distributing papers to the class, for having students get their books, and for writing on the board. The routine is one way the teacher demonstrates that he or she

    (A) uses class time efficiently.

    (B) has good problem-solving skills.

    (C) is a rigid and unreasonable teacher.

    (D) expects his/her students to do their best.

30. Assertive Discipline involves all of the following EXCEPT that

    (A) the students establish clear guidelines for their behavior.

    (B) the teacher creates and establishes clearly defined rules.

    (C) the teacher establishes clear consequences for violating the rules.

    (D) the teacher establishes a reward for appropriate behavior.

31. Recent research on the relationship of time and student learning defined engaged time. Which definition is correct?

    (A) Engaged time is that part of allocated time in which students are actively involved with academic subject matter.

    (B) Engaged time is the amount of time a student spends in independent study.

(C) Engaged time is the amount of time allocated for each subject, for example, 45 minutes for math.

(D) Engaged time is the allocated time in which students are involved with academic subject matter and have a high rate of success (80% or higher).

32. Which of the following two arguments accurately supports the use of *cooperative learning* as an effective method of instruction?

    I.   Cooperative learning groups facilitate healthy competition between individuals in the group.

    II.   Cooperative learning groups allow academic achievers to carry or cover for academic underachievers.

    III.   Cooperative learning groups make each student in the group accountable for the success of the group.

    IV.   Cooperative learning groups make it possible for students to reward other group members for achieving.

(A) I and II.   (C) I and III.

(B) II and III.   (D) III and IV.

33. After asking a question, the amount of time a teacher waits for a response should

(A) depend on how uncomfortable and humiliated the student may appear to be.

(B) bring a negative response from the student called on to answer.

(C) serve to stimulate improved student responses.

(D) not vary according to the student's intellectual ability.

34. If there is a tornado warning, your class should be

(A) evacuated from the building.

(B) on the top level of the building.

(C) in your classroom.

(D) in a first-floor room away from windows.

35. The time needed to learn is a consideration in mastery instruction. Another factor to consider is

    (A) teacher's attitude.   (C) student's characteristics.

    (B) school environment.   (D) teacher's knowledge.

36. Segregation that occurs as a result of school policies, laws, or government actions is

    (A) de jure segregation.   (C) integration.

    (B) controlled choice.   (D) semi-integration.

Answer Key

1.	(*)	13.	(C)	25.	(A)
2.	(*)	14.	(B)	26.	(A)
3.	(*)	15.	(B)	27.	(D)
4.	(*)	16.	(A)	28.	(C)
5.	(*)	17.	(B)	29.	(A)
6.	(*)	18.	(C)	30.	(A)
7.	(*)	19.	(A)	31.	(A)
8.	(*)	20.	(C)	32.	(D)
9.	(*)	21.	(B)	33.	(C)
10.	(*)	22.	(D)	34.	(D)
11.	(*)	23.	(D)	35.	(C)
12.	(*)	24.	(D)	36.	(A)

*Constructed-Response Item. See sample essays in Detailed Explanations of Answers section.

Detailed Explanations of Answers

PLT 5-9

PRACTICE TEST 2

Case Study I

Constructed-Response Items

1. **Essay 1**

Brian needs to investigate the thoughts and feelings of his students, determine the social relationships among those he teaches, and motivate his class about their research in order to enhance learning.

First, Brian should find out why the five girls did not want parents to attend the presentations. He will first of all want to talk with the girls individually to try to find out their reason for not wanting their parents in attendance. The answer may be simple; for instance, their parents may have to work, and they fear that they will be left out. The reasons may be even deeper, however. Perhaps the girls do not have a traditional family situation; they may not want their friends to know that they live with grandparents, instead of with parents. Perhaps they have foster parents. Perhaps they have a fear of performing in public. The best way to find out may be to ask directly.

The second step, after Brian asks the students about their primary reasons for not wanting the parents in attendance, is to get everyone—even the students who were originally not in favor of the audience—to work together on the event. Trying to involve everyone in the event may help with the social relationships in the class.

A third step is to emphasize the importance of the sharing of the research with other people. Brian can even suggest recording the event with the use of a video camera so that other classes and groups can profit from their work. Hopefully this enthusiasm from the teachers, parents, and others in the class will increase the motivation of everyone in the class.

I think it is important for Brian to find out as much as possible about the sociology of the classroom, to understand the "whole student," and to emphasize the importance of the research that his class has done. Only when Brian understands the students he teaches and the networking within his classroom can he motivate and teach most effectively.

Essay 1 Analysis

This essay would receive a score of 2.

This essay is an exemplary response to question one because it responds with specifically detailed answers directly to the question at issue. The essay describes 1) what Brian should do about the situation, 2) the steps he should use, and 3) why the writer responded as he/she did.

The thesis is clearly stated: "Brian needs to investigate the thoughts and feelings of his students, determine the social relationships among those he teaches, and motivate his class about their research."

The language is accurate and articulate. The steps and central ideas are clear. The writer suggests professional actions for Brian and demonstrates a sense of purpose. The essay is proficiently written.

Essay 2

Brian should call the students who protest attendance by the parents into a group. He should ask them the reasons for their opposition. Brian should tell them that the class has voted and that he expects no more discussion of the issue. The majority has ruled, and he wants to hear nothing further.

Brian should take control of the situation and should exert his authority as teacher. This should end the matter.

Essay 2 Analysis

This essay would receive a score of 1.

Essay 2 presents an authoritarian view. The teacher TELLS the students what they must do. Even though the writer does suggest that Brian should ask the students who protest the attendance of parents the reason for their actions, the writer suggests that Brian should ask for this information in a group setting; it does not seem that Brian can get all the details in such an atmosphere.

The essay does not really answer the question about the steps Brian should use—except to say that he should TELL the students what to do. The only explanation as to why the writer answers as he/she did is that the teacher "should exert his authority" and "end the matter."

The essay, then, does not answer all the questions adequately and presents a very authoritarian—not really professional—view of the matter. The essay is simplistic. The essay is weak in organization and structure. It is not as conceptually strong as Essay 1.

Essay 3

It's not unusual for folks to disagree over issues. These girls seem set in their ways. This happened at our church. One group wanted a new church auditorium. The other group wanted to build a new gymnasium instead. The final outcomes were that our church divided and a new church was built down the street with a big gymnasium. Our church now has a big auditorium, but there are not enough people to fill it up. The message is obvious.

Essay 3 Analysis

This essay would receive a score of 0.

The writer has ignored the questions on 1) what Brian should do about the situation, 2) the steps he should use, and 3) why the writer answered as he/she did. Instead of answering the questions asked, the writer answers on a totally different tangent. He/she begins to discuss a situation in his/her church.

Even though the writer tells us, "The message is obvious," the relationship between the church breakup and the steps the teacher should use to help the children who object to presenting research in front of visitors may not really be so obvious. The whole point of the treatise is not clear.

Because the organization is poor, the structure unsound, and the whole question unanswered, the essay is inadequate in all respects.

2.   Essay 1

Brian should respond by stating the following: "Thank you for asking me about my work with students. Like you, I believe reading is extremely important. We are doing better with education today than ever before, but we can use all the help we can get. We in education always appreciate the interest of others."

"Most people do not realize that only about 30% graduated from schools in the 1930s. We have only just about reversed these figures—we have only about 30% NOT graduating today. I love to remind others of these wonderful statistics. They make me proud."

"These games that I am checking out all involve reading. They are a wonderful way to motivate some of my students who might have been dropouts in a previous decade. Could you come by my class? I would love to show you how the games work sometime after school. Why don't you call me sometime and set up an agreeable time for both of us? In fact, our school could probably use your help with our after school homework program. We can talk more about that when you come."

Essay 1 Analysis

This essay would receive a score of 2.

The writer has done an exceptional job in answering the woman in the library. He was able to stay calm and interested; this was a good public relations tactic. He cleared up some misconceptions—but only after the woman asked for his opinion. He was able to perhaps gain a volunteer for the school and to demonstrate his own knowledge, his belief in the importance of reading, and indicate the educational significance of the audio-visual materials he was checking out of the library.

The answer is clear and to the point. The speaker was able to present his points quickly without seeming to lecture. What a good representative the school has in Brian!

Essay 2

Brian should respond by stating the following: "One of the disadvantages of teaching is that everyone thinks he/she can do it and likes to give advice. I have trained for four years to teach, and I do not like to hear anyone bad mouth education and me—especially in front of my students."

"I am busy now. I have a group of students I must supervise. I do not have time to talk with you further now. I can meet with you by appointment with my principal in attendance whenever you care to set up a time through the school office."

Essay 2 Analysis

This essay would receive a score of 1.

Although the answer is a well-structured one, the response that Brian gives is not an acceptable one. He has succeeded in alienating a member of the community and has done so before the library staff and his students. Whereas the first respondent has succeeded in perhaps recruiting a volunteer for the schools, the second respondent has created an enemy—in the presence of witnesses. This answer is inappropriate and unacceptable.

Essay 3

Brian should respond by stating the following: "You are right. Our kids can't read. We are ending up entertaining them. The schools are doing a worse job than in the past. The kids I often am expected to teach should not have been passed and should not be in my grade. If I did not have these audio-visual materials to help me, I would not even be able to keep some of them quiet during the day."

Essay 3 Analysis

This essay would receive a score of 0.

This response to the question does not alienate the woman in the library, but it is unacceptable because it perpetuates some misinformation about the school system and education. Brian, in this response, has not corrected the belief that the schools are performing more poorly than ever before. He has failed to explain his use of the materials he is securing, and he succeeds in speaking negatively about the teachers, the students, and the school system.

The content is totally unacceptable. This response is not one of a professional educator.

3.   ## Essay 1

The four most important objectives, in my opinion, for Brian to achieve during the conference are to (1) list the practical jokes that the student has played, (2) impress on the parents the concern that the teacher has for the safety of students, (3) make sure that the parents know that the student is disrespectful of others and disruptive in the classroom, and (4) how to stop the student from continuing to play the jokes. Hopefully the parents will, at this point, promise to talk with the student and work with the school on preventing the continuation of the problem.

Essay 1 Analysis

This essay would receive a score of 2.

The writer has certainly communicated the four major purposes that he/she would like to achieve during the conference. The writer has used good sentence structure and has structured the essay in a logical way. This essay is highly acceptable.

Essay 2

The teacher should certainly hold a conference if a letter home does not work. It is essential that the parents know what is going on at school. I would suggest that the teacher send a letter for the parent to sign. This signed letter will release the teacher from any responsibility if a child is hurt in the classroom. I would suggest sending the letter home first. If the situation continues after the parents receive the letter, I would suggest a phone call.

Essay 2 Analysis

This essay would receive a score of 1.

This essay, though well-structured and containing good grammar and punctuation, is not acceptable. The essay does not answer the question: what four objectives are most important for Brian to achieve during the conference? The writer fails to answer the question.

Essay 3

The four most important objectives for Brian to achieve during the conference are: being sure the principal knows what's going on, making sure that the principal attends the conference, being sure that the teacher is released from any blame if a child is hurt, and letting the parents know what is going on.

Essay 3 Analysis

This essay would receive a score of 0.

Essay 3 is not suitable. The writer is primarily concerned with the teacher—not with the students. Letting the principal know what is going on, getting the principal to the conference, releasing the teacher from any responsibility, and letting the parents know what is going on are the four things this writer wants to achieve. Notice there is no mention of solving the problem and ensuring the well-being of the students.

Case Study II

Constructed-Response Items

4. ### Essay 1

    The practice of grouping students by ability in the elementary school has negative social and academic consequences for students. The negative effects of ability grouping overshadow the few positive benefits that may be derived from this practice. Grouping by ability may be appropriate for certain subjects, such as reading, within a particular classroom as long as the group membership changes for instruction in other subjects. However, I feel that grouping by ability is an inappropriate practice at the elementary school level if all students remain in that group throughout the day.

One of the negative effects of ability grouping is that it contributes to the development of a poor self-image for many students. Children of all ages are very adept at recognizing and correctly identifying high-, middle- and low-ability groups. Assigning non-threatening names to the groups has no effect on children's ability to identify these groups. This is apparent when observing or talking with students in schools that use ability grouping. It does not matter whether the teacher calls the top group "Red Birds," "Group 3," "Triangles," or "Mrs. Smith's class," students are keenly aware of their membership in the group and the perceived ability of that group.

Students make comparisons among the ways teachers interact with different groups, the types of assignments groups receive, and the privileges different groups enjoy. Students in the high-ability group may look down on other students and may refer to students in other groups as "stupid" or "dumb." Name-calling may result. Students in the low-ability group may resent their placement in that group. Students in the middle-ability group may feel ignored or may even resent being labeled "average." The naturally occurring friction among the groups creates a climate in which teachers will have difficulty building positive self-images for all students.

Ability grouping also necessarily limits peer interaction, both in and out of the classroom. Elementary students need to interact with many students to develop mature social and intellectual skills.

An additional negative effect of ability grouping is the stilted instructional environment that is created within the classroom. Teachers of high-ability students are encouraged to feel privileged to teach this group and usually prepare creative, challenging lessons. Teachers of the low-ability group may provide many drill and practice worksheets. The result of these practices is that only the high-ability students are challenged to work to their capacity.

The negative consequences of ability grouping are experienced by students of all ability levels. For these reasons, the practice of ability grouping in the elementary school should be abandoned.

Essay 1 Analysis

This essay would receive a score of 2.

This essay addresses the topic directly. The topic of ability grouping is narrowed in the first sentence to the use of this practice in elementary school. The author's point of view and the focus of the essay (the negative social and academic consequences) are also established in the first sentence. Specific negative effects are named and briefly discussed. The last paragraph restates the author's point of view.

Several sentences in the essay are wordy and seem to ramble. Some of the issues raised (peer interaction) are not fully discussed. The author mentions the "positive benefits" of ability grouping but does not specifically name or discuss the benefits. However, the author demonstrates the ability to state a topic clearly and present a specific point of view.

Essay 2

Most teachers prefer ability grouping. I know I would. Ability grouping allows teachers to plan assignments for specific groups of students. In this way, teachers can make assignments fit the needs of specific groups of students, instead of just making one assignment for everybody. Teachers can spend additional time helping slower students because the advanced group will be able to complete their assignments independently. Teachers can also give the advanced students extra work or projects to keep them busy. This gives the teachers more time to work with students who really need help.

Schools that group by ability can plan smaller classes for slow students and larger classes for average and advanced students. This is better for the students because those who really need extra help have a better chance of receiving it. Smaller classes for slow students also helps the teachers give more attention to slow students.

Ability grouping is especially important in math and reading because these subjects give many students difficulty.

Essay 2 Analysis

This essay would receive a score of 1.

Although the essay is satisfactory given the time limit, it is flawed for several reasons. The major error is the lack of a controlling central idea or theme. The topic stated in the first sentence, that most teachers prefer ability grouping, is never fully developed. Instead of developing this topic, the writer discusses the advantages of small classes for slower students. The last two paragraphs seem tacked on and are not smoothly connected to the first paragraph.

Essay 3

Ability grouping is terrible. It's awful to be in the slow group because everybody in the whole school knows it. Average students don't like ability grouping either because teachers don't pay any attention to them. Only the smart kids receive any attention. Even then it only shows how different they are. Some kids in the slow class like it because they never have homework and the teachers don't expect them to finish assignments; they get lots of time in class to do everything.

I observed in a school that has ability grouping, and I would not want to teach there. They would probably assign a new teacher to the slow class.

Essay 3 Analysis

This essay would receive a score of 0.

This essay does discuss the topic, but the opinions stated are never developed. Although the writer gives several specific examples to support his/her point of view (that ability grouping is terrible), he/she does not develop any of these examples so that the reader can understand the reasons behind his/her conclusions.

5.   Essay 1

When I think of what specific characteristics a person must possess in order to be an effective teacher, I think of these characteristics: upstanding values, compassion, and a thorough knowledge of their subject matter.

First, people who become teachers must keep in mind that they are a role model to the children in their midst. Their private and professional life must be beyond reproach. A teacher is responsible for setting values as well as teaching values. A teacher has a big influence on a child's life; therefore, a teacher must be careful about the kinds of signals he/she sends out to the children. Today, it is hard to tell teachers from students because they dress alike, wear their hair alike, associate together, and act the same. A teacher should set him/herself apart if he/she is to be a positive influence on the students he/she encounters. Once a teacher loses his/her credibility and/or self-respect, he/she is no longer effective in the classroom.

Compassion is a quality that allows a teacher to have a sense of humor, get to know students' qualities, and be supportive of students' efforts. A teacher must be able to laugh with his/her students. This creates a relationship between learner and teacher, shows the students that the teacher has a human side, and tells the students that the teacher is approachable. A good teacher will get to know each of his/her student's learning abilities and styles. This will allow the teacher to get the most from each student. Compassion allows the teacher to empathize with the students who are having problems in school or at home by being supportive and by providing a positive direction. Students can be turned off if they perceive that a teacher does not care.

Finally, if a person is going to be an effective teacher, he/she must have a thorough knowledge of his discipline. This gives the teacher a sense of confidence and allows the teacher to be well organized. An effective teacher knows and likes what he/she teaches, and the enthusiasm will show and will become a part of the students. Without a good mastery of the subject matter, a teacher is unable to make well-informed decisions about objectives to be covered.

In conclusion, by possessing and demonstrating upstanding values, showing compassion, and exhibiting a thorough knowledge of his/her subject area, the right person can make a good teacher. If students are to learn, they must be influenced by persons who have all three of these characteristics.

Essay 1 Analysis

This essay would receive a score of 2.

This essay is well written, as evidenced by the clarity, organization, and mature language.

The writer adequately introduces the topic "Characteristics of an Effective Teacher" by outlining the three characteristics to be discussed. Each of the three paragraphs of the body contains a characteristic as the main idea and details to explain and/or support it. The conclusion is a summary of the essay and an explanation of why these characteristics are important. The reader should have no difficulty understanding the message the writer is conveying.

Essay 2

An effective teacher must have the following characteristics: dedication, knowledge of the subject matter, and versatility. A dedicated teacher is one who is always willing to go that extra mile to help a student to learn. A dedicated teacher is not one who is just looking for a paycheck every other week. This type of teacher will find the students' weaknesses and start building on those points day-by-day. A dedicated teacher is also a caring person who will help build confidence in students' ability to learn. Without this type of dedication, there will be a decrease in effective teaching because if the teacher does not show his/her dedication and concern for the students to learn the material, then the students will not reflect that initiative to learn.

Teachers must be knowledgeable in the subject areas that they are teaching. Teachers with more formal education, teaching experience, and hours of training are more successful in helping students achieve educational goals. Now, without this knowledge and education, there will be a reduction in the effective teaching method. Teachers who do not know the academic subject that they are teaching cannot make clear presentations or use effective teaching strategies. They cannot answer questions fully and must be very evasive in their answers.

Another characteristic that a teacher must possess is the versatility to teach slower and advanced learners in a manner that both will be able to receive and retain the given information. A teacher must be able to make the subject matter come alive, demand quality work meeting personal as well as academic needs of students, and add humor to the classroom. With the absence of this versatility, a teacher will only reach a small number of students in the classroom.

All of the above characteristics are important. Teachers who do not possess them will have difficulty reaching their students, and the drop-out rate will continue to climb.

Essay 2 Analysis

This essay would receive a score of 1.

The writer of this essay addresses the topic well, and the essay is without major errors. Nevertheless, the essay lacks clarity in organization and presentation of ideas. No introductory paragraph exists. This is very important because the introductory paragraph sets parameters for the remaining parts of the essay. The writer, in this case, combined the introduction and the first paragraph of the body. The introduction should have read: "A teacher must have the following characteristics in order to be effective: dedication, knowledge of subject matter, and versatility." In earlier years, a one-sentence paragraph was not allowed. That, however, is no longer true; "A dedicated teacher..." should have been the beginning of the next paragraph.

The remaining paragraphs are well organized. Each is introduced by a characteristic (the main idea), and that characteristic is explained and supported by adequate details. However, a bit of ambiguity exists in paragraph three: "A teacher must be able to make the subject matter come alive, demand quality work meeting personal as well as academic needs of students and adding humor to the classroom."

Some awkward expressions exist throughout the essay, but considering the time factor, this essay is considered adequate.

Essay 3

If you pick up a newspaper, turn on your radio, you will hear, see, and read about the decline of education. Discipline is a problem, test scores are down, and the teacher is being slained. Society has asked the perplexing question: What makes an effective classroom teacher?

First, to become an effective classroom teacher, there has to be an internal love within self, along with external love of the art of teaching. Secondly, devotion, dedication, and discipline among self and the environment in which you are entering will demonstrate the first procedure of effectiveness in the classroom and set up the essential elements involved in teaching. Thirdly, carrying the three "P's" in your heart will produce an effective classroom teacher, being "Proud" of what you are, being "Patient" with whom you are teaching, and being "Persistent" in what you are teaching. Finally, I think the most effective characteristics of an effective classroom teacher, are staying beyond your paid time, getting emotionally involved with your students after your paid time, living beyond the classroom, and the ability to cope with the stress of the educational process before your paid time. In order to endure effectiveness, there is long-suffering, perservance, and understanding any situation at any given moment to entitle all children to a worthwhile education of an effective classroom teacher.

Essay 3 Analysis

This essay would receive a score of 0.

The writer of this essay partially addresses the topic, but the essay itself is totally unacceptable. The initial paragraph, which should have outlined the characteristics to be discussed, leads one to believe that the essay will address "decline of education," "test scores," and "slained teachers." To identify problems that demand effective teachers is an acceptable way to introduce the topic, but the writer of this essay does it very poorly. Additionally, the past participle of slay is slain, not slained.

The writer does present the characteristics of an effective teacher, but these characteristics are all contained in one paragraph, and they are very unclear due to poor word choice, ambiguous expressions (awkward), and poor sentence structure. Three paragraphs should have been used, one for each characteristic; and each should have contained details to explain and support the characteristic.

This essay is filled with awkward expressions that suggest an inability to effectively use the language: "decline of education, internal love within self," "external love of the art of teaching," "demonstrate the first procedure of effectiveness in the classroom," "set up the essential elements," "staying beyond your paid time," and others.

The writer excessively uses "you" and "your"—second person. Essays should be written in the third person—he, she, or they. For example, the noun "teacher" or "teachers" should have been used as well. Third person creates a more scholarly essay.

6.   Essay 1

Expecting students and the family to give up their culture and their language in entirety is unreasonable. Most people are proud of their language, their culture, and their families; rejecting their language and their culture implies rejecting them and the people that they hold most dear.

Rather than asking a student and family to discard beliefs and traditions that are a part of their culture, the teacher might ask the students to share with the class some of the things that are most important to them. The teacher must be prepared to ensure a climate of acceptance and cooperation among those in the classroom; he/she might even want the students to give their presentations to other classes or even to parents on PTA/PTO night. Knowledge may increase acceptance of one another and may encourage the cooperation that will help the school, family, and the students within the classroom to work together in harmony.

Essay 1 Analysis

This essay would receive a score of 2.

Essay 1 very clearly expresses the view that teachers should take in their classrooms. Teachers must accept the students and their families for what they are: unique individuals with worth. Disseminating knowledge can only improve the situation and not worsen it. The suggestion of presenting at the PTA/PTO meetings is one that has merit. Hopefully, as the writer stated, the result will be working "together in harmony."

The writer makes a statement, supports it in the essay, and presents the ideas clearly in the writing.

Essay 2

The teacher demands only English in the classroom. The teacher is building blockades to cooperation and learning in the classroom. The teacher fails to acknowledge that belonging and safety are in Maslow's Hierarchy. Unless the basic needs are met, the students will not reach what Maslow calls "Self-Actualization."

Essay 2 Analysis

This essay would receive a score of 1.

The test-taker has some good points to make, but he/she does not make them in an acceptable way. It is true that demanding only English be used builds blockades in the classroom. It is true that the teacher fails to recognize the needs that we all have for safety and belonging. Three sentences is not an adequate essay.

Essay 3

I would tell the teacher that using only English is important. Like her, I would make the use of any other language unacceptable during class. Like Mrs. Breen, I would ignore any comments or questions from students who forget to speak English; only by realizing that they do not fit in will they ever begin to give up their native language and culture.

Parents, too, must discard their native language and traditions. If parents come to meetings and do not try to communicate clearly with teachers in English, the teachers should not waste their time trying to decipher their failure to speak in the language of the country in which they reside. I think they must learn to speak English now or not receive the benefits of living in the United States.

Essay 3 Analysis

This essay would receive a score of 0.

This essay presents an unacceptable way of treating the students and the parents. Only by recognizing the students and their families for who they are and accepting them as students to be taught can learning proceed in the classroom. The elitist view that the writer expresses in the essay is totally unacceptable.

The content of Essay 2 indicates an unaccepting view of the learners in the class.

Case Study III

Constructed-Response Items

7. **Essay 1**

Homework assignments can be an important part of the instructional program, or they can be meaningless, busy-work activities. Quality, meaningful homework assignments have several characteristics. First, they are appropriate for the age and grade level of the student. No more than 20 minutes of homework should be assigned to students in grades 1 to 4. As a student matures, longer and more complex homework assignments are appropriate. For students in grades 5 to 8 assignments that require 30 or 40 minutes to complete are appropriate. High school students are able to concentrate for longer periods of time; consequently, longer homework assignments are appropriate for them.

Second, homework assignments should be directly related to classwork. Homework quickly becomes busy-work if the teacher simply hands out another worksheet to complete. However, homework becomes a valuable learning experience if the assignment is designed to provide an additional opportunity for students to practice a new concept introduced in class.

Third, students should be able to the complete the assignment independently. An exception to this characteristic of quality homework is that teachers may occasionally ask students to complete a project or poster as homework. Students may need to consult reference books, parents, or friends in order to complete some projects. This can also be a valuable learning experience.

A fourth characteristic of quality homework assignments is that the teacher must evaluate the homework in some manner. The teacher may want to grade the assignment, have the students put answers on the chalkboard, display the papers on the bulletin board, or discuss answers as a form of evaluation. The key issue is that the teacher must acknowledge the work the student has done and give credit and recognition for a completed assignment.

The fifth characteristic of quality homework is that the teacher needs to inform parents early in the school year that homework will be assigned regularly. Parents need to be supportive of the educational plan.

Too often, teachers assign meaningless, repetitious, drill and practice activities for homework that are not specifically related to classwork. Students quickly identify these assignments as busy-work and may become resentful of future homework assignments.

Carefully planned homework assignments not only reinforce classwork but also teach responsibility and independent work habits. Each school needs to develop a clearly defined homework policy that recognizes the necessity of making homework assignments meaningful, appropriate to the student's age and grade level, directly related to classwork, and evaluated by the teacher upon completion.

Essay 1 Analysis

This essay would receive a score of 2.

This essay is well-planned and organized. The main idea is clearly stated in the first sentence. The author lists five characteristics of quality homework assignments and explains each. The last paragraph summarizes the writer's main points. Nevertheless, there are some problems with the essay. Several sentences in the essay are long and seem to ramble. The author does not clearly explain how parents can "be supportive of the educational plan" in relationship to homework. The writer, however, has demonstrated the ability to focus on a specific topic and write an organized essay with a definite introduction, body, and conclusion.

Essay 2

All students need homework—it is an important part of the educational process. The school day is too short to allow teachers to provide time to complete all the activities students need to do. Some of these assignments must be taken home for completion.

There are two major problems with homework assignments. The first is that teachers often assign too much work to be completed at home. Homework assignments should not require any more than thirty minutes to complete. If the assignment will require more time, then it should be split into two parts. The second problem is that teachers often make an assignment at the end of class. This does not give students a chance to begin the assignment during class so they can ask questions if they need to. It also does not give teachers a chance to see if students have started the assignment correctly.

Homework is important. All teachers should assign homework regularly. Students need to become accustomed to working on their own. Parents expect homework. It keeps students busy after school and helps develop self-responsibility.

Essay 2 Analysis —————————————————————————————

This essay would receive a score of 1.

The length of the essay is satisfactory for the time period. However, the essay does not have a clearly stated main idea. Many topics are discussed (students need homework, the school day is too short, problems with homework), but the writer's position on these topics is never fully explained. The last paragraph introduces three new ideas (homework should be assigned regularly, parents expect homework, and homework develops responsibility). None of these topics are completely discussed. The essay lacks a definite introduction and conclusion.

This essay is clearly inferior to Essay 1.

Essay 3 ———————————————————————————————————

Students need homework, but generally teachers give too much. Assignments are usually too long and don't allow any time for students to participate in outside activities. Schools need to develop a system so that students would not have homework in more than one subject everyday. That way students could concentrate on one subject and not have to worry about remembering assignments in other areas.

Teachers need to plan homework assignments that are easy to grade. Everyone knows that teachers have too many papers to grade already. Homework assignments should be short and easy to grade.

Teachers should also remember to look at the football and basketball game schedules to avoid giving homework on game nights. It is not fair to team members and cheerleaders to have homework on game nights. Besides, teachers can always give class time to do homework.

Essay 3 Analysis —————————————————————————————

This essay would receive a score of 0.

This writer has focused on the problems related to homework. The issues raised are important (assignments should not be too long, be easy to grade, and not interfere with team sports). However, the writer discusses these issues from only one point of view—that of the students. He/she fails to consider or even acknowledge the goals of teachers in assigning homework. The essay seems to take the opinion that "teachers don't understand." If this is true, the writer does not explain why he/she has this opinion. Frequent repetition reflects a lack of organization.

8. **Essay 1** ———————————————————————————————

The cynic in me wants to react to the idea of universal public service for the young with a reminder about previous complaints aimed at the military draft. These complaints suggest that wars might never be fought if the first people drafted were the adult leaders and lawmakers. Still, the idea of universal public service sounds good to this concerned citizen who sees everywhere—not just in youth—the effects of a selfish and self-indulgent culture.

One reads and hears constantly about young people who do not care about the problems of our society. These youngsters seem interested in money and the luxuries money can buy. They do not want to work from the minimum wage up, but want instead to land a high paying job without "paying their dues." An informal television news survey of high school students a few years ago suggested that students had the well-entrenched fantasy that with no skills or higher education they would not accept a job paying less than $20 an hour. Perhaps universal service helping out in an urban soup kitchen for six months would instill a sense of selflessness rather than selfishness, and provide the perspective necessary to demonstrate the flaw in this perception.

The shiny gleam of a new expensive sports sedan bought on credit by a recent accounting student reflects self indulgence that might be toned down by universal service. That self indulgence may reflect merely a lack of discipline, but it also may reflect a lack of purpose in life. Philosophers, theologians, and leaders of all types suggest throughout the ages that money and objects do not ultimately satisfy. Helping others—service to our fellow human beings—often does satisfy. Universal public service for that accounting student might require a year helping low income or senior citizens prepare income tax forms. This type of service would dim that self indulgence, give the person some experience in the real world, and also give satisfaction that one's life is not lived only to acquire material things.

Universal service might also help young people restore faith in their nation and what it means to them. Yes, this is the land of opportunity, but it is also a land of forgotten people, and it is a land that faces outside threats. Part of the requisite public service should remind young people of their past and of their responsibility to the future.

Essay 1 Analysis

This essay would receive a score of 2.

Essay 1 uses a traditional structure: the first paragraph states the topic, the second and third present development with specific examples from personal observation. The fourth ends the essay, but it is not as strong a conclusion as it could be. The writer probably ran out of time. The essay as a whole is unified and uses pertinent examples to support the opinion stated. The sentence structure varies, and the vocabulary is effective. Generally, it is well done within the time limit.

Essay 2

In the U.S. today, when a boy turns 18, he is obligated, by law, to register for the military draft. This is done so that in case of a war or other catastrophic event, these boys and men can be called upon for active duty in the military. It is good to know that we will have the manpower we need in case of a war, but my opinion on the military draft is negative. I don't like the idea of forcing someone to sign up at a certain age for something that they don't want to happen. Of course, I know that we need some sort of military manpower on hand just in case, but it would be so much better if it was left to the individual to decide what area to serve in and at what time.

When a boy turns 18, he's a rebel of sorts. He doesn't want someone telling him what to do and when to do it; he's just beginning to live. In Switzerland, when a boy turns 18, he joins some branch of the military for a time of training. He is given his gun, uniform, and badge number. Then, once a year for about two weeks he suits up for retraining. He does this until he is about *65* years old. In a way this is like a draft, but the men love it and feel that it is honorable. I think that they like it because it does not discriminate and their jobs pay them for the time away. Switzerland seems to give the 18-year-old some choice regarding what division to join, and whether or not to join at all. They're not as strict on joining as we are so it's more of an honorable thing to do.

Of course, I'd love to see this decision be strictly up to the individual, but it can't be that way. We have too many enemies that we might go to war with, and we would need a strong military. Switzerland's neutrality provides more options than we in the United States have.

Essay 2 Analysis

This essay would receive a score of 1.

Essay 2 displays competence in overall thought. It does not state its topic quite as well as Essay 1. The extended example of Swiss military conscription is the main strength of the essay. The writer hedges a bit but manages to convey an opinion. Sentences have some variety, and the vocabulary is competent. Even though the writer leads the reader to think he will oppose the draft, he concludes by saying it is not possible.

Essay 3

I agree with the many leaders who suggest we require young people to serve the public in some way, rather than the military draft.

There are several reasons this could benefit our country. The first is to give the young people, perhaps just out of high school with no job experience, an opportunity to give something to their community. In return for this, one gains self-respect, pride, and some valuable experience.

Whether it be taking flowers to shut-ins or just stopping for a chat in a rest home, a young person would have gained something and certainly given, perhaps hope, to that elderly person. I can tell from my own experience how enriched I feel when visiting the elderly. They find joy in the simplest things, which in turn, teaches me I should do the same. This type of universal service would also strengthen the bonds between the younger generation and the older generation.

Another advantage of doing voluntary type work is gaining a sense of caring about doing the job right-quality. If you can't do it for your country, what else matters? Maybe, if a young person learned these lessons early, our country would be more productive in the global economy.

Essay 3 Analysis

This essay would receive a score of 0.

Essay 3 has major faults, not the least of them the lack of a clear sense of overall organization. The thoughts do have some coherence, but the writer does not seem to have a plan, except to express agreement with the statement. Examples from personal observation do help, but the paragraphs are not well developed.

9.   Essay 1

The two students who remain at the school because of religious reasons can still profit from the day. The teacher might leave some work for them related to the project. They might, for instance, figure out how many booklets they have, how much they will charge per booklet, and determine the total amount they might make for the playground equipment.

These students might also begin to write up an article for the local paper; the article might describe how the class researched the information, wrote the articles, and laid out the pictures and information in the booklets. The students can do this assignment in the principal's conference room to add some special events to their day. They might spend a block of time in the first-grade classroom; they can read to the students there and help them with their classwork.

The two students can spend the time before lunch with the sixth-graders who are going to do an experiment to determine heartbeat rates before, during, and after exercise.

Essay 1 Analysis

This essay would receive a score of 2.

The essay is very precise. It tells exactly what the students will be doing and when. The activities planned should help to ensure a successful day for the two students—even though they do not attend the celebration. The students will have many learning experiences.

Essay 2

The best thing that the school can do for the two students who do not have permission to attend the celebration is to place them in a classroom. The sixth-grade classroom should challenge them. The other fifth-grade class will be attending the celebration also; the students cannot go there. It should be satisfactory to the parents to keep them in a classroom situation.

Essay 2 Analysis

This essay would receive a score of 1.

Merely placing the two students in another classroom—even if it is a sixth-grade class—does not ensure that the students will learn. The two students will be in a math class for which they may have an inadequate background. The essay is well-written, but the planning for the students is not the best. The essay is not acceptable.

Essay 3

I think the best way to handle the situation is to tell the parents to keep their children at home for the day that the rest of the students go to the celebration. This way the teacher does not have to plan for the two students. It is the parents' fault that the students are not attending the trip; let the parents contend with them.

Essay 3 Analysis

This essay would receive a score of 0.

The content of the essay suggests that the teacher should tell the parents not to send the children to school. It is illegal for children of this age NOT to attend school; the teacher is telling the parents to break the law. This three-sentence essay with its inappropriate content is unacceptable.

Case Study IV

Constructed-Response Items

10. **Essay 1**

It is important for Juan Pesaro to take the focus of the conversation off himself and back to the problem: the academic performance of Phillippe. Mr. Pesaro must not get defensive, become angry, or ask the parent not to go to the superintendent. Mr. Pesaro might begin by saying, "I, too, am concerned about Phillippe. As you know, I send home Phillippe's papers each week for you to sign. When the students return the papers with the adult's signature, we keep a portfolio in the classroom with the papers. Why don't you come by the classroom and let's look at his work together? Please call me at this number, and we can set a time this week to talk. As a teacher, it is encouraging to have a family to take a special interest in the education of the child. I look forward to working with you and helping Phillippe to have a good academic year."

Essay 1 Analysis

This essay would receive a score of 2.

The writer of this essay has done well to turn the conversation back to the child and away from the teacher. The advice for the teacher not to become defensive, angry, or suppliant is good. Juan Pesaro changes the location of the conference from the market to the classroom; this change of venue is appropriate. Reminding the parent of the portfolio and the availability of the teacher for a conference—in a professional atmosphere—are valuable information for the teacher to present. The content of the essay is good. This essay is a good example of an excellent response.

Essay 2

Juan Pesaro should immediately tell the parent that he will not talk with her in the grocery store and that he will be happy to meet her in the superintendent's office when she wants. When the superintendent will meet with them, perhaps the principal will be there also. If the teacher does not remain stern in this situation when the public is observing, he will lose all respect.

Essay 2 Analysis

This essay would receive a score of 1.

The tone of this essay suggests that the child's academic progress is not as important as the teacher's pride. The teacher has sacrificed an opportunity to win the cooperation of the parent and to help the student. The challenge to meet the parent in the superintendent's office will probably come to pass with this "dare." The essay is unacceptable because of the content and because of its presentation.

Essay 3

Juan Pesaro should immediately tell the parent that he is trying to make a living, that he needs a job, and that he hopes that she will not go the superintendent. He should begin to give his qualifications, the colleges he attended, and his desire to do a good job.

He should suggest that the parent meet with him in the principal's office the very next day. Hopefully, Mr. Pesaro will be able to keep his job.

Essay 3 Analysis

This essay would receive a score of 0.

One of the main issues in this confrontation is Phillippe—not just the teacher's job. The writer of this essay has totally forgotten the academic progress of Phillippe. The beseeching attitude of Pesaro is not attractive or desirable; the defensiveness is not appropriate either. Setting up an appointment with the principal for the next day is not advisable without the permission of the principal. In fact, with a good teacher-parent conference it may not even be necessary to bring the principal into the interview. The essay is not acceptable.

11. Essay 1

Juan Pesaro should be careful to be professional. Pesaro should not say anything to one parent about another. Pesaro might say something like, "All teachers, like caregivers, want to help their children. I am looking forward to working with you and with Mrs. Hammett. Please feel free to call me if you have any questions or if you need a conference."

Essay 1 Analysis

This essay would receive a score of 2.

The content of the first essay is fitting for a professional teacher. The teacher remains supportive of both Mrs. Goodwin and Mrs. Hammett. Juan Pesaro offers no confidential *information about Phillippe to another parent. The essay is a well-structured one. The essay is one that would receive an above-average score.*

Essay 2

Juan Pesaro has found a friend in Mrs. Goodwin and someone in whom he can confide. Mrs. Goodwin has some knowledge about Mrs. Hammett and Phillippe. She will be a good supporter if news about the confrontation with Mrs. Hammett surfaces. This is a good time for Mr. Pesaro to ask if Mrs. Goodwin will vouch for his behavior should there be a problem with the encounter. He should also ask Mrs. Goodwin to verify the fact that Phillippe has learning problems if the situation should come before the superintendent.

Essay 2 Analysis

This essay would receive a score of 1.

Juan should NOT even suggest to Mrs. Goodwin that he suspects that there will be a problem from the encounter. He certainly should not pit one parent against another. Juan would do well to try to get along with both parents. He should certainly steer away from discussing Phillippe with outsiders; this is very confidential information. The teacher should not share information about the child with third parties. Although the writing itself is good, the content is not. This essay is not appropriate.

Essay 3

Juan Pesaro should immediately return to his home and call his principal at his home to describe the scene in the grocery store. He should reveal that Mrs. Hammett may go to the superintendent and that she may ask for his job. Ideally, Juan should call the superintendent at his home to describe the encounter. Juan should also tell both the principal and superintendent about the problems with Phillippe. Juan should tell both administrators about the appearance of Mrs. Goodwin and about the possibility that she will defend him if the occasion arises. To end the conversation, Juan should express his pleasure in his job and his desire to continue in the position.

Essay 3 Analysis

This essay would receive a score of 0.

This essay is an overreaction to the situation. If Juan could handle the situation by bringing Mrs. Hammett into his classroom and discussing Phillippe's progress with her in a professional way, it would simplify the situation considerably. The principal and the superin-

tendent have more to do in their homes than to discuss the encounter with Juan. Perhaps he may wish to mention the upcoming conference to his principal when Mrs. Hammett comes to the classroom. Hopefully Juan can handle the situation with the parent who seems to want the best for her child. Neither the content nor the handling of the situation is appropriate.

12. Essay 1

Mr. Pesaro should respond to Margelo's aunt by stating the following: "How fortunate Margelo is to have an aunt who is interested in her education! I send home a calendar for the upcoming week each Friday. The calendar gives the plans for the week, project assignments, suggested ways that parents can help, and even some suggested readings and activities for the family. I will be sending home the second of these tomorrow—Friday. You might want to ask Margelo for your copy when she arrives home.

"Margelo probably gave the first of these letters to her grandmother, with whom she was staying last week. I know she will be responsible about getting the information home in the future. Just give her a gentle reminder if she doesn't immediately share it with you.

"Please know you can call me at school, and I will call you back at my planning period or in the evening if that is more convenient. In addition, you are welcome to arrange to visit our class through the principal's office. We all have Margelo's best interest at heart."

Essay 1 Analysis

This essay would receive a score of 2.

The content of this essay is reassuring to the aunt to whom the teacher is addressing the information and to the reader of the essay. The teacher seems well-planned and interested in the well-being of the student. The teacher appears to be an educator most of us would want for our child. The essay is literate, clear, and to the point. It is a good example to follow.

Essay 2

Mr. Pesaro should respond to Margelo's aunt by stating the following: "I'll be sending home assignments for the students each night. Ask Margelo what her homework is; this'll give you an idea as to what is going on. There are special days to visit the class. Margelo'll let you know."

Essay 2 Analysis

This essay would receive a score of 1.

The teacher has given a minimum answer. Juan has placed most of the responsibility on the child to communicate with the parent/caregiver. There is apparently no plan for Juan to communicate regularly with the families. Juan does not volunteer to develop a plan nor does he invite the parent to communicate with him or the school.

This essay is inappropriate in content and in its tone. Three sentences are too short for a sufficient essay.

Essay 3

Mr. Pesaro should respond to Margelo's aunt by stating the following: "I encourage the students to take responsibility for their own education. I will contact you if I need you. If you do not hear from me, you will know that things are going as they should. I suggest that you keep the communication lines open between you and your niece. I wish you luck."

Essay 3 Analysis

This essay would receive a score of 0.

This response from Juan is a discouragement to the adult who expresses an interest in supporting the school and in helping Margelo. Most teachers welcome this family involvement and do not seek to suppress the adult help. Juan has seemingly uninvited the adult participation. The content makes the response a tasteless, badly chosen one. Cooperation between home and school would be best for the child—always the ideal.

Multiple-Choice Answers

13. **C**

Students can internalize what a teacher expects of them and will perform at that level, whether it is positive or negative.(C) is, therefore the best answer. (A) could be true if personal was changed to teachers. A teacher cannot predict progress (B), but a student might perform up to the teachers' expectations. Because students do seem to know what the teacher expects, (D) is false.

14. **B**

The learning activities in class should be based on specific objectives, preferably ones that are closely related to the recent objectives of the class. Students should not always select the activities nor should objectives always be knowledge-based; (A) and (C) are not good choices. The educator may not use ALL learning activities DAILY; (D) is unacceptable.

15. **B**

Canter and Canter's assertive discipline is a system for teachers to maintain a positive classroom while managing misbehavior situations constructively. One of the fundamental ideas is that proper behavior in a classroom should result in positive consequences, which in turn promotes a positive classroom environment. Neither ignoring (A) nor failing to reward (C) positive behavior is a good choice. Positive behavior (D) should have its own good, positive results. (D) is unacceptable.

16. **A**

Transitions allow students to be aware of future events, topics, and expectations (A). Transitions are not evaluations, so students cannot be classified as either performers or non-performers (B). Transitions set up events rather than questions (C) and are generally supplemented by formalized instructions for each topic or event (D).

17. **B**

"I" statements begin with the word "I" and express the individual's thoughts or feelings. They are not statements of goals and/or expectations (C). "I" statements are not incomplete statements (D), nor are they called "I" statements because eye contact is involved (A).

18. **C**

The teacher should allow the students to evaluate the list and add some names to show that they do recognize the diversity of individuals who have contributed to America's greatness. Answer (D) is sarcastic, and answer (A) is too harsh. Answer (B) does not allow the students to participate and amend their list.

19. **A**

A positive statement of encouragement will boost the confidence of some students and will not undercut anyone's self-esteem. Answers (B), (C), and (D) are almost certain to generate anxiety that will interfere with test performance for some students.

20. **C**

Since a teacher will be working with students of all levels and abilities, it is important to select materials that can be useful to all students. Looking solely at the ratio of pictures to text (A), the size of the font (B), or the size of the material (D), alone is unacceptable.

21. **B**

This question is related to implementing instructional design and conditions that facilitate learning. Option I is generally thought of as a quality that students like in a teacher, so it is likely to be chosen. The other options, II, III, and IV, may be not as well known as qualities which a well-liked teacher possesses. It is important to note in these other three choices that students need only perceive the qualities listed. The teacher need not actually possess them. In any case, only choice (B) lists all four options, so (B) is the best answer.

22. D

This question is related to issues of sex equity in the curriculum. Since this question asks you to identify the "best example" of a sexually nonbiased curriculum, you should assume that there may be several correct answers to this question. To answer this question, you should read carefully through all of the answers and choose the one that is the best example of the ones that are given. Choice (A) can be eliminated because the teacher is making statements that are solely directed to girls, and it does not indicate any classroom practices to reinforce that belief. Choice (B) could be the correct answer since this teacher obviously devotes an entire month to the study of women. Choice (C) is another move toward integrating women as it emphasizes the women who are perceived as being different—"uncommon"—in the fields of writing, politics, and sports. Choice (D) is another possible correct answer since teacher D has integrated the contributions of women into both his/her lecture information and additional readings. At this point, choice (A) can be eliminated and the best choice from (B), (C), and (D) can be made. Choice (B) represents only one month of the curriculum and does not truly integrate the contributions of women throughout the entire curriculum but separates them into one unit of study. Choice (C) implies the fact that the only women who make worthy contributions to society are "uncommon women" and perpetuates a negative stereotype. Choice (D) is the best choice because it indicates that women are consistently represented throughout all areas of the science curriculum and that additional effort is being made to include women through the supplementary readings.

23. D

This question is based on recognizing cultural influences and expectations. This question asks you to recognize which of the given verbal and nonverbal communication patterns are culturally based. The answers give you combinations of two or three options as well as one choice including all four options. To answer this question, you should read each option and decide which of these patterns can be attributed to cultural expectations. All of the behaviors listed in I-IV are culturally determined patterns of communication. Therefore, the correct answer for this question is (D).

24. D

An inspection of students' work is the most effective way to check their understanding. Asking questions (A), (B), (C) rarely provide the feedback the teacher needs to assess students' understanding.

25. **A**

When points are not given for inappropriate behavior, but points are given for positive behavior, it is known as withholding reinforcement from the negatively reacting student. Thus, response (A) is the correct one. If you gave positive reinforcement, it would encourage the student to continue with the misbehavior, so response (B) is incorrect. You cannot use reinforce-ignore strategy if you plan to withhold points for misbehavior. Thus, choice (C) is incorrect. Averting control is not the answer either. It needs to be clear why points are given and why they are taken away in the classroom, so response (D) is also incorrect.

26. **A**

This lets the student know what she has done correctly. The other answers (B), (C), (D) are affirming, but vague.

27. **D**

Guided practice helps you to identify the students' individual weaknesses and strengths. It allows one student to work on his/her low skills area, while another works on his/her own weakness. Thus, response (D), guided practice, is the correct choice. Instruction, strategy, and motivation are factors to consider with groups as well as individuals, but guided practice is more nearly a perfect example of one-to-one. Thus, responses (A), (B), and (C) are incorrect.

28. **C**

The classroom can have an effect on the behavior of the students, and should be taken into consideration as an important factor when managing student behavior. Being able to hear, is important, but volume would not affect behavior at only one time a day; (A) is incorrect. Misbehaving only once a day would not be a "phase"; (B) is incorrect. Changing one's seat would not usually affect attitude during only one period, so (D) is incorrect.

29. **A**

Using class time efficiently is an important part of successful teaching. Answers (B) and (D) are irrelevant to the situation described. The information provided is insufficient for concluding that the teacher is rigid or unreasonable (C).

30. **A**

Assertive Discipline does not mean that students can do whatever they want and establish guidelines for however they want to behave. Thus, response (A) is the exception and correct answer. Assertive Discipline is a plan to establish appropriate rules for the classroom, with consequences for violating rules, or rewards for appropriate behavior, with the teacher in charge. The plan does include (B), (C), and (D), so they are not the exception and are incorrect responses to the question.

31. **A**

An important part of the research on academic learning time is the amount of student engaged time. Engaged time is the time the student is actively engaged with academic subject matter. Engaged time might include independent study, but is not limited to independent study (B). The total amount of time a teacher spends on each subject is allocated time (C). Including a level of achievement, as in response (D), has changed the statement to a definition of academic learning time.

32. **D**

The correct response is (D), III and IV. The question asks for examples of arguments that support cooperative learning as an effective method of instruction. Statement I does not support cooperative learning and, in fact, argues against it. Cooperation between group members, not competition, is essential for successful learning groups. Statement II supports one of the "pitfalls" of cooperative learning; that is, if cooperative learning groups are not properly facilitated, an academic achiever might attempt to carry or cover for an academic underachiever's learning experience. This is counterproductive to cooperative learning where the success of each individual benefits the group. Statement III is a supportive argument, thus, a correct response. Each member of the cooperative learning group must do his or her part (i.e., learn) so that the group can be successful. Statement IV is a supportive argument and a second correct response. Cooperative learning groups give students a reason to support and reward each other for achieving because each individual's success is also dependent upon the success of other group members.

33. **C**

By waiting for responses, a teacher will motivate and stimulate the students to improve these responses. Thus, response (C) is correct. If a teacher causes the students to feel uncomfortable and humiliated, they will not want to respond next time, so (A) is incorrect. Wait-time could bring a positive or correct answer, while not allowing wait-time may bring a negative response. Thus, response (B) is incorrect. Wait-time after asking a question must vary according to the student's intellectual ability, so response (D) is incorrect.

34. **D**

In case of a tornado, you should evacuate everyone to the first floor of a building and then place students near walls that are away from windows. Everyone should crouch on the floor and then cover their heads with their hands. The teacher should evacuate students to the first floor of the building, but not outside the building (A). Students should also not be on the top level of the building (B) or in a classroom (C) unless the classroom is on the first floor and students are away from windows.

35. **C**

Mastery instruction time is not based on teachers' attitudes (A), school environment (B), or teaching knowledge (D). (A), (B), and (D) are incorrect. The students' characteristics are the greatest factor to consider in mastery learning, as well as the time needed, so the correct response is (C).

36. **A**

De jure segregation is defined as resulting from laws, school policies, and/or government actions that are designed to specifically bring about separation, so response (A) is correct. Controlled choice and integration may occur, but they do not cause segregation, so choices (B) and (C) are incorrect. Response (D) is incorrect, since (A) is a correct choice.

Index

A

Absenteeism, 66–67
Abuse
    drugs and alcohol. *See* Substance abuse
    physical, 95–100
    sexual, 98–99
Academic learning time, 125–126
Accelerating factors in risk of violence, 148
Accommodation, 29, 74–75
Activities
    human resources, 275–276
    motivation and, 53
    organizing, 277–279
    outcome-oriented, 279–280
    overview, 269
    procedures for success, 276–277
    teacher planning, 282–283
ADA (Americans with Disabilities Act), 74
Addictions. *See* Substance abuse
Administration of PLT, 5, 158
Adolescence, 27, 87–88
Affiliation as human need, 36
Affirmations, 44, 56
Alcohol abuse. *See* Substance abuse
American Council for Drug Education, 93
American Psychological Association, 148
Americans with Disabilities Act (ADA), 74
Analysis, Bloom's taxonomy, 107
Anecdotal records of student assessment, 163, 193
Angelo, T. A., 303
Anger, 65–66, 68
Anger: The Misunderstood Emotion, 65
Answer sheet, 305
Anticipatory set, 252–253
Antithesis, 234
Anxiety disorder, 129
Application, Bloom's taxonomy, 106
Art inductive teaching strategy, 293
Assessment. *See also* Tests
    authentic, 161–164
    checklists and scales, 191
    classroom, 302–303
    narrative reports, 194
    overview, 157–159
    parent-teacher conferences, 194
    performance-based, 167–168
    permanent student records, 195–197
    postassessment, 40
    preassessment, 40
    purpose, 159
    report cards, 193–194
    software, 206–207
    student and class progress, 190–193
Assimilation cycles or processes, 29
Attendance in class for academic achievement, 66
Audiovisual aids, 271-272
Auditorial learning, 81
Auditory learners, 249
Ausubel, Davis, 51–52
Autism, 129–130

B

Background material, 212
Backup computer copies, 207–208
Bandura, Albert, 47–48
Baxter-Magolda, M. B., 43–44, 52–57
Behavior
    classroom, 126–128
    modification therapy, 47
    patterns, 128–130
    reinforcement, 45-46
    risky, 28
    student. *See* Student classroom behavior
Behaviorism, 45–47
Bell-shaped curve, 165
Blanchard, K., 143–144
Bloom's taxonomy, 106–108
Blueprints for tests, 170–172, 173
Body language, 139, 250
Boys, maturation milestones, 27
Brophy, Jere, 251
Bruner, Jerome, 49–50
Bulletin boards, 122
Bureau of Justice Statistics, 147
Business inductive teaching strategy, 293

C

Call-outs, 111–112
Camaraderie building, 53–54
Career Days, 61
Categories
    feedback, 216–217
    teachers, 296
CBT (Computer-Based Tests), 4
Certification, 6
Chamber of Commerce community information, 59

Characteristics
adolescent development, 27
substance abuse, 87–92
Checklists for student assessment, 163, 191
Churchward, Budd, 144–146
Classroom assessment, 302–303
Classroom Assessment Techniques, 303
Classroom environment
academic learning time, 125–126
behavior patterns, 128–130
overview, 121
physical, 121, 122–123
social and emotional climate, 123–125
student behavior, 126–128
Cognition, defined, 28
Cognitive development
metacognition, 41–42
moral decision-making and, 133–136
sample multiple-choice question for testing, 33–34
social interaction and, 48
theory, 28–30
Cognitive psychology theory, 28–30, 33, 37–38
Cognitive skills, 40
Coles, Robert, 53–54
Collegial learning, 52
Communication
body language, 139, 250
eye contact, 248–249
media, 250
nonverbal, 248
overview, 245
planning processes, 251–253
self-directed learning, 254–255
summary, 251
verbal, 214, 246–247
voice, 247–248
Community
learning about local makeup, 58–60
problems, 62–64
stabilizing strengths, 60–62
substance abuse factors, 89
substance abuse resources, 92-93
Comparison teaching strategy, 295
Comprehension of material
Bloom's taxonomy, 106–108
overview, 103–104
questioning, 104–105, 106–108
retention of information, 111–113, 115–116
seatwork, 113–115
tests of mastery, 182
variety in activities, 108–110, 112–113

Computer and information-processing theory, 38–40
Computer-Based Tests (CBT), 4
Computer science inductive teaching strategy, 291–292
Computers in the classroom
classroom management, 200–201
displaying of large visual materials, 274
instruction, 202, 204–205
interactive video, 275
media center, 201
primary classroom exposure, 199–202
secondary, 202–207
software copyrights, 207–208
software selection and evaluation, 206
software tools, 202–204
Concrete operations, 30, 34
Connected discourse, 218
Context of material, 212
Contrast teaching strategy, 295
Control, 54–55
Cooperative learning, 237–239
Cooperative strategies, 294
Correcting student's errors
ask questions, 230–231
explanations, 229–230
overview, 227
provide information, 230
simply give correction, 228–229
Covey, Stephen, 139–141, 145
Crime. *See* Violence
Criterion-referenced tests (CRTs), 164–165
Cross, K. P., 303
CRTs (criterion-referenced tests), 164–165
Cultural diversity
eye contact and, 249
impact on learning, 69–71
questioning, 108
risk factors for substance abuse, 89

D

Databases, computer, 203
Decision-making by students, 139–141
Deductive teaching methods, 288–290, 294
Depression, 129
Design in learning environment, 78–79
Desk arrangements, 122–123
Development
adolescent, 27–28
cognition. *See* Cognitive development
dynamic view, 65
information processing, 38–40
moral, 133–136

physical, 26–27
psychosocial, 31–33
zone of proximal development, 48
Dewey, John, 50
Dialogues, 230
Diffusion, 31–34
Digressions, 216, 217–218, 283
Directions for tasks, 298–299
Disabilities legislation. *See* Special education legislation
Disability services for test-takers, 6
Discipline
defined, 144
one-minute reprimand, 143
positive, 147
stages, 144–145
Discourse
connected, 218
scrambled, 220
Discussion teaching strategy, 294–295
Disequilibrium, 29
Disorders, 128–130
Distributed activity, 116
Diverse learners
Americans with Disabilities Act (ADA), 74
educational environment, 74–75
Individual Education Plan (IEP), 75–77
Individuals with Disabilities Education Act (IDEA), 72–74
Public Law 94-142, 72–74
Diversity, 69–71.
See also Cultural diversity
Drug abuse. *See* Substance abuse
Drug therapy for emotional disorders, 128
Dunn, Kenneth, 78, 79–82
Dunn, Rita, 78, 79–82, 206
Dynamic view of human development, 65

E

E-mail, 203
Education for all Handicapped Children Act, 72
Education, purpose of, 140
Educational scaffolding, 50–51
Educational Testing Service
contact information, 6
registration bulletin, 7
Electronic mail, 203
Elkind, David, 27
Emotional classroom environment, 121, 123–125
Emotional disorders, 126–128
Emotions
anger, 65–66, 68
fear, 65–66

guilt, 65–66
learning factors, 79–82
Employment
family stability and, 63–64
substance abuse risk factor, 89
Empowerment, 54–57
End-of-the-lesson recap, 236–237
English teaching strategy, 291, 295
Enrichment, 253
Environment
classroom. *See* Classroom environment
classroom design, 78–79
impact in information-processing approach, 39
learning style and, 77–79
light, 78
stress and, 67
temperature, 78–79
testing, 158
Equilibration of accommodation, 29
Erikson, Erik, 31–33
Errors. *See* Correcting student's errors
Escalante, Jaime, 131–132
Ethnocentrism, 69–70
Evaluation. *See also* Assessment
Bloom's taxonomy, 107
of goals, 262
Expectations, unfulfilled, 66
External factors, 35
External motivators, 54–55
Eye contact in communication, 248–249

F

Facial expressions, 139, 248
Family characteristics of substance abuse, 88
Feedback
categories of, 216–217
classroom assessment, 303
formative, 158, 189
marking tests, 224
providing clear feedback, 220–224
from students, 211–213
teacher statements about students' responses, 225–227
Field trips, 276
Fixed ratio scheduling, 46
Flavell, J. H., 41–42
Formal operations, 30
Format of PLT, 8–10

G

Gagné-Ausubel pattern of lecture (GAP), 51–52
Gagné, Robert, 51–52, 252
(GAP) Gagné-Ausubel pattern of lecture, 51–52

Gardner, Howard, 48–49
Gender bias
    auditorial learning, 81
    classroom, 69–71
    moral development differences, 136
    research study, 69–70
Gilligan, Carol, 136
Girls, maturation milestones, 27
Goal-setting
    Board of Education or curriculum
        specialists, 260
    evaluation of goals, 260–262
    incremental, 278
    modeling by teachers, 254
    one-minute, 143, 144
    teacher. *See* Teacher goal-setting
Gordon, Thomas, 295
Grade books, 190–191
Grading scales for tests, 180–181, 191
Graphics computer programs, 204, 207
Gregorc, Anthony, 206
Guessing factor on tests, 178
Guilt sense, 31
Gun-Free Schools Act of 1994, 150
Guns in school, 92

H

Hall, G. Stanley, 50
Hanson, J. R., 296
Hawthorne effect, 70
Hierarchy of needs, 35–36
Honor Level System: Discipline by Design, The,
    144
Housing for teachers, 59
Human resources for information, 275–276
Hunter, Madeline, 251, 252–253

I

"I" messages, 146
IDEA (Individuals with Disabilities Education Act),
    72–74
Idea scaffolding, 277
Identity achievement and diffusion, 31–34
IEP (Individual Education Plan), 75–77
Imaginary audience, 27–28
Incompatible responses, 139
Individual Education Plan (IEP), 75–77
Individualism and change moral development
    stage, 134
Individuals with Disabilities Education Act (IDEA),
    72–74
Inductive teaching methods, 252, 289, 290–
    293, 294

Industry sense, 31
Infantile autism, 129–130
Inferiority sense, 31
Information-processing theory of human
    development, 38–40
Infraction slips, 144–145
Initiative sense, 31
Instruction
    aspects of, 49–50
    computer-assisted, 202, 204–205
    goals, 262
    objectives, 40, 299–300
    outcomes, 40
Instrumentalism, 50
Intelligence
    eight types, 48–49
    triarchic theory of intelligence, 38–40
Interactive video, 274–275
Internal
    factors, 35
    motivators, 54–55
    voices, 55–56
Interpersonal conformity, 134
Intimacy in adolescence, 32
Intuitive personality type, 137–138
Isolation, 28, 32

J

Johnson, Elaine M., 85–86
Johnson, S., 143–144
Jointly constructed meaning, 52–58
Journal writing, 237
Justice, principles of, 135

K

Kinesthetic learners, 249
King, Martin Luther, Jr., 135
Knowledge
    Bloom's taxonomy, 106
    metacognitive, 41–42
Kohlberg, Lawrence, 134–136

L

Language
    community, 62
    effective use in classrooms, 214
    inclusive use, 53
    test accommodations, 7
Laws, copyright, 207–208. *See also* Special
    education legislation
Learners, types of, 249
Learning
    cooperative, 237–239

factors, 34–35
lifelong process, 44
outcome-oriented, 279–280
personality types and styles, 137–138
self-directed, 254–255
steps for success, 276–277
styles, 287–288
Lecture learning method, 51–52, 289–290
Legislation, copyright laws, 207–208. *See also*
Special education legislation
Lesson cycle, 252–253
Licensing of computer software, 208
Light in learning environment, 78
Low-key interventions, 146

M

Macrorie, Ken, 123–124
Magazine resources, 272
Maintenance scheduling, 122
Marker expressions, 218–219
Maslow, Abraham, 35–36
Massed activity, 116
Mastery, 182. *See also* Comprehension of
material
Materials
class requirements, 301–302
educational resources, 271
overview, 269–270
planning, 271–272
print resources, 272–273
for taking test, 17
videodisc and interactive video, 274–275
visual, 273–274, 289
Mathematics inductive teaching strategy, 293
Maturation and student development, 26–28
Measurement. *See* Tests
Media center, 201
Media communication, 250
Metacognition, 41–42
Methods of teaching
classroom assessment, 302–303
comparison/contrast, 295
cooperative strategies, 294
deductive, 252, 288–290, 294
discussions, 294–295
giving directions, 298–299
individual styles, 296–297
inductive, 252, 289, 290–293, 294
objectives, 299–300
overview, 287–288
performance standards, 300–301
supplies needed, 301–302
Misbehaving behavior
parent-teacher communication, 153–154

reasons for, 126–128
solutions for, 138-139
"with-it"-ness by teachers, 151–152
Mobility needs during study, 80–81
Modeling, 47–48, 139
Monitoring by teachers, 146
Monthly reviews, 239–241
Mood disorders, 129
Moral development and decision-making, 133–136
Morris, George Sylvester, 50
Motivation
activities and, 53
computers and, 202
empowerment, 54–57
external, 54–55
extrinsic, 79
internal, 54–55
intrinsic, 79
for learning, 42–44, 298–299
MSAT (Multiple Subjects Assessment for
Teachers), 4
Multiculturalism, 71
Multimedia system, 275
Multiple-choice question
sample, 33–34, 57-58
tests, 160, 172, 174, 176–178, 184–185
Multiple Subjects Assessment for Teachers
(MSAT), 4
Music inductive teaching strategy, 293
Mutual interpersonal expectations, 134

N

Narrative reports, 194
National Center for Education Statistics, 147
The National Center on Addiction and Substance
Abuse at Columbia University, 93
National Clearinghouse for Alcohol and Drug
Information, 93
National Institute on Drug Abuse, 93
Nature, 36, 65-68
Nature vs. nurture debate, 36, 65–68
Neglect, 97, 99–100. *See also* Physical abuse
Neo-Piagetian theory, 37–38
Newspaper resources, 272
No Child Left Behind Act, 244
Nonverbal
communication, 248
signs of not understanding, 246
use of language, 214
Norm-referenced test (NRT), 165–166
Note-taking skills, 290
NRT (norm-referenced test), 165–166
Nurture, 36, 65–68

O

Objectives, instructions for, 299–300. *See also* Goal-setting
Observation assessment, 162–163
One-minute goal-setting, 143, 144
The One Minute Manager, 143
One-minute praise, 143
One-minute reprimand, 143
Operant conditioning, 45–46
Outcome-oriented learning, 279–280

P

Paint computer programs, 204
Paper and pencil tests, 158, 160
Paralingual use of language, 214
Parent-teacher conferences, 153–154, 194
Parents' community groups, 60–61
Percentile scores, 165–166
Perception and reality, 65, 68
Perceptual strengths, 81–82
Performance standards, 300–301
Performance tests, 158, 167–168
Permanent student records, 195–197
Persistence as emotional learning factor, 79
Person knowledge, 41–42
Personal fable, 27–28
Personality characteristics and substance abuse, 87–88
Personality types and learning styles, 137–138
Physical abuse
        overview, 95–96
        reporting suspicions, 99–100
        symptoms, 96–97
        visible signs, 98–99
Physical changes in student development, 26
Physical classroom environment, 121, 122–123
Physiological changes in student development, 26–27
Physiological learning factors, 80
Physiological needs, impact on learning, 35–36
Piaget, Jean
        cognitive psychology theory, 28–30, 34, 37–38
        moral decision-making, 133
        reveal thinking process, 52
Planning processes
        classroom communication, 251–253
        organizing activities, 277–279
        outcome-oriented learning, 279–280
        resource, 271–272
        student activity, 282–283
        time management, 280–281
        transitions, 284–286

Plato, *Dialogues*, 230
Portfolios for student assessment, 163–164, 191–192
Positive discipline, 147
Post-conventional morality, 135
Postassessment (post-test), 40
PPST (Pre-Professional Skills Tests), 4
Practice activities
        duration, 110
        long-term retention, 111–113, 115–116
        recitation, 109
        seatwork, 113–115
        skills practice software, 204–205
        test-taking tips, 15–16
        variety, 108–110, 112–113
Pragmatism, 50
Praise
        one-minute, 143
        student interaction, 241
Praxis Series, 4
Pre-Professional Skills Tests (PPST), 4
Preassessment (pretest), 40
Preoperational stage, 29–30
Principles of Learning and Teaching (PLT) tests, Praxis II test category, 4
Print resources, 272–273
Proactive students in decision making, 139–140
Problem-solving computer programs, 205
Proctor, 188–189
Professional Assessments for Beginning Teachers, 5
Projects in student assessment, 162
Psychosocial development, 31–33
Psychotic disorders, 129
Puberty, 27
Punishment and obedience moral development stage, 134

Q

Questions
        authority, 43–44
        for material comprehension, 104–105, 106–108
        overload, 220
        Socratic method, 230
        test questions by students, 241

R

Reading skills acquisition, 39
Reagan, Ronald, 131
Recapping significant points
        end-of-lesson, 236–239
        purpose of, 232, 234–236

questions to ask, 232–233
Reciprocal determinism, 47–48
Recitation, 109
Records
     anecdotal, 163, 193
     permanent, 195–197
References
     assessment and testing, 198
     classroom environment, 130
     communication, 255
     comprehension of material, 117
     computers in the classroom, 208
     feedback and review, 244
     goal-setting, 266–267
     human resources, 275–276
     materials and activities, 286
     methods of teaching, 304
     physical abuse, 101
     student classroom behavior, 155
     students as learners, 82–83
     substance abuse, 93–94
     time management, 286
Registration Bulletin, 7
Registration fee, 7
Reinforcement of behavior, 45-46
Relationships between teachers and students,
     214–215
Repetition and retention of information, 112–
     113, 115-116
Report cards, 193–194
Reprimand
     one-minute, 143
     warnings, 144–145
Research skills, practicing of, 123–125
Resources. *See* Materials; References
Responsibility as emotional learning factor, 79–
     80
Retention of information, 111–113, 115–116
Revelation of self, 53–54
Reviews
     methods, 242
     for PLT, 11
     of previous material, 211–213, 234–236
     purpose of, 241–243
     weekly and monthly, 239–241
Risky behaviors, 28

S

Sadker, David and Myra, 69–70
Safety
     classroom rules, 147–150
     community, 64
     contributing factors, 148

Departments of Education and Justice
     recommendations, 150
     impact on learning, 36, 141
Scales for tests, 180–181, 191
Schedule for PLT study, 19–22
Schizophrenia, 129
Science inductive teaching strategy, 292–293
Score report, 13
Scoring tests, 12–13, 165–166, 180–181
Scrambled discourse, 220
Seatwork, 113–115
Self-direction, 140, 254–255
Self-efficacy, 54, 55
Self-esteem, 54, 55
Self-knowledge, 57
Self-respect, 55–56
Self-revelation, 53–54
Sensorimotor stage, 29
Sensory personality type, 137
Sequencing short-range objectives, 265–266
The Seven Habits of Highly Effective People,
     139–140
Sexual abuse, 98–99
Silver, H. F., 296
Simulation computer programs, 205
Skills practice software, 204–205
Skinner, B. F., 45–47
Social classroom climate, 123–125
Social interaction and cognition development, 48
Sociological learning factors, 80
Socratic method, 230
Software
     backups, 207–208
     copyright laws, 207–208
     databases, 203
     electronic mail, 203
     graphics or paint, 204, 207
     selection and evaluation, 206–207
     simulation or problem-solving, 205, 271–
          272
     skills practice, 204–205
     spreadsheets, 204
     tutorials, 205
     word processing, 202–203
Special education legislation
     Americans with Disabilities Act (ADA), 74
     Individual Education Plan (IEP), 75–77
     Individuals with Disabilities Education Act
          (IDEA), 72–74
     No Child Left Behind Act, 244
Special interest groups, 61
Spreadsheet computer programs, 204
Stage theory, 29
Stand and Deliver motion picture, 131

Standardized tests, 158, 164–167
Standards of behavior, 134, 138–139
Sternberg, R. J., 38–40
Strategies for teaching. *See* Methods of teaching
Strategy knowledge, 41
Stress, 67–68, 96, 126–127
Structure as emotional factor, 79–80
Student classroom behavior
    behavior standards, 138–139
    learning styles, 137–138
    moral decision-making, 133–136
    overview, 131–133
    parent-teacher communication, 153–154
    personality types, 137–138
    safety issues, 147–150
    student decision-making, 139–141
    teacher's role, 142–147
    "with-it"-ness, 151–152
Students
    development and maturation, 26–28
    interest assessment, 206
    learners. *See* Students as learners
    participation, 211–213
    relationship to teachers, 214–215
Students as learners
    aspects of instruction, 49–50
    behaviorism, 45–47
    educational scaffolding, 50–51
    instrumentalism, 50
    intelligences, 48–49
    lecture method, 51–52
    reciprocal determinism, 47–48
    social interaction, 48
Study schedule, 19–22
Studying for the PLT test, 7–8, 14
Subject Assessment/Specialty Area Tests, 4
Substance abuse
    characteristics of students under the
        influence, 91–92
    community problem, 63
    family characteristics, 88
    individual characteristics, 87–88
    overview, 85–86
    prevention, 86
    referrals for help, 92
    risk factors, 87–90
    social and cultural characteristics, 89–90
    teaching of dangers, 93–94
Suitability of goals, 262
Summarizing of information, 213, 242
Supplies, 17, 301–302. *See also* Materials
Synectics, 295

Synthesis
    Bloom's taxonomy, 107
    recapping material, 234

T

Tardy students, 284–285
Task attraction and challenge, 219
Task knowledge, 41
Tavris, Carol, 65–66
Teacher
    categories, 296
    classroom management, 142–147
    effective instruction, 37–40
    goal-setting. *See* Teacher goal-setting
    knowledge of psychosocial stages for
        teaching, 32–33
    promoting motivation, 42–44
    relationship to students, 214–215
    styles of teaching, 296–297
Teacher goal-setting
    evaluation of goals, 260–262
    importance of, 261
    long-range goals, 262–263
    overview, 259–260
    short-range goals, 263–266
Teacher-made tests, 158, 160–161, 165
Technology. *See* Computers in the classroom
Temperature in learning environment, 78–79
Test questions
    essay, 160–161, 172, 175–176
    fill-in-the-blank, 160, 179
    listing, 172
    matching, 160, 172, 174, 179–180
    multiple-choice, 33–34, 160, 172, 174,
        176–178
    multiple-choice analysis, 184–185
    recall, 172, 174, 178–179
    sentence completion, 172
    by students, 241
    true/false, 160, 172, 174, 176, 178
Tests
    administration, 5, 158, 187–189
    after, 19
    analysis, 183–184
    before, 17
    blueprints, 170–171, 173
    classroom, 168–169
    construction, 169–170
    during, 18
    evaluating and revising, 182–185
    formative feedback, 158, 189
    marking objective items feedback, 224
    objectives, 171–172

overview, 157–159
paper and pencil, 158, 160
performance, 158
practice, 12–13
Praxis Series, 4–5
preparation for testing, 158, 185–187
proctor, 188–189
questions. *See* Test questions
scoring, 165–166, 180–181
standardized, 158, 164–167
teacher-made, 158, 160–161, 165
test items, 172–175
tips for taking tests, 15–16
Textbooks, 272–273
Theory
behaviorism, 45–47
cognitive development, 28–30, 34, 37–38
moral development in women, 136
Neo-Piagetian, 37–38
psychosocial development, 31–33
reciprocal determinism, 47–48
social interaction and cognitive
development, 48
stage, 29
triarchic theory of intelligence, 38–40
zone of proximal development, 48
Thesis, 234
Time management
overview, 270
prompt beginnings, 281–282
references, 286
teacher planning, 280–281
transitions, 284–286
Tips for taking the test, 15–16
Total Quality Management (TQM), 140
TQM (Total Quality Management), 140
Transformations, 30
Transitions, 284–286
Triarchic theory of intelligence, 38–40
Tutorial computer programs, 205
Twain, Mark, 246

U

U.S. Department of Education, 148–150
U.S. Department of Justice, 148–150

V

Vagueness, 220
Validating students as knowers, 43, 44
Values
classroom behavior, 138–139
community, 62
Verbal communication, 214, 246–247

Videos and films, 272, 274–275
Violence
accelerating factors, 148
community, 64
contributing factors, 147–148
prevention, 149
school statistics, 147
warning signs, 148–149
Visual learners, 249
Visual materials, 273–274, 289
Visual perceptual strength, 81
Visualizations, 56
Voice
communication, 247–248
internal, 55–56
Vygotsky, L. S., 48

W

Wall space usage, 122, 273
Warnings signs for violence, 148–149
Watson, John B., 45
Web sites
Educational Testing Service, 6
goal-setting, 267
No Child Left Behind Act, 244, 267
physical abuse, 101
substance abuse information, 93
time management, 286
Weekly reviews, 239–241
"With-it"-ness in the classroom, 151–152
Women, moral development theory, 136
Wong, Harry K., 123
Word processing programs, 202–203, 207

Z

Zero-tolerance laws, 150
Zone of proximal development (ZPD), 48
ZPD (zone of proximal development), 48

Installing REA's TESTware®

SYSTEM REQUIREMENTS

Pentium 75 MHz (300 MHz recommended) or a higher or compatible processor; Microsoft Windows 98 or later; 64 MB available RAM; Internet Explorer 5.5 or higher.

INSTALLATION

1. Insert the PRAXIS™ PLT 5-9 CD-ROM into the CD-ROM drive.

2. If the installation doesn't begin automatically, from the Start Menu choose the RUN command. When the RUN dialog box appears, type d:\setup (where d is the letter of your CD-ROM drive) at the prompt and click OK.

3. The installation process will begin. A dialog box proposing the directory "Program Files\REA\PLT 5_9\" will appear. If the name and location are suitable, click OK. If you wish to specify a different name or location, type it in and click OK.

4. Start the PRAXIS™ PLT 5-9 TESTware® application by double-clicking on the icon.

REA's PRAXIS™ PLT 5-9 TESTware® is **EASY** to **LEARN AND USE**. To achieve maximum benefits, we recommend that you take a few minutes to go through the on-screen tutorial on your computer. The "screen buttons" are also explained here to familiarize you with the program.

TECHNICAL SUPPORT

REA's TESTware® is backed by customer and technical support. For questions about **installation or operation of your software**, contact us at:

> **Research & Education Association**
> **Phone: (732) 819-8880 (9 a.m. to 5 p.m. ET, Monday–Friday)**
> **Fax: (732) 819-8808**
> **Website: *www.rea.com***
> **E-mail: info@rea.com**

Note to Windows XP Users: In order for the TESTware® to function properly, please install and run the application under the same computer administrator-level user account. Installing the TESTware® as one user and running it as another could cause file-access path conflicts.